REMEMBERING
Bob

REMEMBERING Bob

SUE PIETERS-HAWKE

Project management by Louise Swinn

First published in 2019

Allen & Unwin
83 Alexander Street
Crows Nest NSW 2065
Australia
Phone: (61 2) 8425 0100
Email: info@allenandunwin.com
Web: www.allenandunwin.com

A catalogue record for this book is available from the National Library of Australia

ISBN 978 1 76052 739 6

Set in 12/17 pt Baskerville MT Pro by Bookhouse, Sydney
Printed and bound in Australia by Griffin Press, part of Ovato

10 9 8 7 6 5 4 3 2 1

The paper in this book is FSC® certified. FSC® promotes environmentally responsible, socially beneficial and economically viable management of the world's forests.

'The essence of power is the knowledge that what you do is going to have an effect, not just an immediate but perhaps a lifelong effect, on the happiness and wellbeing of millions of people, and so I think the essence of power is to be conscious of what it can mean for others.'

Bob Hawke

Contents

FOREWORD

Tom Keneally

THIS IS NOT going to be a dull book! Hawke was a vivid fellow, and entertaining by his very nature. His very contradictions made him so. A Congregationalist minister's son who revelled in the profane Australian tongue. From a Temperance tradition he seemed bent on letting abstainers know what they were missing out on, until in the interests of the polity of the Commonwealth he himself renounced liquor. A Rhodes Scholar whose weekend Bible was the racing guide and who spoke in the most energetic Australian demotic. The face that launched many a strike, but from whose lips came the words of Accord. The man who opened Australia to the world and wanted to maintain, as an essential mark of our society, the Social Wage. In speaking of such things, he had some of the marks of a prophet. He blazed with certainties. And when his lips formed that potent rictus of denunciation, everyone around, particularly journalists he considered snide, went pale. For his eyes could flash with a hawkish savagery.

I don't need to say: he wasn't perfect. Everyone knew it, for he admitted to his flaws on television. As well, he changed uranium policy to help a Labor South Australian government, and he let the Western Australian Premier Brian Burke chase him away from creating Commonwealth-wide land rights law. He might have had a weakness for the spivs of the 1980s, but at the apogee of the new Australian capitalism, the winning of the America's Cup, he sat in his bodgie jacket and famously invoked the proposition that workers were entitled to take their leisure too.

By his own admission a less than model husband, he nonetheless recognised the competence of women and the authenticity of women's voices, and appointed Susan Ryan to the position of Minister Assisting on the Status of Women. I could go on for thousands of words about Hawkie's contradictions. He wore his paradoxes boldly and with an unrehearsed exuberance that captured the people's imagination and affection in a way no subsequent PM has done. There was no formula to it. It was just Hawkie!

Anyone, any citizen who ever spoke to him, was astounded by the way he stopped, fixed his gaze on you, and—unless you were an utter fascist screamer—seemed absorbed by your observations. This always appeared to be a huge gift of attention, an electoral compliment to the voter. And he did it because he saw us as more than mere integers in an economy, and more than mere clients of the state. He convinced those to whom he spoke that they figured as an inheritor of a special and utopian society, and he was emphatic that that special society had not been reduced to a mere market, just because we had entered the global market. Thus, his demeanour grew out of his convictions about the Commonwealth, beliefs bred in him by a strong mother and a kindly father, members of a church that emphasised Christ's social statements; and, after his motor bike accident when he was seventeen, the same year his brother Neil died, reinforced by the influence of the Labor Party. In the Australia of his boyhood, there was a sense that though we lived in the back-blocks of the world, we had the dignity of belonging to a society that would never abandon its children.

Hawke was scorned when in 1987 he declared that by 1990 no Australian child would be living in poverty. His speech notes on the day he made this pledge said: 'No Australian child *need* live in poverty.' In any case, neo-conservatives had conniptions at the whole concept. The market, the great God and Moloch of the modern age, decreed who was poor, who wasn't. The poor were leaners, not lifters. Modern market economics came near to confirming the nineteenth century Tory concept that poverty could be blamed on the poor themselves.

What was wrong with such a hope, prayer, aspiration? It is an aspiration negated by the tendency of recent governments to limit the commitments between the state and the people, to wave a big stick at unemployed and the aged. I prefer Hawke's vision.

Hawkie really got the arts. He saw every Australian film that gained the world's attention, every book, every work of art, every song performed, as part of a great communal enterprise. Hawke escaped the limits of our post-colonial mind. The urgency to get out there ourselves and be actors in our own stories has diminished since Hawke's era.

My own stories of Hawkie?

I remember a night in the late 1970s when, at a party in the Rose Garden of Old Parliament House, he complained to a press baron whose newspaper had been condemnatory of his union activism—he said the baron was proving to be 'a geriatric fuckwit'. There are no such voices raised in precisely those terms to press barons now, and we are the poorer for it.

'How do you like your tipster?' he shouted with that Hawke exuberance once at the Sydney Football Stadium after the team he had unfashionably predicted as victors won a Rugby League Grand Final.

One afternoon when Hazel Hawke called me in to Kirribilli House to discuss writing a book, Hawke sat by in tracksuit and with the racing guide, half-listening, and suddenly it was like visiting any couple who were getting on a bit. And I must record the two women of his life! Hazel, the great, enduring pilgrim in her own right, has left her children and grandchildren a legacy of amiability, intelligence and adaptability. And then Blanche D'Alpuget, gifted writer, whose work on Hawke is the best political biography written in Australian history. Blanche had, despite her notable literary talent, all the disadvantages of beauty, particularly the popular suspicion that the beautiful are shallow. I was always fascinated by her interest in monasticism and similar matters—I remember receiving from her a bottle of chutney, a gift she bought during a time of reflection in a Benedictine monastery. Both of these women were and are remarkable in their own right. I salute them for taking on and adjusting their lives to the meteor that was Hawke.

I was chilled when earlier this year he predicted his own death. Demigods aren't supposed to do that. However, demigods are always right, and he's gone. But the silence sings of him.

INTRODUCTION

Sue Pieters-Hawke

ONE OF THE first points to make is that I've not written this book, I've been the facilitator. The authors are the wonderfully diverse people who have very generously written and shared their stories at short notice with tight deadlines.

I'd never planned on writing a book about Dad. I've done two about Mum, and surely two about one's parents is enough! Besides, Dad has had so much written about him. He had his favourite biographer, whom he married, and while I, of course, had so much knowledge and behind-the-scenes experience, it didn't seem that any gaps in the story were big or interesting enough to bother.

But in the last few years of his life I felt that as he mellowed and his reflections crystallised and became more succinct, some of these thoughts were relevant to the public domain. And so, he and I talked about the possibility of a conversational and reflective book that didn't cover familiar ground. These conversations between us were interesting in themselves—and I'd talked to my previous publisher, signed a contract, was paid an advance, and even bought a microphone ready to go, when Dad had a turn and became unwell. We later understood it to be a mini-stroke. It became clear that asking him to talk too much was going to be onerous, but he and I continued to have mellow and interesting times together. We'd still chat but simply hanging out with him was my priority now, so I put aside the idea of a book, and Allen & Unwin kindly put the issue of the advance on the backburner. Some time before Dad's death we talked about other people's memories. This loose idea of a book with Dad and me in conversation and featuring other people's input was the last idea we'd had before he died. After his death, the book was the last thing on my mind.

At the memorial and the wake, it was wonderful how many people had stories about Dad that others mostly hadn't heard before. There were hours of boisterous reminiscing by many of the wonderful raconteurs who had known Dad—as well as being a great storyteller, he was the object of many a good story. Later, it occurred to me that sharing stories of Dad more widely might now be the book that could replace the earlier one we'd envisioned. So in some ways I feel as though this book, a collection of those stories and more, is a people's eulogy. I hoped that in being open in calling for public submissions, people who I didn't know would hear about the book—and that is indeed what happened, which has led to some delightful contributions.

Doing this at a time of grieving, while still getting used to the idea that Dad's not here anymore, is strange. I can still glance at a photo of him, and feel a tangible flash of his presence, that he is just down the road for me to visit and sit with as he does his cryptic crosswords or chats with the kids, or as we watch golf on television. Then the moment passes. In an odd way though, it has been very therapeutic reaching out to his friends and colleagues and friendly strangers. As well as peoples' generosity and goodwill, the shared sadness and fondness, and the inevitable tales of his 'flaws', amusing or otherwise, hearing repeated stories of his kindness and his willingness to go out of his way for others was very affirming of my sense of him as a human being. But it has gone further than that.

As is usually inevitable when families have broken a bit, a shadow of the pain can linger and subtly colour the nature of relationships—and whilst I certainly had a good, mellow, loving relationship with Dad in his last years there was perhaps still a touch of shadow in us both.

What I had fully restored to me and loved in putting together this book was the magnificance of who he was. A large part of this had happened when I was researching Mum's biography—his ebullience, the sense of fun and joy, tenderness, irreverence, that kindness, his lack of respect for most conventions, but also his deep respect for humanity re-emerged vividly. The person, who as a teenager I sometimes wondered why I'd hero-worshipped as a child, was mostly restored to me. In processing his death, and compiling this book, I came to fully understand as an adult why he meant the world to me. Anything I'd held against him in some subtle way fell away, tranformed into a sense of fully loving the man, where 'the yuck stuff' was a minor part of the imperfectly human whole.

Piles of guff has been written about Dad not being a perfect father, a far from model husband, and being at times a nasty drunk, and I in no way deny the sound kernels of truth therein. But a writer is lucky if they come away from doing a book with something of deep personal value. Amongst other things, I came away from writing Mum's biography with a sense of Mum and Dad's love for each other and the love, optimism and enthusiasm on which our family was founded. Immersion in Dad's life over the last six months has reiterated that I was deeply loved by a dad who sort of became problematic at times. In sifting my own memories, and hearing observations from others, I see how much he did, how much he loved and played, hoped and wanted for us. I am reminded that the only compensation in his own mind for his deficit in fathering was his absolute belief that Hazel was an excellent mother doing a great job. Which she was.

And about the husband thing—I was over at his and Blanche's on what happened to be Valentine's Day. A glorious bouquet of crimson roses was on the table, which Dad was quick to point out was entirely due to him (always the irrepressible child within . . .). 'I thought of it and went and got them all by myself!' he proudly exclaimed, failing to realise as usual that this might be a slight barb to some of us, given his fairly profound lack of any romantic gestures towards Mum—at least any that we saw. Despite myself, I smiled, and complimented him on being a good husband second time around. He grinned and looked at me, faltered over how to take the backhander, then with his usual optimistic self-confidence decided that he would take the compliment.

They say not to speak ill of the dead. I don't think that's a convention that Dad would have insisted on observing. But I did make it clear to contributors that this book was not the place for gratuitous sniping, either at Dad or at anybody else (despite which, the odd bit of editing was required—mostly in relation to others!) Circumstance maybe render this remembrance 'unbalanced', not necessarily because of rose-coloured glasses, but from the desire to preserve the best of someone we have loved and whose memory we honour in this telling of his life. This book focusses on the positive—and my god, there was so much positive to focus on!

Just as Dad could so charm and impress people in life, engendering in many a tendency to forgive or tolerate occasionally atrocious behaviour, so he clearly has done in death. What was called complexity has been whittled down by cliché to flaws, but I personally find this less important to focus on than the breadth of contributions and joy Dad generated in eighty-plus years. Life is maybe best analysed backwards, but can only be lived forwards. The act of memorising becomes a choice, not of denial but of what one chooses to take with you and to share. There is a luxury afforded in looking back, especially when someone has died, that could be called biased in life, but is allowed for in death.

People used to ask me what it was like growing up with a dad who was Prime Minister of Australia. And I would say that I didn't—I grew up with a dad who was a trade union official. Some of the pieces in this book are about the early times and give a sense of life in the ACTU, which is how I grew up knowing Dad. But in other respects what was it like to live with him as his daughter?

This book is about Dad, and not the place to recount details of the extraordinarily rich, varied and mostly happy childhood I had, but there's plenty you can infer from these pages. I will admit to having some identity issues growing up. My parents, were raised in Perth, didn't know Melbourne but wanted to live near the beach when we first moved there from Canberra in 1958. With an advance from the ACTU they kept looking further along the coast south of the city until they found and bought a little weatherboard they could almost afford. A few years later we moved to a home they couldn't really afford on the other side of the tracks in the same suburb. Dad was proud that the local bank manager had said that he was 'a bloke on whose future I reckon it's worth taking a gamble' and knew it would be a great place for us kids. It was hard yards for Mum, but we loved the freedom to roam both inside and outside the house. The downside, apart from financial pressure, was that the social environment was not easily welcoming for trade unionists and fellow travellers. But Mum, of course, gradually made a good home and friends everywhere, and we formed enough local friendships for it to work.

Then I won a scholarship to a 'ladies college' a few suburbs away in blue-ribbon Tory territory, and my father was now the 'class enemy': the parents thought he was a communist intent on stealing their money and their daughters, and the principal was somewhat befuddled as to how to deal with the hornet/s in the nest. For a thirteen-year-old girl it was very confusing, and I spent a year in horrified silence, but it was there that I slowly found the means to articulate and debate ideas in an environment that may not have been conducive to my world view, yet perversely reinformed it. Grounded in values transmitted by my parents, and excited by many of the new ideas that emerged in the 1960s and 1970s, I found the snobbery about wealth and self-interest, the compulsion towards conformity, and the narrow view of religion both distasteful in their expression and damaging in their implications. But I was lucky enough to have a few friends and a few great teachers, and I started to learn courage, albeit with a horribly righteous teenage twist.

One of the great things about living life around Dad was that his curious and gregarious nature, together with my mother's flexible, welcoming, inclusive bent, meant that our life was full of interesting people. I grew up amidst a library of ideas and people, a cauldron of folk who were not all pointed in the same direction—although there was a common kindness and humanity and effort and humour that threaded through this diversity. That might mean waking up to find a stranger asleep on the floor, a cricket team barbecue at half an hour's notice, or a hoary old unionists making our first dilapidated house fit for habitation in a way that Dad's education had never taught him to master. The barbecues in the backyards from earliest times, the optioned tennis court we could never afford until a libel case took care of that, and later a swimming pool, ditto, were all convivial playgrounds for people of all ages. Our New Year's Eve parties throughout the 1970s were awesome!

One lesson I learned when Dad became Prime Minister was how easy it could be to forgive someone for a sense of accumulated hurts or slights when you see that person is giving themselves two hundred per cent to something bigger than themselves. Not that that wasn't the case earlier—but I was younger then. Between being able to spend more time with Dad and constant media coverage, it was in an odd way closer up this time. I was also having kids myself, which can render you much more appreciative of the impossibility of being a perfect parent. My parents had these values about it being pointless to hold resentments, which I certainly felt made sense in theory, but in practice when Dad was PM I learnt the dynamics of this more personally. In doing so I better understood both him and my mother.

Having harboured, and to a large degree, still harbouring lofty lefty hopes and ideals, it was sobering indeed to have the opportunity to observe the realities of government. Amongst other things, I saw not the popular clichés, but the constraints and subtleties that operate against achieving what you are committed to. I marvelled at these people who kept their faith and optimism and maintained punishing workloads to achieve what they knew could only ever be a part of the world they hoped for. I saw what it took to maintain that optimism in the face of naysayers. I could see that principled pragmatism was not always 'selling out', but was essential to getting many things done. I started to understand why leaders went grey and faces aged quickly. It wasn't that it was burdensome, because there such privilege and joy to be governing for a greater purpose, but there was no doubting the weight of the responsibility. They were the bottom line in terms of the lives and choices available for millions of people. As a family we never discussed, never peeked at or breached the 'Top Security'-stamped papers Dad always carried, some of which seemed to weigh heavily on him. We simply knew that this responsibility went deeper than we would ever really know.

A book cannot capture the immediacy of the beautiful, poignant bittersweetness of a wake where harmony and grieving co-reside, often fuelled by alcohol, but this grieving and celebration is something that many have gone through in relation to a loved one, or perhaps even in relation to Dad. So, it might be that these memories of will be read aloud with a few tinnies in the Australian sun or they might be something dipped into occasionally at night. This book will be a lot of different things to a lot of different people, as was Dad himself, but the feeling confirmed in me is how completely fortunate I have been, not only to have had Dad as my father but to have grown up surrounded by commitment and reflective conversation and debate for most of my life and to have had the opportunity to meet so many good people who knew him. You will find something of all that between these covers.

In the early days of talking about the book I asked Dad what, with the distance of time, he regarded as his proudest achievements, his deepest regrets, and his fears for the future. He mentioned several achievements referred to in the pages of this book that he was proud of for himself and for his governments including: preserving the Antarctic as wilderness for peace and science, contributing to the end of Apartheid, significantly raising the high school completion rate, strengthening the social contract between people and government, and elevating environmental issues in political decision-making.

I approached the discussion of regrets not knowing how it would go because Dad had always said, 'Arrhhh, I don't do regrets', but at the private reception after Mum's memorial he asked me shyly if he could say a few words. He said some good things about Mum, then paused and became very sombre. 'Hazel and I had a great life together for many years,' he said, 'but I unreservedly apologise for all the pain I caused her at times.' You could have heard a pin drop in the room. This most sincere and authentic acknowledgement and apology was healing both for many of us and for Dad himself.

So when I asked him about regrets in his public life, he did come forth and without hesitation he named his failure to stand stronger on the issue of a treaty with Indigenous Australians. Expressing great disappointment most bitterly at himself, he said, 'I was swayed by false arguments and some of the conmen from Western Australia and I shouldn't have been.' You'll find elaboration on this issues in these pages. We also discussed the sense that there was a failure of good government in Australia and elsewhere, and that there remained significant 'unfinished business' which was vital to pursue in the interests of Australians as a whole, and particularly in relation to some cohorts. More of this in the Afterword.

I knew he had never been one to feel or indulge personal fear much at all, but when it came to discussing it, he said: 'Well, I've had a great life, and I'm not scared of dying but I am fearful for the future of the planet. Some are trying but too many are being blind and selfish and risking our children's and grandchildren's future. Both in Australia and globally it's the issue that requires the most concerted response and I am fearful for future generations if it doesn't happen effectively.' He talked, as he had thirty years ago, about the need for intergenerational equality and care. As it happens, my daughter was to take this as the theme of her speech at his public memorial, and to commit to contributing towards effective action on the issue.

There are other small things that don't get a mention here that are in my memories of Dad: his love of animals; the bows and arrows he made us from green stems and string when we were little and running riot in what seemed the huge backyard of our first home; the aviary he made me in our second house after Mum and I had measured up and bought all the materials, cut them to size and laid them out; our trip together to Israel and the USSR when I was a teenager; the regular weekend tennis doubles games Mum and Dad played for years with friends, as we (again) ran riot or 'umpired' and then joined the happy post-play conversations as the adults sipped beer. I still love watching tennis. Then there were regular dinners at home with the ACTU national executive, who were all 'uncles', where the conversation ranged from deeply serious to hilarious. And the singing! Every year on my birthday, Dad would ring and sing a rousing 'Happy Birthday' to me, leave a message I knew would be there when I checked my phone, as I always did. But now he has gone . . . There are so many memories . . . and in this book you will find so many more, and perhaps bring to mind some of your own.

Of course, this is not a biography or a complete portrait of Dad, but on the whole I think it captures him well. I hope you enjoy.

REMEMBERING
Bob

Rawdon Dalrymple

My relationship with Bob began in 1953 or '54 at Oxford where I was the Rhodes Scholar from NSW for 1952. My opposite number from Western Australia was a brilliant economist, John Stone. Stone was succeeded the following year as the scholar from WA by Bob Hawke. It is (or was) customary for a senior academic scholar to be assigned at Oxford to guide and help the Rhodes Scholar from far away at least for the first year. In what must have been one of the most spectacular misalliances of the period, Rhodes House arranged for Bob to be assigned to a Catholic economist famous for his orthodox religious and economic doctrinal views. From Bob's point of view this was a bridge too far and I recall him consulting me about the problem. I have no recollection of what advice or help I gave (which suggests I was not much use on that occasion). But he was able to get the arrangements changed and over the next couple of years produced a thesis (on what, I no longer remember*) which Hazel typed in her unacknowledged position of consort and helper.

My general recollection is that Bob did not really settle down in Oxford. He had friends, and would presumably have attended lectures, but perhaps it was a time for exploring new intellectual horizons and thinking through new positions on a range of issues including possibly politics, although I don't have a clear recollection of discussions of politics at that time. He and I were in the same college, University College, and Bob would have had responsibilities there preparing for his research degree. This was, I think, for him not a very demanding assignment and he probably spent more time meeting real live politicians and following Labor contacts. But he would have presumably had to attend to whatever requirements his supervisor asked of him.† I recall that Bob and Hazel had a close friend who was a member of the Oxfordshire Constabulary and I think they sometimes stayed with that family.

In the vacation time, he and Hazel went travelling in a little Ford van which they had bought. This was the Hawke version of the Great European Tour, which is a theme of

* Dad's thesis was on the history of wage determination in Australia.

† Dad's story contrasts to a degree with Rawdon's here. 'I worked like a dog all winter, played cricket all summer,' he would say, and as Mum backed this story, I tend to believe it. He was never work-shy, whether it was 'work' or sport or anything else he took on. Default setting 200 per cent effort seemed normal to us.

American literary fiction. What Bob and Hazel lacked in wealth and comfort I am sure they compensated for with contentment and mirth. They were a pretty happy couple in those days. Back in Australia, Ross and I often saw Bob and Hazel, and then afterwards when we were sent to London occasionally Bob came by, so we were always in touch.

My relationship with Bob next went into a more intense phase after I was appointed Australian ambassador to Israel, which was my first ambassadorial appointment. I had not been aware that Bob had a close interest in Israel and significant contacts there. But he had a close relationship with a major Jewish ALP figure in Melbourne, and this spread in predictable ways so that it was not long before Bob visited Israel on our watch, and our old friendship was continued. As always with Bob there were no half measures and his support for Israel was full on. He had a plan for engaging the Soviet Union in a grand scheme, the details of which I have, I'm afraid, forgotten.*

Years later when he was Prime Minister, Bob appointed me ambassador to the United States and I will close

---

* Grand, I don't know, but optimistic, yes. Dad had good contacts with people in the Soviet Union from his extensive involvement over years with the ILO (International Labour Organization). I was with him on his first trip to Israel, when I was fourteen, and together we took an unplanned detour to Moscow and other cities, where he put his case for the Soviets to ease their ban on allowing 'dissident' Jews to emigrate to Israel. Over several years, he was to have both disappointments, and later as PM, noteworthy success on this front.

Years later, Rawdon and Rossi's son David became a boarder at Geelong Grammar, and spent many a weekend as part of our family.

this note by recounting an episode of high protocol in the White House. Ronald Reagan was President and someone (I'm sure it was George Shultz) told him that Bob would be responsive to an exchange of amusing stories. After 40 minutes or so of serious talk with Reagan making use of his memo cards, he set those aside and gave Hawke his Irish grin. 'Mr President, have you heard the one about the old Irish Lady?' Bob was a world-beater at this game and responded in kind. It was a vintage display by two master players.

I am sad Bob has left us.

James Baker

When I was a young lad, my Uncle Bob and Aunty Hazel always made time for family and would regularly appear at our home in Coogee Street, Mt Hawthorn. Family members would gather to catch up and enjoy time together, sharing news of children, discussing current affairs, and having a laugh. Bob would often contribute to singing, accompanied by my mother or her sister, Hazel, on the piano.

Bob had fun with his 'party tricks' and took great pleasure in teaching me some of them. One involved tossing a box of matches into the air whilst simultaneously lighting a match and then catching the box whilst holding the latter—all done with one hand. I remember his delight that I was able to repeat his trick on the first attempt. He always took an interest in my development. On learning that I was a chess enthusiast, he was quick to challenge but he was definitely miffed at being beaten by a thirteen-year-old! Three years later, he left me in no doubt about his superiority on the tennis court!

Christmas 1963 was spent with the Hawkes in Melbourne, after we drove from Perth. The luncheon dessert was ice-cream cake but it was frozen so solidly that it resisted all attempts to be cut. Typically, Bob took on the challenge and adjourned to the back lawn where he took up an axe. The ice-cream cake was submitted to a fierce assault and ice chips flew in all directions. Bob did not seem to appreciate the hilarity of the witnesses.

My Uncle Bob shaped my values. Together with my mother, he nurtured an appreciation of the importance of education and the power of knowledge, as well as recognition of the plight and rights of those less fortunate. It took me longer to emulate his respect for the dignity and wisdom of many who did not have the advantage of a formal education. I remember him and his parents with gratitude, affection and much respect.

Jeff McMullen

My memories of this complex man span fifty years and remarkably different settings.

In the 1960s, as ACTU leader, Bob's confidence and intellectual clarity were striking. He had an engaging openness.

Even when I was a young ABC journalist I found that he liked to debate ideas and had a willingness to empty his head of his own assumptions. To me, this was a mark of his intellect—and something I observed in other memorable encounters with leaders such as Lee Kuan Yew and Nelson Mandela.

When Bob came to Washington DC not long before toppling Bill Hayden for the ALP leadership, he had an entertaining joust with a group of us Australian foreign correspondents. The handful gathered in a Washington garden for drinks, and conversation included the economist, Dr John Edwards, Brian Toohey, and other good friends who have since passed away.

I have never forgotten Hawke's glowing sense of destiny. In his view he was describing a political inevitability that was akin to Divine Intervention.

I asked, 'Well, you don't think Bill Hayden is just going to roll over for you, surely?'

'Yes he will,' answered Bob, straight-faced.

We all watched it happen.

That ebullience shone through in his personal style as Prime Minister and in the swagger of his Cabinet colleagues as they came to visit President Ronald Reagan in the White House.

I was the ABC's White House correspondent and I had married Kim Hoggard, a senior presidential staffer in the West Wing. I know that the Americans were struck by the

Hawke team's independence of thought and confident world view that verged on cockiness.

I recall Hawke's sure-footedness when interviewing him at length in a live national television broadcast as Australian armed forces joined the UN-sanctioned push to drive Saddam Hussein's forces from Kuwait in the first Gulf War. He managed leadership by mastering the art of listening to bright colleagues whose talents he genuinely respected.

Many years later, after he had left politics, he came to try his hand as a reporter on the Nine Network's *60 Minutes*. You can imagine how that went over with Richard Carlton with whom Hawke had clashed over that 'blood on your hands' encounter, a taunting piece of television melodrama. Bob was not much of a reporter, but of course he thought it would be easy—just like smashing a cricket ball for a six.

I came to appreciate Bob's warmth over his final twenty years when I was a director of the Engineering Aid Australia Indigenous Engineering School. Retired engineer Jeff Dobell asked Bob to be patron, and each year, Bob would engage wholeheartedly with helping build this small contribution to the education of young Indigenous people who went on to form the first cohort of Indigenous engineers in our era.

This, of course, was small compensation for Bob's own profound disappointment that he and his government had failed to deliver the promised Treaty with Australia's dispossessed First Nations. I had similar conversations with Malcolm Fraser before he died, and both former leaders pointed to their own party dissenters for undermining the long overdue negotiation of a just settlement with Aboriginal and Torres Strait Islander people. While his political reforms are now history, this failure to deliver genuine Indigenous Land Rights was a dark cloud over his record time as a Labor prime minister.*

When addressing a large dinner audience including Bob and Blanche one evening, I improvised some thoughts on why some men were hesitant to speak aloud of love. To speak of love of country, love of a partner or even love of our children, so often we find it hard to find the words. I looked out to see Bob crying and Blanche's eyes glistening too. Bob said to me later, 'Now those were words that mattered. One of the best speeches ever given.'

As so many of us said on his death, he loved generously—and the country loved him in return.

Jeff McMullen is a journalist, author and film maker.

Paul Munro

Bob Hawke was about thirty-six when I first met him in 1966, and I was twenty-six. Although by that time he was known widely in Australia through his representation of

* There are other contributors who refer to Dad's failure and disappointment in himself on this issue, as I do in the introduction.

the ACTU in National Wage cases, he was an unknown quantity in Papua New Guinea. The ACTU had agreed to his leading a case before the Public Service Arbitrator to seek pay increases aimed at overcoming newly introduced discriminatorily lower pay rates for indigenous members of the PNG Public Service compared with the salaries paid to expats.

I was to be Bob's assistant, effectively his junior counsel. I was a lawyer of some five years in PNG, but a cleanskin so far as industrial and party political matters were concerned. I had never heard of Bob before I met him.

He turned up a short time after I started on the case. The PSA leadership thought it a good idea to have me take Bob on a familiarisation tour of parts of the territories. He was enormous fun to be with. He was inspirationally informative about the case, and about his objectives as an ACTU employee and as a member of the ALP. We formed a quick and close rapport. Over the course of a couple of weeks we met with an array of local officers, took preliminary evidential statements and socialised. The last day of the tour was in Wewak, where we spent some time with Michael Somare, then a public servant but later to be the first Chief Minister of an independent PNG.

We were to fly the next morning on a 6 a.m. flight back to Port Moresby for a 9 a.m. conference with the PNG Administration's legal team, headed by Hal Wootten QC.

We hoped to set a timetable for the public hearings and also to try to persuade the administration to offer an interim increase in salaries pending final determination by the arbitrator. A few drinks on the evening before the flight developed into a session, Bob leading the way at his expansive and boisterous best. Around midnight, as mentor and guide, I did what I could to wind up the proceedings in Bob's motel room so that we could be ready for a 5 a.m. Land Rover to catch the flight. When I got to sleep at around 2 a.m., in the room next door to Bob's, he was still in full flight with a couple of other players.

I was no teetotaller but, as a legal professional, I was pretty unimpressed by the idea of anyone getting a skinful the night before an important conference. At 5 a.m. I responded to the alarm, got myself going and, somewhat grumpily, dug Bob out of his bunk. By then I was thinking that I would need to resign from the job if I was to be led by anyone I thought to be so undisciplined and irresponsible to those we were to represent.

Feeling the after-effects of the night myself, I was only a bit mollified when, on the plane, Bob, by then bright as a button, turned to me and cheerily said, 'You're looking a bit poorly Paulie, what's up?'

Still expecting the worst, I sat with Bob and other PSA reps at the conference. Wootten immediately went on the front foot to insist that our local officers' case be postponed to allow Ian Macphee to complete a case for an increase in the allowances paid to expatriate officers;* any consideration of an interim increase should also be deferred.

I cannot now recall whether Bob took a short break to consult with PSA advisors. I am certain that what he came up with was completely his own invention. Grasping completely the likelihood that local officers would feel themselves betrayed if the PSA went along with the administration's proposal, Bob launched into the administration with gusto. He told them he would brook no delay in either starting our case or in securing an interim increase. He told them to switch the venue for the completion of the allowance case to Melbourne, out of sight and out of mind of PNG. When the administration rebuffed that suggestion he said that if they didn't adopt it, the PSA would withdraw the process upon which the case was before the arbitrator. I was startled almost breathless by the boldness of the threat.

After a short break, the administration capitulated, agreed to a timetable and undertook to table an interim increase.

Hawke's negotiation style and brilliance was so effective, so dramatic, so different from anything I had witnessed

---

* I remember when I first met Ian Macphee, who went on to become a minister in the Fraser government. I woke up one morning at home in Royal Avenue, Sandringham and there was a noise. I looked around to discover there was a strange man asleep on my floor! Now this was not entirely unusual in our home, through which many and diverse people flowed much of the time. If beds were full, we had camping mattresses. Ian explained that he had just come in from PNG, and I figured Mum and Dad must like him if they put him on my floor. He stayed two or three nights as my 'floor guest'.

before then, I was immediately converted. Confident, completely assured, steely, he had displayed a mastery of the facts, off-the-cuff innovation and an ability to conjure up a suspension of belief about alternative options that carried the day. In later years I came across similar displays of his truly outstanding persuasive capacity. It was those moments in Port Moresby that caused me to realise how lucky and privileged I was to get to work with a person of such capacity.

Working with Bob Hawke

In 1966 I was no stranger to putting a lot of effort into court hearings. Working with Bob stretched even the limits I had been used to.

Typically, hearings finished each day at around 4 p.m. Bob's practice was then to drop into the tavern next to our office and have a beer or two until we had a meal at around 6 p.m., often fraternising with witnesses or opposition. Around 8 p.m., Bob would get the effort for the next day started. Often we worked through till 2 a.m. and he would bounce back in early the next morning for a continuation.

He was the first person I saw master the appearance of speaking *ex tempore*, all the while reading from notes. He took in his long-hand crib with a passing glance, his eyes on the tribunal or audience.

A less endearing feature of his advocacy stance was a habit he had developed of allowing his left hand to work its way under his trouser belt into the vicinity of his buttock crack, while standing on one leg, the other propped on a chair. Seated at the Bar table next to or near the star advocate regaling a Bench, his underlings were often puzzled by what was being explored in his nether regions. The view from the seated audience often provoked chuckles, and Hazel would get good laughs from the spectacle.

In all my dealings with him, he was the most effusively generous person with his recognition and praise for work contributed by staff working with or for him. I never heard him claim credit for work that one of us had performed for him, indeed he would introduce whoever it was to all and sundry as though the sun shone out of us.

He was the most ready delegator of jobs, ready to trust the person allocated the task, and expect performance without direction. Peter Matthews, having been appointed Education Officer for the ACTU, spoke to me some months later, making a soft impeachment of Hawke as president for not coming anywhere near him to guide him as to what the job entailed; I remember telling him something to the effect: 'You have to work it out for yourself, and Bob will give you a free hand unless you stuff it up.'

While Bob could be intense with finishing off a task against a deadline, it was internalised. The sense of humour was always close at hand, as was his ridicule of the opposition, he could spot the funny side of word plays, and had an inexhaustible set of anecdotes about barristers, judges, and labour or union figures.

Bob could listen. I recall two occasions in Port Moresby, socially, where Bob sat through an entire evening almost silent, hearing accounts on one occasion of a catastrophe at sea, on the other occasion of life in immediate post-revolution Shanghai.

The reciprocal attraction of Bob to women and of women to Bob was not a secret from me after a few months working with him. Although he did not shrink from disparagement of women and men, it was gender balanced; I saw no evidence of misogyny. Certainly, for the women who were high achievers that I came across with him in the sixties, his treatment of them was exemplary, long before Australian men generally adjusted to accepting the equal status of women in the workforce.

Hawke's framing of a political perspective for newcomers

In 1966, I had no party-political alignment. I had not registered to vote in Australian elections. I took the work on the local officers' case because I saw it as a means to redress more remuneration injustice than I could ever hope to achieve through conventional litigation.

Bob brought within my purview settings of his political and union views that transformed my own perspective and values. As we travelled around, his ambition to succeed Albert Monk as president of the ACTU was often discussed.

The objective of that ambition was even more clearly articulated; it was to develop a much more unified and much better resourced union movement and to achieve through it and the labour movement generally a much better quality of life for working people. Central to those broad propositions was always the necessity for the labour movement, especially the federal level ALP, to overcome the dearth of economic understanding bedevilling its electoral policy positions.

From when I first spent time with him in the mid-1960s, Bob was determined to do what he could to bring about economically well-informed policy at national level. I would not dispute that there were occasions, perhaps especially during the Whitlam years, where he did little to encourage that outcome,* but it was unquestionably an abiding value and force for him.

I had no room for cynicism about what Bob meant by pursuing a *better quality of life* for working people. I knew a fair bit about the quality of life deficits for many of the local officers we were representing; I knew how even small pay increases lifted those I knew best out of poverty and hardship; and I personally witnessed, and was swept up in, the intensity, industry and zeal that Bob applied and expected of us in attempting to use the union to win improvements for those

* He argued forcefully with Whitlam and others about the need for economic literacy if reform was to be sustained. That a worthy social agenda increasingly fell victim to economic incompetence saddened and maddened him.

we represented. Through my exposure to him, his objectives became my own and influenced much of my subsequent career.

Mention should be made of Hawke's convivial relationship with many, but by no means all, of the people against whom he appeared or opposed in industrial arenas. He avoided cant about the 'class' enemy; his friendship with Jimmy Robinson, top advocate for the employers over many years, was genuine inside and outside court. An even more important relationship in my view was with the inimitable and great George Polites, the effective planning and strategic guru of the employer councils for decades. Through association with Bob and later, I got to know George more than slightly; he was masterful and very approachable.

Bob Hawke as workmates and friends knew him

I was among those who held very much to the view that the Bob Hawke people saw on their TV screens was very close to the person that those close to him got to know. There was very little artifice or affectation in his manner. He let it pretty well all hang out, saying what he thought, asked or unasked. He had different styles of address according to his audience, but so should any advocate or public speaker. The gusto, the readiness to laugh, the pungent counter-punching wit, and the delight in his sport were all absolutely authentic and full-throated.

Bob, as soon as awake, tended to get the house moving. 'Hazelllll . . .' was bellowed as he might search for a lost sock, his newspaper, or whatever, striding across the house, lounge room, or wherever, sometimes stark naked, the first naked man I ever saw who acted oblivious to the houseguest, children and whoever happened to be there at the time.

Among the perks of high ACTU office in the seventies was an annual Christmas gift from Ansett to contacts or opponents in industrial relations matters. In Bob's case there would arrive at Royal Avenue, Sandringham a half-dozen or so bottles of Grange Hermitage wine. In those days there was not the reverence for Grange that now applies but even so, it was considered a stately drop. Not at the Hawke table! On several occasions I remember Bob producing a bottle and polishing it and another off with whoever was drinking, as though it was no more important than a bottle of Jimmy Watson's one-dollar dreadful cleanskins.

When Jane and I were newly arrived in Melbourne and newly wedded, we purchased a terrace in Middle Park. Bob, no doubt at the instigation of Hazel, organised a working bee to tidy up the place. I think it was the closest most of us ever saw Bob come to doing actual physical work around a house. Amidst a lot of talk and plenty of libation, he painstakingly removed the nails and tacks that had fastened the putrefying lino to the stairs. He and Ralph Willis did a good day's work, Ralph unearthing, literally, under the lino floor of the bathroom a foundation of plain soil.

Bob was a good and capable fisherman, quite astute at it when in his favoured territory, rueful when not. Once at

Manus we were in a profusely productive spot but all either of us could land was the head of a fish—the rest had been amputated by a reef shark as we hauled in; much cursing. Back in Australia, we had a trip with the family to York Peninsula South Australia in 1969, fishing mostly for whiting, rambling the coastline, playing cards and relaxing for a month away from the rest of the world. As we were leaving, we spotted two large great white sharks, very close to shore, where we had spent the last month swimming. They were probably drawn by the month's worth of fish debris we had put out as we cleaned up to leave. Spotting them, Bob decided we should try to catch one. Jane caught and supplied a living rock cod. I was put on the oars, rowing a tinny around as Bob stood in the bow, in his swimmers, casting the fish toward an apparently drowsy, disinterested shark. Had it taken the bait, Australia's political history may have been very different, as there was no way that the shark would not have towed the tinny or Bob as far as it wanted. The gleeful, reckless holiday bravura of that close encounter with danger still comes to mind as emblematic of Bob at play.

The Royal Avenue living room as I remember it was always very alive with noise and movement and articulate, vociferous debate; rarely hostile in character but vigorous, especially where Bob and daughter Sue were involved, although Stephen on matters radioactive could be goaded into some intensity. Bob regularly tested and debated his offspring and I saw no ill-intent, it was part and parcel of the personality and certainly had educative and training effect—none of the kids were ever short of a word or likely to die wondering.*

Patti Warn

On Bob Hawke's confirmation as ACTU leader: My overwhelming memory of that occasion is of witnessing the absolute pride and joy of hoary old unionists that their boy had got up in the ballot.

They saw a son of the manse from Bordertown, South Australia, who had been educated at Perth Modern School, and who had gone on to the University of Western Australia. They saw a kid from a state school who had won a Rhodes Scholarship to Oxford when the Rhodes meant something. They saw someone who was prepared to accept paltry pay as the ACTU Wage Case Advocate and Research Officer who could confidently face off against the employers and the lawyers and achieve real results.

---

* My recent text exchange with Jane Munro.

Me: Do your kids EVER get over thinking they know more than you about everything??!!

Jane: Well darling, I can remember when you knew more than your father!!! You had a huge row with us there . . . about uranium. You gave each other the business, you left the room in tears. He turned to me and said, 'Isn't she magnificent?!'

Such was life in those days . . . nothing has changed, it appears. Same genes!! You challenged so many things as a girl and young woman. So straight! I think he was making you tough! He adored you, no doubt! I think he saw himself in you.

They saw Hawke as a kind of antipodean Kennedy—someone who asked not what his country could do for him, but what he could do for his country. They saw him as the best and the brightest in Australia. They saw all this, and they loved him for it.

Patti Warn, then a researcher for the ABC's Four Corners, *later worked for both the Whitlam and Hawke governments.*

Patricia Edgar

The first time I met Bob Hawke was at a dinner at the Wentworth Hotel in Sydney in the early 1970s. I was a member of the board of the Australian Film and Television School. By then he was the ACTU President and a well-known public figure. He was seated at an adjacent table. I was introduced and sat down beside him. He turned and gave me his undivided attention; he asked me about myself and we spoke for some time. It was striking, as men in that era didn't ask women anything unless they were trying to pick them up, and that was not his agenda. I was more used to being ridiculed and patronised by my male colleagues, as I taught Film Studies, a discipline which most male academics of the time thought had no place in a university. That encounter made an enduring impression on me, for Bob Hawke had seemed genuinely interested in me as an individual.

It would be more than ten years before I met him again. In the meantime, he had been elected Prime Minister, and

Hazel had joined the board of the Australian Children's Television Foundation (ACTF) in December 1983, where I was the founding director. Over seventeen years as a member of my board, Hazel was a staunch supporter of my work, and she became my friend.* She told her husband about my programs and at one time took home, for him to see, a tape of *Top Kid* from a script by Bob Ellis about a precocious quiz kid. Bob invited Barry Jones, Australia's eminent quiz kid, to come to The Lodge to view it with him.

One day I was having lunch with Hazel at The Lodge. The Prime Minister swept in with his entourage, gave me a cheery greeting and went upstairs to change into bathers to lie in the sun for half an hour. It was a warm Canberra day. From the dining table where I was seated, I had an excellent view of the chestnut brown body and the PM's taut backside swinging up the stairs in a snug, pale-blue, shiny, swim costume. An interesting sight, I thought.

As wife of the Prime Minister, Hazel opened multiple events for the Foundation and, when she travelled, she took along ACTF programs as gifts, introducing them to the King and Queen of Jordan, First Lady Nancy Reagan, Prince Charles and Princess Diana. But the most important contribution she made to the children's television production industry, and the greatest opportunity for the ACTF,

---

* My kids loved the ACTF video cassettes 'Nan' gave them. They filled many a rainy day and the kids learnt a lot.

was to set up and attend, as a board member, a meeting for me with Michael Duffy, the Minister for Communications. The meeting was to convince the minister he would need to change the Broadcasting Act to ensure the Australian Broadcasting Tribunal had the power to enforce Children's Television Content Standards.

On 21 May 1985, the High Court had handed down a decision in the Herald Sun TV Pty Ltd case that held the Children's Television Standards relating to quotas and C classification were invalid. I reported to the minister on the threat to the television production industry and was given a good hearing. Bob Hawke's government moved quickly and introduced an amendment bill, strengthening the Broadcasting Television Act and affirming the tribunal's powers. Taking on the commercial industry was not something Australian governments had been eager to do in the past, so this was a significant decision. Without this change in legislation the Children's Television Standards and drama quota would never have succeeded.

Bob Hawke would come to my aid again five years later. Robert Holmes à Court had invited me to be a trustee of his charitable foundation, which he established following the stock market crash of 1987. He encouraged me to make an application for funds, expressing some interest in taking over the ACTF. But I saw an opportunity to create an important program for early childhood development. I took a proposal to Robert's board to develop a comprehensive program to support the education of young children nationwide. It was called *Lift Off.*

I came away from the meeting with a commitment from the trustees to invest $2 million in the project so I set about investing heavily in wide-ranging script and character development for the series, consulting widely to ensure the best quality. But, try as I might, I could not get Robert to agree to hand over any of the proposed funding. He loved to play games. For him a contract was the beginning of a negotiation, and I was an easy target. Finally, he told me that if the Prime Minister would announce his investment of $2 million at a public function then he would attend.

What else to do but seek Hazel's help? It took some engineering, but the Prime Minister obliged and at a launch for *More Winners* (the third anthology of children's television programs I had produced), Bob Hawke announced the $2 million investment in the *Lift Off* series. He spoke of Robert's generosity and of his own personal support for the ACTF. I sat beside the Prime Minister at lunch in the Great Hall of Montsalvat with Robert attending, and journalists could not believe their luck to be face to face with both the Prime Minister and Robert Holmes à Court at the same gathering.

Bob Hawke had played his part, happily, and spoken with genuine enthusiasm, 'I get so much excitement, both directly and residually, through Hazel's comments to me and my knowledge of what the Foundation does. Clearly, my friends, this is no ordinary TV series.'

Despite this, Robert still would not agree to the funding, and as I pushed him hard he did not like it. He told Janet, his wife: 'No wonder Phillip Adams called Patricia a Centurion tank.'

The Montsalvat launch on 14 June 1990 would be Robert's final public appearance. Strangely and unexpectedly, a letter arrived on 29 August, two days before Robert's death from a heart attack, agreeing with no further argument to the investment in *Lift Off*.

When US President George H Bush and his wife Barbara were to visit Australia in January 1992, Hazel was consulted about a program for the President's wife: she would have time to visit one organisation only. Hazel suggested this should be the ACTF, and the planners liked the idea. The publicity was huge and *Lift Off* was the program I presented to Barbara Bush. As it happened, Bob Hawke would not receive President Bush as Prime Minister and Hazel would not be able to attend the visit to the ACTF by the First Lady, for by January 1992 Paul Keating would be PM.

On 1 December 1996, my husband Don turned sixty. As it was a significant benchmark I hired a paddle steamer, the *Coonawarra*, and invited thirty friends to travel over a weekend from Mildura, my home town, to the Murray–Darling River junction. The river was in flood, and as the steamer sailed under the Wentworth Bridge we drifted and hit a pylon. The paddle was smashed and we were immobilised on the river. Bob happened to phone Hazel at that point and she told him she was shipwrecked on a paddle steamer on the Murray River. In typical Hawke speak he asked, 'What the F**k are you doing there?' Hazel laughed.

Bob Hawke and Hazel were a vibrant partnership in the years when he was at his peak. Directly and indirectly they had a significant impact on my life.

Dr Patricia Edgar AM, writer and producer, is best known as the founder and director of the Australian Children's Television Foundation, 1982–2002.

George Campbell

I have known Bob for fifty years. I was twenty-six and Bob would have been in his thirties when I first met him in the John Curtin Hotel.

The John Curtin was a small pub and everyone gathered there on a Friday night. The ACTU drank in the back, saloon bar. The Victorian Left drank in the same bar but on the other side of the room. And the Builders Labourers, the BLs, drank in the front bar.

I became the Secretary for the Shipwrights Union, and Bob became the President of the ACTU, we spent a fair bit of time together, and he helped our union with some major campaigns.

Shortly after the election of the Whitlam government in 1972, rumours were swirling that the Whitlam government was contemplating cutting defence expenditure, which would have seen many metalworkers and defence shipyard workers lose their jobs.

Bob as ACTU President, and Harold Souter as ACTU Secretary, led the multiple delegations that went to Canberra to meet with Gough Whitlam and Defence Minister Lance Barnard. Bob argued very forcefully, actually very aggressively, with Gough. He argued for alternative civilian work to be found for these workers. We were successful and, as a result of our negotiations, the naval dockyard in Williamstown built sections for the Westgate Bridge, and the aircraft factory at Fishermen's Bend became engaged in making medical instruments.

He was so good at advocating that even when Bob lost the prime ministership, the ACTU called on his services to advocate before the Industrial Commission on behalf of mining workers.

George Campbell is former National Secretary of the AMWU, more commonly known as the Metal Workers Union.

Kate Faulkner

I was a producer's assistant on *This Day Tonight* at the ABC Ripponlea studios in Melbourne in the 1970s. Bob Hawke, then President of the ACTU, was coming into the

Melbourne studios to speak live on air with Richard Carleton in Canberra on his return from the Middle East.

On that night's show, Richard was interviewing Phillip Lynch (a Liberal minister) in the studio, and he also wanted Mr Hawke's assessment of the situation. Mr Hawke agreed to answer Richard Carleton's questions but, at the same time, expressed that he did not want to debate Phillip Lynch.

However, as Richard crossed to the Melbourne studio, he asked Mr Hawke to debate Phillip Lynch. Because it was live-to-air, Mr Hawke was forced to enter the debate, but he made his displeasure clear to Richard. He then proceeded to debate Phillip Lynch with typical Hawke attitude and style.

When the program finished, Mr Hawke was still angry and insisted that we arrange a replay of the interview. This was in the day of 2-inch video machines that were very slow to cue and required intricate handling. While they were lining it up, Mr Hawke needed to go to the toilet. I waited for him and, after he was finished, he sat down next to me on the stairs. He just wanted a bit of peace and quiet for a few minutes. We chatted away, and I mentioned to him that I was from Perth too.

We returned to the viewing room and watched the replay of the interview. At the end of it, he and his entourage agreed that he had won the debate, so we all relaxed with a few beers. It was a delicate situation because of the 'betrayal' by Richard Carleton. Mr Hawke asked me about my favourite Perth beach and I replied that it was City Beach and that

I used to surf there in the mornings before starting work at midday.

He responded with, 'Ah, City Beach . . . I had my first kiss in those sand hills when I was sixteen—Sarah (---) I'll never forget it.'

I jokingly said, 'She is my mother!'

Mr Hawke was a bit taken aback until I laughed and said, 'No, she wasn't . . . but, she could have been.' He then threw his head back and laughed that gorgeous laugh and said, 'Got me!'

From then on, when I had to call him to see if he would be available to appear on the program, he would always ask, 'Aaah Kate, how's your mum?' and then laugh.

A post-script to this story: Phillip Lynch also insisted on seeing a replay of the interview when he returned to Melbourne the next morning. After he had seen it, he was very happy; he and his entourage thought that HE had won the debate.

Jan and Peter Marsh

In the early 1970s we were asked by Bob and Hazel to take over from Ralph and Carol Willis to mind their Sandringham house when the Hawke family went on holidays. Ralph had recently entered federal Parliament and Jan was working at the ACTU. The minding chores included caring for Chindi, the Siamese cat, and Flash, the Border Collie-cross. Chindi was notorious for licking Bob's armpits.

The relative silence of the house was smashed when the Hawke family returned. We always had our car packed but were never allowed to leave until after the evening meal. Highly energised by the holiday, the family wanted to either pile down to the beach or play tennis on their court. On one occasion, a journalist and photographer turned up, so a picture of all of us at the beach was in *The Age* the next day! The tennis matches between Bob and Hazel were intensely competitive. Hazel was good and Bob could be described as energetic. Our recollection is that Hazel used to win.

Occasionally, we would be asked to stay for a meal. Invariably Bob had asked other guests that he wanted to bounce ideas off. Bob tended to dominate the discussion, but we recall on one occasion when somehow the discussion turned to Robbie Burns' poetry. Everyone fell silent as Bob and Hazel went hammer and tongs about what the true import of certain poems was, and the atmosphere was electric. Often, though, Hazel would play the piano and we would all sing in convivial enjoyment. Bob was warm and loving to his young children. Sue was always gregarious and intensely interested in her father's activities, while Stephen was reserved in his views. Ros was just so affectionate and would spend as much time as possible cuddling her father.

The family doctor became a good friend of Bob's. The doctor had a beef cattle farm at Yarram.* Bob invited us to visit the farm and we spent the time helping out with the chores. We recall that Bob enthusiastically took to drenching the cattle, but in his enthusiasm he narrowly avoided a bad accident in the cattle crush. We never saw Bob as relaxed as he was on the farm. He yarned late into the night with warmth and charm.

As Bob began positioning himself to enter politics, there were often large gatherings of the ALP's Labour Unity faction at Sandringham. Bob was always at the centre of everything, often in his Speedos, making sure everyone was enjoying themselves. It was on these types of occasions that Bob was at his best. He loved company and he engendered love and commitment back to him.

After Bob became Prime Minister, we were asked to provide our house for a meeting between him and some of the ACTU executive members that had mentored him and opened up the path for his union career. Apparently there was a feeling emerging that he had left his old friends

---

* We often went down to the farm near Yarrum, Gippsland for weekends and holidays. When our friends bought some extra grazing land, they offered us the use of the broken-down shack on it. We patched it up, and it became a favourite refuge for our family and friends for years. We would help out on the beef and dairy farms, pick mushrooms and blackberries, chop wood and ride horses. We had a small put-put motorbike to explore the area. Dad would shoot rabbits, but after a try, I decided it was not for me. Most seasons, we would have blazing fires at night. (Dad and I were the pyromaniacs who would keep adding logs until everyone was sitting around the outer walls, even in the depths of winter.)

behind, and the point of the meeting was to ensure that he mended any fences that needed it. The night was very successful, and it demonstrated his ability to generate loyalty and support from people. Bob was courteous and respectful, and this was appreciated.

Deborah Homburg

Mr Hawke, as he was to me nearly fifty years ago, was my school friend's father. He taught me, at a family dinner, how to tell what was a good red wine (no aftertaste) and what was not (mouth/throat feels mucky after a sip). So, for over forty years, I have been able to have one glass of really good wine and be happy enough to get up and go on.

I remember with pleasure that the Bob Hawke I knew taught a young woman to enjoy one glass of good red wine.

Ralph Willis

I had the unique experience of working with Bob in both his ACTU days and his time in Parliament. At the ACTU I was his research assistant through all of the 1960s and then after Bob became ACTU President at the beginning of 1970 I was ACTU Research Officer and Advocate (Bob's old job). In Parliament, as shadow Treasurer, I was involved with Bob in determining the ALP economic policy and we were in the shadow ministry together after he was elected to Parliament at the 1980 election. His shadow ministry office was next to mine at the back of the Old Parliament House. Once he was elected leader of the Opposition in 1982, I was in his shadow ministry until we were elected to government in early March 1983. Thereafter, I was in each of his Cabinets.

I worked with Bob in various degrees of closeness—from very close in the 1960s at the ACTU, through to the still cordial but more distant relationship in his prime ministerial days. At the ACTU I worked with him on a daily basis in the preparation and presentation of National Wage Cases to the Arbitration Commission and accompanied him on much of his mainly pub-based socialising, and even undertook occasional child-minding duties whilst he went out with Hazel.

What struck me most about Bob was his absolute self-confidence and belief in himself, his exceptional articulateness, his determination to win whatever contest he was engaged in, from the trivial to the most important, his ability to relate really well to people at any socio-economic level, his passionate belief in a more equitable and tolerant society, his love of an argument, and his ability to persuade people to accept his point of view.

These personal attributes stood him in great stead as the union advocate in National Wage Cases. These advocacy skills, along with a more thorough knowledge of the history of wage fixation in Australia than anyone else in the country, and his economic literacy, made him an extremely formidable advocate for the unions before the Commission.

He also had an exceptional physical capacity for long periods of advocacy—these National Wage Cases could go for months, with 4–5 hours of hearings each day. And when the day finished in court, there was usually more work to do back at the office. The whole process was physically and mentally exhausting for the advocate, but Bob seemed to thrive on it.

In one case in the early 1960s he spoke for three weeks in reply to those who were opposing our claim. Some of this involved spirited interaction with the Bench, but rather than being daunted by it, Bob relished the challenge to convince his interlocutors of the correctness of his arguments and the justice of his case.

He was also quick to seize an opportunity to put down an opposing advocate. One such occasion arose in the mid-1960s when our claim was, as usual, being opposed by an array of employer organisations, including, as usual, the Wool Growers and Graziers Council. The difference this time was that the wool growers had employed a leading QC to put their case.

This QC was a large, pompous, arrogant individual who clearly had it as part of his role to put down the union advocate upstart, who wasn't even a member of the Bar! In making his case that the wool growers were in dire circumstances and couldn't afford a wage rise, he adopted a sneering, dismissive attitude to the union case and to its advocate. But Bob was able to very effectively puncture this balloon of pomposity by, apart from effectively dealing with the details of his arguments, also pointing out that if, as the QC claimed, his clients were in such dire straits, he wasn't doing much to assist them by wearing a synthetic suit! This was at a time when non-natural fibres were beginning to make their mark and suits from such material were quite rare. Bob's put-down caused great laughter in the courtroom, with most, including members of the Bench, enjoying seeing the QC's embarrassment and his blustering attempts to regain his composure.

Subsequent events give this moment an added piquancy in retrospect, as the QC involved was John Kerr, who later as Governor-General in 1975 betrayed the Whitlam government.* But no matter how fierce the battle in the courtroom had been, at the end of the day Bob was always keen, when he had time, to have a few beers with his principal opponents (but never including Kerr!). I was always intrigued by how easily he could 'flick the switch' from fierce opponent to pleasant drinking companion once the day was done. It

* I remember being on holiday overseas with Dad when he received the news that Kerr had been either appointed or announced as the new Governor-General. He was apoplectic: 'There's no way we can trust that man or the requirement he be impartial' was the gist of it. Despite the complications of an overseas phone call from some remote corner of Greece, he managed to get through to Gough, but failed to persuade him of his view that it was a dangerous appointment. Ironic.

was a transition that I struggled to make but Bob's innate sociability was a key part of who he was.

Later, when he was ACTU President and representing Australian workers at the International Labour Organisation (ILO), the principal employer advisor in National Wage Cases, George Polites, was also there for the Australian employers, and they continued their association as industrial opponents but social friends at that level throughout the 1970s.

But although Bob was exceptionally good as an industrial advocate there was always a feeling about him that that was not enough. A good indication of that came with his acceptance in late 1963 to be the ALP candidate for the federal seat of Corio. Once he was endorsed for it, he gave it, in typical style, everything he had—taking leave from the ACTU, renting a house in the electorate and moving the family there, and working flat out to overturn the incumbent, the former world champion cyclist, Hubert Opperman. One of the concerns Bob (and I) had about the ALP national campaign was the vagueness about how it would be able to pay for its promises. A few days before the election the Labor leader, Arthur Calwell, came to Corio to support Bob's campaign. At the town hall style election rally, Bob spoke for about an hour; as he sat back down, Arthur leaned over and said, 'Congratulations Bob, that's the best explanation I've heard as to how we can pay for our promises.'

Although Bob lost that election, he had a few per cent swing to him in an election where Labor lost ground nationally. When he finally stood for Parliament again in 1980, he had a fuller range of experiences and an extraordinarily favourable national reputation.

In all my time with Bob I can only think of one occasion when he was literally lost for words. That was in the early 1960s after a marathon National Wage Case which had gone on for several months, at the end of which he came with me to a football match: North Melbourne versus Melbourne. I was a North Melbourne supporter and North was a struggling team from an inner-city working-class area in which I had lived in my earlier years.

Somehow, when Bob had moved from Canberra to Melbourne to join the ACTU he'd become a Melbourne supporter. Melbourne was the antithesis of North Melbourne—a highly successful team that had won a string of premierships in the 1950s and that was very much the team of the well-to-do.*

* True, Dad loved sports in general and some in particular. He had deep respect for sportsmen and women—their athleticism, commitment, hard work, their competitive spirit—across the sporting spectrum. But having grown up in WA, and then living for years in Victoria, when it came to football, AFL was his personal code of choice. When we lived in Portarlington during the 1963 preselection campaign in which he stood for the federal seat of Corio (and lost), it included regular attendance at the Cats' home games at Geelong, a team that included the brilliant Polly Farmer, who sadly died whilst we were putting this book together. Dad and my brother's hearts were captive to Polly and the Cats for many years thereafter. It was only after the code was nationalised and Dad and the Swans had left Melbourne for Sydney that he then became a keen Swans supporter.

As the game progressed, to the surprise of everyone, North was doing very well and was right up with Melbourne, which caused much excitement in the North crowd. Bob was barracking enthusiastically for Melbourne when a chap in front of us started to barrack even more enthusiastically for North. His impassioned cries of 'Come on North!' eventually progressed to 'come on the working class!'. Bob was flummoxed to find himself on the wrong side in the football class war and was very subdued for the rest of the game! Later on, when he stood for Corio, he sensibly transferred his football allegiance to Geelong.

One element of Bob's life that totally mystified me was his love of betting on horse races. For someone who was so intelligent and so incredibly busy it seemed to me to be an unnecessary addition to his busy schedule and even an utter waste of time, but clearly he relished what he saw as an intellectual challenge.*

It was an interest that he also shared with the President of the Arbitration Commission, Sir Richard Kirby, with whom he established a friendly relationship. One day when Bob was presenting a case before the Bench which included

---

* I remember that some time after we returned to Melbourne, a chance conversation with author Frank Hardy (remember *Power Without Glory*?) led to them running a betting syndicate of two. It involved Frank in Sydney and Dad in Melbourne attending the races at the track, placing doubles bets with the best odds they could get from the bookies, and sharing their tips and their winnings. I loved it because I often went to the track with Dad on a Saturday and it was great, if slightly unconventional, father–daughter time.

'Dick' Kirby, Bob developed an irritating cough in the mid-morning. As the case wore on his cough became worse and worse until Kirby asked him if he would like a short break. Bob readily agreed and rushed outside just in time to listen to a race in which he had a considerable interest—as, I was later informed, did Dick Kirby. On resumption, Bob's cough had miraculously disappeared!

Even as Prime Minister, Bob often swapped information with ministers who shared that interest, such as Michael Duffy and Gerry Hand. I am not aware that Bob ever stopped a Cabinet discussion so that he could listen to a race, but I wouldn't rule it out! Overall, however, Bob was an extremely diligent and competent chair of Cabinet and ministerial meetings, and indeed it was this that helped greatly to bring the previous Hayden supporters in Cabinet to acceptance of him as Prime Minister.

One area of great tension in Bob's life concerned his relationship with his family. His 'work hard, play hard' lifestyle did not leave a great deal of time for his family and was very hard on Hazel, but he clearly loved his family and greatly valued the time he had with them, as I personally witnessed at various family functions over the years. Indeed, he never seemed happier than when he was spending time with the family. That family should have been four children, but the youngest, Robert, died soon after birth. Bob was really traumatised by that and by the fact that Hazel was extremely ill in hospital following the baby's birth. I attended the baby's funeral with Bob at Melbourne Cemetery. Hazel, too ill to attend the funeral, eventually recovered, and Bob returned to his previous lifestyle. His award as Victoria's Father of the Year in 1971 was one of the great ironies of Bob's life—as for all that he loved and was proud of his family he had hardly been a model father, a fact that Hazel forcibly related to him when my then-fiancée, Carol, and I drove him home on the day of the announcement.

A key aspect of Bob's character was that whatever he was involved in he strove to win. Whether it was sport or games or an argument or an arbitration case, he was always determined to win. That absolute determination to succeed was exemplified by his giving up alcohol once he was elected to Parliament. Drinking in the pub had been such a central aspect of his lifestyle that it seemed inconceivable that he could just stop. Admittedly, the time he spent in the pub was not just about drinking but also the social interaction that he seemed to need at least as much as the alcohol, and through which he forged relationships with many people, including some who were central to his progression to the ACTU presidency. On the downside, he could become very verbally pugnacious and on a few occasions that I witnessed it was only through the protection of friends that he was able to avoid being physically assaulted. So his decision to stop drinking when he entered Parliament was an absolute testament to his determination to succeed. He clearly recognised that in his parliamentary role he could not afford to engage in the kind of excesses of the past that had periodically blotted his career. The will to win was the predominate characteristic and it was that which drove him to successfully challenge Bill Hayden for the leadership of the Labor Party, and which continued to drive him throughout his prime ministership.

A major factor in the success of the Hawke government was its ability to avoid a wage/price spiral of the kind that had been so damaging to the Whitlam government and indeed to the Fraser government. The principal reason for that was The Accord, which Labor, in opposition, had negotiated with the trade unions.

Another important factor in Labor's success in the Hawke government era was the establishment of an Expenditure Review Committee (ERC) of Cabinet. This committee was chaired by Bob, and included the key economic ministers. Its initial development was in response to the budget deficit blow-out we had unknowingly inherited from the Fraser government, which provided a real challenge to our ability to responsibly implement the election promises that we had made, and deliver an appropriate budget bottom line. The ERC's job was to comb through existing expenditures to see what savings could be made as well as ensuring any new expenditures were constrained to appropriate levels. This task was extremely difficult and time consuming but Bob was a competent, well-briefed and fully focused committee chair, not just initially but over the years when the task never seemed to get any easier or be less necessary.*

SPH

Dad and the horses

I include an excerpt from my biography of Mum where I wrote about how Dad started following the horses, which was a big departure from his previous complete disinterest.

> Final preparation and conduct of the case [in Papua New Guinea in 1965, see Paul Munro page 10] was to take several months, so it was decided it would be a good idea, and a good experience for us, to spend that period up there with him, based in Port Moresby . . .
>
> The main hub there for many larrikin ex-pats was the home of colourful journalist Don Hogg. Here, most weekends you would find progressive advisors, academics, journos and the like gathered, with their families and various indigenous activists—all heartily engaged in issues involved with agitating and preparing for independence for the territory, which was to eventuate in 1975.

* I remember one night when visiting Mum and Dad in Canberra, I was going downstairs at The Lodge at about 2 a.m. to get something I'd left in the living room. Dad came home, looking weary and weighed down. I asked him if he was okay, and he answered a bit sadly to the effect: 'Yeah, but just come from a marathon ERC meeting. It's so tough—you have to turn down some really good proposals, trim others—and they are often things that would be good policy and beneficial for people. I hate that part of the job. But the figures have to add up to a dynamic workable budget, or nothing works . . .' I gave him a hug, and we both headed for bed.

As well as the boundless hospitality tirelessly provided by 'Hoggie' and his then-wife Gayle, he was famous, or infamous, for being the territory's unofficial SP bookmaker. The afternoons would be punctuated by discussions of form, placing of bets, and races run in Australia played on the radio, during which conversation stopped and children were hushed. Dad, until then completely uninterested in horses or gambling, figured that 'if you can't beat 'em, join 'em'. He asked a few questions, chanced a few bets, had a few wins and became hooked for life.

He never became a compulsive gambler, but certainly a committed one! He remained fascinated by the enormous complexity of mastering odds and, in time, with the colourful characters of the racing world. He went on to be good at it, with his occasional winnings becoming [along with the odd libel win] a welcome part of the family finances.'

Hazel: My mother's story, Sue Pieters-Hawke, Pan Macmillan, 2011

Bill Kelty

Springbok tour

It was early 1971. We crowded into the ACTU boardroom in Lygon Street, a room designed for eighteen but crammed with over fifty. It was a time when smoking was prevalent and there were no rules. As we waited, the room took on a hazy glow as idle chatter became progressively louder. After a long delay Bob walked in with Harold Souter and Charlie Fitzgibbon. They went to the top end of the table.

Bob was armed with papers, books and photos to which he never referred—they were for warmth rather than reference. He started with a touch of emotion: 'As you know, I would normally get your views but this is something we feel strongly about so before I go around the table let me put my views.'

He talked first about Nelson Mandela, he told of his discussion with him, his plight and his cause. It was as if Nelson Mandela was in the room. Bob made the point that it was not about Mandela, it was about the cause. He took us through the history of Apartheid and the impact on black people. He took us to South Africa, the township of Soweto, the beaches of Cape Town, and the streets of Johannesburg.

He went through the argument about politics and sport being separated. 'They say that politics and sport should be separated but they select a team based exclusively on race.'

He concluded with a strategy. The call for action was quietly and emotionally delivered but at the time it sounded like an army of trumpeters. There was plainly a tear for all to see. They were not the tears of weakness but the tears of determination. He spoke for close to forty minutes, never looked at a note, and there was hardly a murmur.

I think it was the best speech that Bob made. It was the best speech I had ever heard. It still is the best speech I have ever heard.

When he finished, people brushed away the emotion, including some of the toughest union officials in history.

There was no real dissent and, unusually for a union meeting, there was not the normal need for positioning or posturing.

When you walked out of the room you knew that this was a meeting for the ages. The unions and the community took the case to the ships, the ports, the depots, the warehouses, the offices and the streets. Bob Hawke was everywhere a warrior and a fighter.

It did nothing for his standing in the opinion polls [and led to a few death threats*] but it strengthened his position not just in unions but in history.

Racing bets

Bob asked me to go to his home in Sandringham to discuss a submission about the oil industry. I duly arrived at about 11 o'clock on a Saturday morning.

---

* We became used to living with death threats to Dad and came to regard them as a bit of a lark, which is probably a testament to how my parents explained and managed them with us. I remember conversation with Dad about them, when he spoke words to the effect, 'I don't take them very seriously, love. I'm not scared of dying—you go when you go—but we have to let the cops and security do their thing and check them out. If they say I need protection, I suppose I'll have to go along with it, but they're not going to change what I think or say or do. Bugger that. The thing that really gives me the shits is any effect on Mum or especially you kids. That makes me angry.' So, if ever the forces assessed any threat might extend to family, we would spend a few weeks being ferried to and from school, friends etc. Once or twice we were 'hidden' down the farm, which would have been tricky to approach unseen. We'd quiz the cops about their lives, their guns, and anything else, play cards with them, and have a drink with any who hung about after their shift. One threat at the height of the Springbok protests caused a plane Dad and I were on to dump fuel and return to Perth, where Dad arranged for me to disembark with the Everly Brothers and their security team, rather than with him, in case there was anything unpleasant in store there. That was pretty cool!

Bob was at his work table with the racing pages spread out, a slide rule, an old calculator, and a long ruler. He explained that the success at winning on races was to reduce the odds in your favour. A scientific approach.

Within a couple of minutes he received a phone call from Tommy. 'Yes, Tommy. Number something in race something,' repeated a few times.

He explained that it was Tommy Smith.

Not long after—'Yes, Colin . . .' The procedure was repeated. He confirmed it was Colin Hayes.

Just before I was ready to go, another phone call. 'Yes, Roy . . .' The ritual continued. Roy Higgins, he told me. I just waited.

'Well,' he said.

'The trainers have called you. The jockeys have called you. When does the horse call in?' I asked.

He laughed. Threw a pillow at me.

As I left: 'I do have one question. What is the slide rule for?'

November 11: the sacking of the Whitlam government

It was Friday 12 November 1975 when Bob returned to his office. It was the most turbulent thirty-six hours in Australia's history. Gough Whitlam had been sacked the day before by the Governor-General. There was an instantaneous outcry, call for massive industrial action.

Harold Souter, notwithstanding how badly he was treated, was all in favour of more sustained action. When Bob sat down behind his desk at the ACTU he was quiet, the quietest I had ever seen him in a crisis. There was just the three of us: Jean Sinclair, Bob and myself.

'What now, Bob?'

'I have thought about it. The reality is that Labor will lose the election and the next one. People will not easily forget, but Fraser will be poisoned forever. He cannot afford to poison the community, wage war with us. The Labor party will win when we are the people of consensus and we demonstrate that we have learnt our lessons. This will be our platform that will deliver us Government. Nobody is better placed to be PM than me.'

I sat there amazed that in a handful of minutes he had outlined the government's strategy, the unions response, the future of the ALP, and his own future. As I look back I am even more amazed at his prescience. Australia is not for revolution but for ballot boxes. We are for protest and rebuilding consensus.

Telling the truth about the drink and other things

We sat in Hawke's room. The good news was that the majority of Australians wanted him to be the Prime Minister. The bad news was that there was a growing doubt about two things – his drinking and his relationship with women.

As his support grew, so did the doubts. I asked Bob what he thought of the news.

'There are times when you have to take a hard look at yourself without rose-coloured glasses. I have been thinking about it and the best is to be honest with yourself and the people who want you to be PM.'

A few days later he told me was facing up to the issues directly. 'I'm giving up the drink, and I accept that I have not always been the best of fathers. People give you marks for honesty but are always disappointed with deceit.'

One thing that stood out

Bob once asked me at a critical time what I wanted from life. I said that, given my father had deserted us, the most important thing for me was to be a good father.

At that point his eyes swelled. He cried with a sense of remorse that I had never seen before. I did not see it as weakness. Not pity. But understanding that he did give up plenty to dedicate his life to public duty.

Margaret Liessi and Lynette Trad

Alex Macdonald, our father, was Secretary of the Queensland Trades and Labour Council from 1952 until his sudden death on 18 August 1969. He was a member of the National Executive of the ACTU. In 1969 Bob Hawke was seeking to be elected to the position of President of the ACTU. Alex believed in Bob's ability and had lobbied among members of the ACTU executive in support. The ACTU Congress, at which Bob achieved that aim, was held shortly after Alex's death. Bob wrote to Alex's wife Molly on the day of Alex's death.

This is an extract from an address by Bob to the Queensland Trades and Labour Council on 3 September 1969.

> I doubt if there is anyone within the labour movement, however far they may be removed from the particular philosophy to which Alex was committed, who would dispute the fact that his premature passing from our ranks leaves the labour movement, not only in Queensland, but in the whole of Australia, infinitely the poorer. He was unquestionably a man who was motivated by a basic determination to do all in his power to improve the lot of the under-privileged in this country.
>
> I believe that from the life and dedication of Alex Macdonald we can draw a lesson which is important for us all at this stage of our careers in the movement. I believe that it is this: that we all have to realise that the labour movement is a movement made up of diverse parts. There are people within the movement who have great genuine differences of opinion as to what is the best way of undertaking the programme. I believe that the life and experience of Alex Macdonald should make us, at this point of time, convinced of the necessity to recognise the integrity of people who may differ in emphasis and degree from ourselves.

> I hope that in the future we may continue to work together to achieve that one thing which, after all, justifies our existence and that is that we will work together to bring about an improvement in the conditions and quality of living of the workers of this country and their dependants, and importantly, to ensure that their children shall have a full equality of opportunity in this country to give expression to all their talents.

•

In around 1972, Margaret met Bob at the Brisbane Labour Day march. She was pushing her small son in his pram. When she introduced herself to Bob, he said to her son: 'You had a wonderful grandfather.'

Twenty years after Alex's death, in 1989, Bob was Prime Minister and Lynette was working in the Office of Multicultural Affairs within the Department of the Prime Minister and Cabinet. At a departmental Christmas event in Canberra attended by Bob, Lynette approached him and introduced herself as one of Alex Macdonald's daughters. Bob's verbal response included the statement: 'I loved that man.'

These sincere and spontaneous reactions years after Alex's death are touching reminders of the special relationship that had existed between Alex Macdonald and Bob Hawke; the fact that Bob continued to remember Alex so fondly has always been valued by our family.

Robert Fennell

Bob Hawke was a wonderful man who I was fortunate enough to meet personally a couple of times in the early 1970s. At that time I ran a small pharmacy, situated in the heart of Melbourne theatre-land in Exhibition Street, dependent largely upon the sale and manufacture of stage, film and television makeup for survival.

The largest supplier of film and TV makeup in Australia was Max Factor, who distributed solely through Myer Melbourne. I attempted to obtain supplies, but Max Factor refused due to the influence of Myer Melbourne's largest retail store at that time.

When I visited Max Factor's head office in Sydney to attempt to change their refusal policy, the general manager said that they could not supply me because of Myer, and demonstrated with a twist of his thumb on the desk.

Through a mutual friend, Bob Hawke was advised of my dilemma. The circumstances were that my father, a taxi driver, had a regular fare booked each Friday afternoon by a well-known bookmaker; they visited the bar at John Curtin Hotel in Carlton (opposite the Trades Hall), and during their visit they regularly shared a couple of beers with Bob, who also placed a bet or two.

Bob contacted me to see if he could assist. When I told him of my problem, he said that he would check with the Attorney-General, Lionel Murphy. On doing so, Senator

Murphy said that it probably contravened the Trade Practices Act. Bob advised me to tell Max Factor that continued refusal to supply would result in them receiving an order from the Bourke's ACTU Store. When I contacted Max Factor, I was told that they would get back to me, and one week later the Australian sales manager of Max Factor was in my pharmacy to take an order.

That same day, Bob Hawke rang me to find out how the matter was progressing. When I told him, he laughed off my effusive thanks and said he was very glad to have helped. In my interactions with others who knew him I was told: 'He is that sort of bloke.'

Several years later, I met him twice and received a 'get well' card from him when I had a serious illness. My proudest possessions were two biographies of his life (one of which he autographed for me) and that 'get well' card. Unfortunately, I lost these when a carton of our belongings went missing when we moved to Queensland.

His generosity and friendliness affected me deeply and I shall never forget him.

Mal Walden

Memories of Bob Hawke, by the late Ron Casey

It was in June 1972. The Australian Council of Trade Unions had just placed a ban on all French shipping as a protest against French nuclear testing in the Pacific. ACTU President

Bob Hawke was also facing intense pressure regarding his support for banning the forthcoming Springbok Rugby tour in protest against Apartheid. That week, the West Australian Transport Workers Union and Hotel Industry workers voted to accept the Rugby players in Perth, opening the way for their controversial tour.

There were also early rumours suggesting Bob Hawke was considering entering politics and possibly running for leadership of the Labor Party. However, reports of his heavy drinking and womanising were not only running counter to his political aspirations but were placing considerable strain on his family life.

Against this background of breaking news and the growing public interest in Bob Hawke, HSV7 Melbourne invited him onto its Sunday night current affair show, *This Week*. The program was loosely based on the traditional *Meet The Press* format hosted by newsreader Brian Naylor and featured a panel of staff reporters and journalists from the Melbourne *Herald* interviewing newsmakers of the week.

I remembered the show well. Every Sunday night we gathered in the boardroom around 7 o'clock, fed ourselves from several plates of sandwiches and prepared to ply our guests with a modicum of drink from the bar fridge. It was a traditional Sunday night routine. However, on this particular night we found the fridge had been locked by Ron Casey, who feared a repeat of a previous incident where all the liquor had been consumed—mainly by the news staff.

An enterprising journalist removed the hinges and opened the fridge, paving the way for a remarkable series of events. The program was scheduled to be recorded around 8 o'clock and then replayed after the Sunday night movie, which varied from 10.30 p.m. onwards, depending on the length of the movie.

Bob Hawke arrived accompanied by his wife, Hazel. He was already primed for the occasion. This was a man who had earned an entry in the Guinness Book of Records for the time it took to skol a yard of ale. On his arrival he appeared to have just competed in another attempt at that record. The last thing he needed was another drink but it was the first thing he was offered, despite a protest from Hazel. This immediately brought a strong rebuke by Hawke who snapped in a withering tirade, immediately reducing Hazel to tears. Humiliated in front of us all, she left and was driven back to their Sandringham home by one of our cameramen.

As tension mounted, Hawke was led to the studio and a short time later, still on schedule, the opening theme began and Brian Naylor introduced his guest and the panel of interviewers. Throughout the program it was a vintage Hawke, cutting down each questioner in much the same way HSV7 News Director John Maher would regularly swipe at me: 'What sort of question is that? I would expect more from you . . . You call yourself a journalist . . . you're not a journalist's bootlace!' And that was just for openers!

However, the program never made it to air and now, twenty-eight years later, Ron Casey, who was station manager at the time, was prepared to reveal what had happened. How he may have helped save the political career of Bob Hawke and ironically his own future as a legend of television. He began his story.

'It was Sunday 4 June 1972. I was sitting at home that night when a call came through around 9.30 from the producer of *This Week*, Sandra Fitzell. She simply said, "Ron, I have a problem. The program is complete but our guest Mr Hawke is pissed and he has slandered and slurred his way through the show and I don't know what to do. Naylor is demanding we run it, but I have my doubts."'

Casey knew that it would be good television, but fearing the implications for the station and for Bob Hawke himself, he made a decision and ordered the program be destroyed and arranged for a movie to replace it.

The following day Casey received a phone call from a very contrite Bob Hawke. 'Ron,' he said. 'I want to apologise for my behaviour last night and thank you for the action you took. I owe you one, I really do.'

Three months later, Ron Casey left for Munich. The Seven Network had agreed to shared rights of the Munich Olympics in Australia, which would be a groundbreaking television event. Millions of dollars had been invested and sponsors were paying record prices, as this was the first Olympic Games to be streamed around the world in vivid colour. Colour had not yet been launched in Australia but special arrangements had been made at the HSV7 studios in South Melbourne to accommodate sponsors and media buyers to witness this historic live colour feed before it was re-transmitted in black and white.

However, a short time before the Olympic athletes began to file out into the stadium, Melbourne's postal technicians went on strike and the video link from Munich was shut down. There was total panic from the master control centre in Melbourne to the Olympic broadcast centre in Munich. The only man to remain calm was Ron Casey.

'I simply picked up the phone in Munich and called Bob Hawke at his home in Melbourne. "Bob," I said, "I have a problem . . . and you owe me a favour."'

According to Casey, Hawke slammed the phone down, jumped into his car and drove directly into the city. He was seen bursting into the telecommunication centre where he physically pushed the plug into the socket himself. That action connected the Olympic studios in Munich to the television studios in South Melbourne with just minutes to spare. HSV7 did not lose one second of the opening coverage or one dollar of sponsors' fees.

In Munich, Ron Casey was not alone in breathing a sigh of relief. Judy Patching, the Olympic *chef de mission* and Victoria's Olympic team boss was so impressed with Casey's calm reaction and the smooth coverage of the opening ceremony that he responded by giving him his personal phone number.

'Judy scribbled a number on the back of a business card and literally stuffed it in the top pocket of my reefer jacket. "Call me," he said. "Any time. It's the direct number to my room." But then I forgot all about it.'

Two nights later Casey says he was woken by the phone in his hotel room. It was news producer Sandra Fitzell back in Melbourne.

'First thing she said was, "What can you tell me of the Olympic massacre?" The fact is I knew nothing about the events that had unfolded near my hotel. Events that would change my life.'

Tuesday 5 September, shortly after 4 a.m., eight heavily armed members of Black September, a faction of the PLO, scaled the perimeter fence and ran towards the building housing Israeli games officials. A short time later they stormed their apartment, capturing a number of Israeli athletes. When several athletes fought back, the Palestinians then opened fire.

'I sat there stunned as she told me that Arab terrorists had killed several Israeli athletes and others were being held hostage. I told her I would call her back, and then hung up. I was out of bed in a shot and fumbling for that business card Judy Patching had pushed into my pocket. I then called his number and he responded almost immediately. "Come straight round to my room, I have the sole eyewitness with me."'

British silver medallist swimmer, David Wilke, and two of his teammates had been returning to the Olympic Village after celebrating a night on the town. They witnessed two people in tracksuits climbing over the perimeter fence and assumed they were athletes. It was the start of the attack.

Another eyewitness, Israeli survivor Shaul Ladany, described how his roommate woke him claiming that Weinberg had been shot and killed. Ladany dressed and left the room. 'I was half expecting to see a war zone outside our apartment. The first person I spotted was a member of the terror squad wearing what I thought was an Australian hat. He was talking to four of the unarmed village guards and a lady who was pleading, "You must let the Red Cross in; be humane," she said. The terrorists simply replied, "The Jews are not humane."'

These eyewitness quotes were exactly what hundreds of international and local reporters covering the 1972 Olympics were seeking. Meanwhile, in negotiations that followed, the terrorists demanded the release of 230 Palestinians jailed in Israel and Germany. In a failed rescue bid, nine Israeli hostages died along with five terrorists and one West German policeman. The Black September assault and subsequent failed rescue attempt was played out on television around the world, becoming the first terrorist attack reported in real time.

However, the behind the scenes hunt for those exclusive eyewitness scoops was won by Melbourne-based sports commentator and HSV7 station manager Ron Casey. He assumed the duties of a journalist by acquiring the first eyewitness accounts.

From that moment on Casey says he never looked back. He cemented his reputation as an Olympic commentator, not just in Australia but also on the world stage. Recognised by IOC delegates as a media player with clout, he not only went on to cover nine more Olympic Games but also became part of the official team that lobbied strongly for the Melbourne Olympic bid in Tokyo. He became President of the North Melbourne Football Club and served three terms as chair on the Board of the Federation of Commercial Television stations and was awarded an MBE.

After returning from Munich in 1972 he was promoted from Station Manager to General Manager of HSV7. However, in summing up his extraordinary story, he simply laughed. 'In all probability it would never have happened had Bob Hawke not got pissed.'

This is an excerpt from Mal Walden's The News Man, *Brolga Publishing, 2016.*

David Poulter

Bob and Hazel were great friends of my parents, and I remember with fondness my visits to their house as a kid. There is a photo somewhere of me wearing Bob's cricket pads and holding his bat. I, of course, had to have the correct stance for the photo, which Bob set up, and this wasn't easy—I was about five and it was adult-sized equipment.

I remember him bowling to me in his backyard. I remember him showing me how to play carpet bowls. And I remember him at the BBQ, cooking steaks and sausages. I remember going for a cruise on his boat, and I remember mucking around in his swimming pool. It was great fun.

Most of all, I remember him having conversations with me as a little kid and being genuinely interested in what I had to say and how I was going. All of my parents' friends were referred to as Mr or Mrs X. Not Bob or Hazel though; it was always first names. Later in life, I became aware that Bob was not perfect (not that he ever pretended to be), but back then he was just amazing, almost superhuman.

A few years ago, Bob was giving a talk in Canberra and I was lucky enough to go. I managed to fight my way through the adoring crowd to catch up. He was warm, funny and interested, as always. After asking after Mum, Dad and my sisters, he felt the need to tell everyone about the first time he'd held me as a baby. Apparently my nappy leaked, or as Bob put it: 'You pissed all over me!' Funny, yes, and also mildly embarrassing. But I loved it.

Joe Feldman

I first met Bob in the late 1970s when he lived in Sandringham. I worked in the area as a general practitioner, and had developed a reputation for thinking outside the box. I was taking a much needed Saturday night off work when my home phone rang. My wife had just spent the last hour being called multiple times by her mother, and thinking it was her again on the other end of the line, she answered with a curt 'What?'. I remember looking at my wife and seeing her startled face, and suddenly I found myself being shoved the phone. I backed away, gesturing 'no way' signs madly with my hands, thinking that my Saturday night relaxation plans did not include having to deal with my mother-in-law. But it turns out that it wasn't my wife's slightly eccentric but brilliant mother on the other end of our phone, but rather our newly minted Prime Minister.

Having not spoken to him since the election, I exchanged pleasantries and congratulated him on his success as I tried to work out why he was calling me. He got to the point quickly.

'Joe, I'm going overseas and the cops tell me I have to take a doctor. You coming?'

'Hang on,' I said. 'I'll ask my wife.'

In hindsight, I should have given more thought to my response. But in that unexpected moment I could not have realised that my answer would be forever etched into Bob's repertoire of favourite quotes and sayings. Never would I be introduced simply as 'this is Joe Feldman, my personal physician,' without Bob then flowing into his account of how this phone conversation unfolded, usually with creative licence added in for good measure. He told the story with passion and laughter, fully intent on everyone within earshot hearing how his personal doctor turned down his offer to travel the world, pending permission and approval from his young wife.

Over the years, he must have recounted this conversation dozens of times all over the globe, including to various foreign dignitaries. He loved all the dimensions of this story, and in particular, how it reflected the strong women behind the men. For someone who earnt his street-cred in the male-dominated union world, and then continued it into the male-dominated field of politics, he relished the opportunity to highlight the hidden reality, and chuckle over the time he almost got stood up on a Saturday night.

•

It was January 1984 and we were partway through a multi-country tour of Asia. I'm not sure who came up with the great idea to fly headfirst into a northern hemisphere winter for a couple of weeks, but no one was owning up. Nor was Mother Nature being kind to our predicament and helping us transition from the humid and rainy summer conditions we had left behind in Australia, to the freezing cold temperatures that seemed to greet us at every stop. So no one was particularly surprised when the RAAF B707 pilot announced that we were flying straight into a snowstorm as we made our final approach into Tokyo.

As we got closer to landing, the pace in the cabin picked up in total opposition to what you normally see on a commercial jet. We knew that waiting for us, upon arrival, would be a full honour guard and procession of dignitaries, media and Prime Minister Nakasone, so we all had to be ready to disembark onto the tarmac in full view of the cameras as soon as the plane came to a stop.

I had a lot to do. I had three suitcases filled with critical life support equipment, and wherever Bob went, I went, and my medical bags had to go with me. As I made sure everything was in order, I noticed a lot of anxious faces peering out of the windows. Behind them, I could make out nothing but white. We were snowed in, as the pilot had so calmly pointed out a few minutes earlier. I started thinking about how we were going to avoid freezing to death and suffering from hypothermia, whilst trying to smile and shake everyone's hands.

Bob, like everyone else, was out of his seat, busy sorting his bags and trying to work out what he might wear during this apocalyptic weather. He reached up to the overheard cabin and pulled out his Russian ushanka hat that he had bought on a previous trip. Made from the finest mink fur, he loved that hat, and being able to wear it was one of the silver linings for him travelling through this nasty weather.

Bob turned to the staff member responsible for protocol and asked if he could check whether Prime Minister Nakasone would also be wearing a hat. Typical Bob. He was willing to brave the freezing conditions and exit the plane hat-less out of respect to protocol and tradition. I watched the protocols staff member disappear off to the cockpit to relay the message to the pilot who would broadcast the question via the radio. But almost as fast as the protocols staffer left the cabin, he returned, and announced that there was a change of plans. 'No hats are needed. We'll be disembarking on the tarmac and then walking immediately into a hanger. It's too cold to stand around outside, fully exposed.'

Good, I thought. I could stop worrying about Bob getting frostbite.

My relief must have shown on my face. Bob gave me a smile, and before I knew what was happening, he had unceremoniously shoved his mink ushanka hat on my head, gave it a good whack so it was on nice and tight, and tied the earflaps down under my chin. 'There you go, Joe,' he said, winking at me. 'It suits you!' And with that, Bob took his seat, stretched his legs out with great satisfaction, and prepared for landing.

Everyone followed Bob's cue and took their seats. We were now minutes away from disembarking, and the frostbite and hypothermia I had been so worried about just minutes earlier were now the least of my problems. Those issues had been replaced by a Russian fur hat situation. I had a large one stuck to my head and I could not get it off. Bob had managed to tie a triple knot that could've helped hold Apollo 13 together on re-entry. If it were my own hat

I would have just ripped it off, but this was Bob's favourite hat, and he wanted to actually wear this to official functions for the rest of the trip.

Fortunately, I caught a glimpse out the window of many other men wearing hats as we taxied to the hanger. Disaster averted, I thought. Even with Bob having intentionally tied the earflaps down firmly against my cheeks, which is not how the hat is traditionally worn, I figured I would easily blend in enough—and besides, the hat was spectacularly warm. Maybe Bob had done me a favour?

I disembarked, like usual, a few steps behind Bob, and took my place in the official line, as a military band began to play a perfect rendition of the national anthem of Japan. But suddenly, as protocol would dictate, all those other men wearing hats reached up to remove them. Even though I was standing still at the time, I froze for a moment as I contemplated the breach in protocol I was now executing in front of the world. I felt like everyone was staring at me, wondering who I was, and why I was so defiant and refusing to take off my expensive hat. With the TV cameras right in front of me, I started side stepping very slowly, like a naughty kid trying to hide in the shadows. By the time the Australian national anthem started playing I had managed to move out of view of the TV cameras. I looked around nervously to assess the likely damage from my actions. And there was Bob, standing tall and proud as the Australian national anthem continued to play, his eyes glistening with laughter, and a smile on his face that only those close to him could identify as an intentional smirk of 'gotcha!'. I wondered what people thought he was thinking and smiling about when they watched him that night on the news. If only they knew he was trying not to laugh about the prank he just pulled in front of the global media.

•

In August of 1984, we were in Papua New Guinea for the fourth Commonwealth Heads of Government Regional Meeting and the opening of the new PNG Parliament House. Given that it was PNG, we were all a little more safety conscious than normal, but like usual, we had been assigned a dedicated floor of the hotel, and it was the one place where we felt we could relax a little, be ourselves, and not worry too much about any threats. Or so I thought.

One evening, while walking down the hallway to my room, I passed Bob's door and noticed that it was slightly ajar. I wasn't particularly concerned, given the clearances of everyone allowed on the floor, but as I continued past the doorway, I suddenly heard loud, painful groaning accompanied by some other shouts in response. I barged into the room, my mind churning through the options and possibilities so that I could render the correct medical aid without delay.

The TV was on when I entered. The 1984 Los Angeles Olympics was in its second week, and a weight-lifting competition was being broadcast live. I quickly swept the room for any danger and instantly noticed Bob on his knees on the carpet, slouched over, moaning loudly, his left arm contorted behind his back. Two of his advisors were kneeling next to him. As I ran across the room to get a better view of what was going on, I recall being slightly confused at the reluctance of his advisors to assist him. In fact, they seemed to be laughing. Their shouts were not ones of distress, but ones of rowdy competition. Whatever Bob was moaning about, they were encouraging it and egging him on.

Bob continued to moan and groan, and now I could see why. In his right hand was the back leg of a desk chair. He was deeply engaged in an impromptu powerlifting competition to see who could raise the chair off the ground whilst holding onto only one of its four legs, a seemingly simple activity that is actually notoriously hard. Bob was struggling to keep the chair parallel to the ground, as per the rules. The remaining three legs of the chair were barely off the ground, and the chair kept tilting in all directions. He kept moaning and straining as he fought the chair and its desire to topple over. He wanted that gold medal. That podium was his. No way was he letting his advisors beat him and having to then face going home with only the silver or bronze medal.

I don't know if Bob even noticed that I was there. I backed out of the room and let the mini-Olympics continue, and started making plans for addressing any muscular injuries that I anticipated would be presented for repair to me first thing next morning.

Dr Joe Feldman OAM is former personal physician to the Prime Minister.

Neil Mitchell

This story has been told many times and it gets better or worse depending on who is doing the telling. I was eye-witness to only a small part of what happened. Others will have different recollections so take this as a personal memory, not on-the-bible evidence.

He could sing a bit, but Frank Sinatra was not a nice chap. Bob Hawke was, mostly, a nice chap, but while Frank was such a big star, he loathed publicity; Bob was on the way up and breathed it. Bob loved the media, and played it like a violin. Sinatra loathed the media and treated it like a wall through which he would crash or break his head trying. When the two came into conflict, it had to be entertaining. And so it was in 1974.

Mr Sinatra, 'Ol' Blue Eyes' to his mates, had said some nasty things about female journalists. They were, he suggested, hookers. Most Australians thought he was talking about women's rugby, which hadn't yet really been invented. But he was comparing the ladies of the fourth estate to those in the oldest profession. And not favourably.

On behalf of the female members, the Australian Journalists' Association took umbrage, and with ACTU support it was decided Mr Sinatra could not leave the country until he apologised.

Now this Mr Sinatra allegedly had Mafia links, and was not familiar with the concept of apology. He attempted to leave the country. His private jet, named 'Ol' Blue Eyes', was on the tarmac at Tullamarine ready to leave. We believed the plan was for a quick trip to Sydney, refuel, and get out of the country. A concert had been cancelled.

So, as a young industrial reporter, I found myself one evening standing next to Bob Hawke, ACTU President, in some strange behind-the-scenes-room at the airport. We had rushed out so that this ACTU President could negotiate directly with this singer to get the apology, sort it out, defend the dignity of the female journalists, and ride into town on his white horse to the applause of all.

When we arrived Ol' Blue Eyes, the aircraft, presumably with the man on board, was on the tarmac with engines running. (There were later suggestions Sinatra had slipped on to a commercial flight and was not on board. The truth is unknown.)

We were admitted somewhere into the depths of the building, an area where now you would need six security passes and four sniffer dogs before you would be allowed through the door. From here, Bob was in direct contact with the control tower which was in direct contact with the pilot in charge of Ol' Blue Eyes. We could hear their conversation through the radio as Bob issued instructions to the tower.

HAWKE: It's Bob Hawke here. Stop that aircraft. It must not be allowed to take off.
MELBOURNE TOWER: Stop the take off, authority of who?
BOB: Me, Bob Hawke.
TOWER: Oh.
TOWER: Melbourne tower to Ol' Blue Eyes, abort take off. I repeat abort take off.
PILOT: Authority of who?
TOWER: Tower to Ol' Blue Eyes. Bob Hawke.
No reply. Just the sound of an aircraft taking off.
BOB: Well, we'd better go and have a beer.

It was not the end, of course. Ol' Blue Eyes got to Sydney but the airport crews, who did as Bob Hawke suggested, would not refuel it. Mr Sinatra seemed trapped in this godforsaken place, which must have caused him more angst than a horse's head in his bed.

Eventually, Bob flew to Sydney on a commercial flight, not a private jet, locked himself in the Boulevard Hotel with several Sinatra minders, and negotiated a deal. Ol' Blue Eyes, the aircraft and the singer, could leave the country after an apology and a benefit concert. An apology of sorts was thrashed out, the concert went ahead, and Mr Sinatra dined out on the story almost as much as Bob.

He reportedly told a New York audience: 'A funny thing happened in Australia. I made a mistake and got off the plane.'

As for the ACTU President, he had sorted it again. Even Gough Whitlam had said he'd fix this one. The man they called 'the fireman', because of his habit of hosing down disputes, was feted again. And loved it.

Neil Mitchell is a Melbourne broadcaster and former newspaper reporter and editor. He first met Bob Hawke in 1972, as industrial reporter for The Age. *He remained in that role until 1976.*

John Mangos

I started my career at the *Melbourne Herald* in 1975. As cadets, we journalists were transferred between the different rounds. It was during a stint at the Trades Hall that I got to know Bob. We often (almost daily) had a drink together after work across the road at the John Curtin Hotel on Lygon Street. By 1981, I had switched to television and the top-rating National Nine News. At age twenty-four, I was a federal parliamentary reporter for Nine in Canberra, alongside the legendary Peter Harvey.

The political climate at the time was incendiary. Labor under Hayden was in ascendency; the Fraser Coalition government was fraying. But having lost a leadership challenge against Hayden already, Hawke was acutely aware of the pressures on his destiny.

Having survived a challenge from the urbane Andrew Peacock, Fraser sought a double dissolution of Parliament and called a federal election for 5 March 1983. He expected to face Bill Hayden.

On the same day, Labor moved to replace Hayden with Hawke. A bitter Hayden would remark in the wake of his downfall, they may as well have elected a 'drover's dog'.

There were now thirty-one days to power. Because of my already established relationship with Hawke, Nine's Director of News, Ian Cook, made a bold decision. He dedicated me to the Hawke campaign for the entire time, and Harvey to the Fraser camp; traditionally correspondents switched leaders every two or three days.

This earned me a 'title' from Hawke, which I am still proud of to this day. On the last evening of the campaign, Hawke held a private dinner for staff at the celebrated Melbourne restaurant Mietta's to thank them for their incredible dedication and effort. I was the only journalist invited because I had been there every step of the way (hence my name was always top of the RAAF inventory as we traversed the nation). That night, his last as federal Opposition leader, he dubbed me 'the ubiquitous Mangos J'. I cherished the new nickname he had given me and thereafter he used this flattering moniker whenever he greeted me.

The next day, 5 March, Hawke became Prime Minister. There was jubilation by the masses. But we reporters needed to keep filing. It was exhausting and exhilarating.

I remember late night drinks at the Boulevard Hotel in Sydney (Hawke's hotel of choice). Amid the aftermath and analysis, I was asked by several people if it was true that Hawke had invited me to become his press secretary. He hadn't. Mischievously, however, I did not deny it.

Several days later, I received a call from the most powerful and feared executive in Australian television—my boss, Nine CEO, Sam Chisholm. I remember it vividly. 'Get here now. I don't care where you are or what you are doing just get here now,' he barked.

I booked myself on the next plane to Sydney and hotfooted it to his office in Willoughby.

'What's this shit I'm hearing that Hawke wants you to be his press secretary?'

I had no idea what he was talking about.

'What the fuck are you doing thinking about working for Hawkie as his press secretary? You are a brilliant reporter. Go to him and you may not have a job in three years. Here's your new contract, sign it.'

My head was spinning. Whoa. I nervously suggested I should get my accountant to check it.

'Don't check. Just sign,' was the gruff reply.

Trembling, I turned the cover page to page two where the salary was stipulated. I was on $34,000 a year. This contract was for the astronomical $70,000. So I signed on the spot.

Did Bob know? He and Sam were good mates. If Sam had checked with Hawke, I am certain Bob would have worked out what was going on and acquiesced, aware that it would be helpful to me.

I ended up with double my pay and a promotion to become Nine's US correspondent, based in Los Angeles. I will never know if Bob engineered the ruse to help me bluff Sam Chisholm. The delicious irony is that a strong part of Hawke's election platform was the Prices and Incomes Accord, a deal struck with the ACTU to restrict wage demands and minimise inflation. Thanks to Bob, I used the huge increase to spend recklessly and boost the economy.

Robyn Steiner

Back in the late 1970s when Bob was the President of the ACTU, they started up two companies: ACTU Petrol and ACTU Travel. I worked for ACTU Travel. I was hired by Jim Clements to work part-time, as I had a five-year-old daughter, Caroline (who is now forty-three). Bob would quite often come up to say hello to Jim, Coral and myself. My name at the time was Robyn Gwynne.

Bob had an amazing memory, and I have always thought that if I walked past him in the street 30–40 years on, he would say, 'Hello Robyn, how are you etc. etc.' My daughter Caroline now lives in Northbridge with her second husband, Frenchman Aurelien, and their one-year-old son Louis, only a short distance from where Blanche and Bob lived.

No doubt, Bob was a character, and I can remember on Andrew Denton's show *Elders* when he was interviewing Bob and halfway through the interview he asked Bob, 'What do you believe in?' and Bob's reply was 'In myself', and I must say I feel the same way.

Stephen

Dear Sue,

I never met your Dad but, like a lot of Aussies, felt that he was one of us. He loved a drink and was a larrikin and liked sports.

The fact that he left your Mum would have been difficult for you kids and Hazel.

I am one of eight kids and am number five on the list. There are five boys and three girls. We all grew up in Engadine and went to Catholic schools. It's a long-running family joke of Mum and Dad's, trying to wrangle eight boisterous kids to Mass in the 1970s.

Our parents are middle/working class who let us grow up pretty much doing our own thing. The old man still drinks at Engadine Inn, as he has done since the late 1950s. Our parents celebrated sixty years marriage recently and are still going strong. They are a couple of years younger than Hazel and Bob.

Our street in 1960s, 1970s and 1980s Engadine had about sixty kids running rampant. A lot of the kids smoked pot and unfortunately used other drugs. Out of us eight siblings, we had two who have had ongoing struggles. I have not used for maybe nine years, and one sister is battling on. As you know, age is no barrier for using.

When your old man was on TV years back talking about addiction, and got emotional, it proves he loved you. I'm sure you know this.

I know a lot of parents would have felt his pain. I know mine would have.

As you know, most Aussies don't worry too much about politics. I think we hope the man or woman in charge is honest and does the right thing by everyone.

I think most people will remember your mum and dad fondly. I know I will. If I'm struggling, I try to remember happy childhood times. I remember Dad coming home from work and kissing Mum and going round the table and kissing all eight of us, circa early 1970s.

I hope this is a help for you and your book.

Mike Carlton

The Big House lay in wait at the start of Sydney's notorious Hungry Mile, that wide, forlorn strip of waterfront road the old-time wharfies used to tramp in the hope of work each day. These days the place is gentrified as the Sussex Hotel—'a multipurpose venue', as it proudly proclaims—with a trendy Thai restaurant and a clientele of the shiny young millennials who work in the new glass towers of Darling Harbour and Barangaroo.

But back in the day it was the wharfies' pub of choice, an early opening blood house where you could get your first schooner at six in the morning and a fight any time you liked. It was where I first met Bob, in the early 1970s it must have been. A new publican had tarted the joint up a bit, put on free beer, and invited no less than the President of the ACTU to officiate at a grand re-opening. The ABC had sent me along to do a colour piece for that night's TV news.

I had to fight my way through a crush of heaving, bellowing bodies and clouds of cigarette smoke. It was lunchtime but the entire Sydney waterfront seemed to have stopped for the day and turned up.

And there was Bob atop the bar. It was an arresting sight. Bare-chested, he was waving his shirt in the air with one hand and gleefully slurping from a schooner in the other as he cavorted to the music throbbing from the PA system. On either side, two equally but far more spectacularly bare-chested go-go girls—yes, I know, but that was the name—were shimmying along with him. Every so often he would plunge his face into the heaving breasts of one of them, then come up with a grin and a guffaw and another slurp from his glass, to a roar of approval from the crowd. As he drained one drink someone would hand him up another.

Later, I managed to stick a microphone under his chin for a few words to the camera. 'I love it, I love it!' he said, voice slurring.

'Love what, Mr Hawke?'

'Meeting the workers, meeting the workers.'

And I'm sure he did. It was genuine, the real deal. Most professional politicians can 'throw the switch to vaudeville,' as Paul Keating memorably described it, but none ever did it with the elan and sheer enjoyment that Bob Hawke brought to the job.

It's a cliché now that he loved Australians and they loved him back but, like most clichés, it rests on bedrock. His critics and political foes would sneer that the fame and adulation massaged his ego and that's probably true, but I'm sure he derived from it the strength and courage to follow the conviction of destiny that eventually took him to the prime ministership. I think it was the journalist Mungo MacCallum who first called him 'The Folk Hero'.

I saw it time and again over the years. Gregarious and inquisitive, he craved company. There was no arrogance to it, no pretence, no condescension. Once, after a radio interview at 2UE I took him to lunch in the beer garden of a pub in North Sydney and he held court there all afternoon, chatting and cracking jokes with all comers and scribbling the occasional autograph. As word spread that he was there, more and more people crowded in just to catch a glimpse or shake his hand.

After studio appearances on the ABC's *This Day Tonight* current affairs program at Gore Hill in Sydney he would lounge around in the Green Room for hours afterwards, skolling the taxpayers' beer and swapping gossip and rumour, grist to the mills of politicians and journalists. 'And I told fuckin' Gough, if you pull that stunt we're rooted . . .'

One night in Melbourne, one of the *This Day Tonight* wives, there with her husband, had had enough. 'Bob, it's high time you fucked off home to Hazel,' she snapped. Startled, he meekly obeyed.

With the extraordinary willpower of a driven man, he shucked off the drinking and carousing to attain the prime ministership and, to the best of my knowledge, he stuck to it. But, happily, he never lost that larrikin touch. Nor his capacity for humanity and compassion, displayed so memorably in his public tears for the dead kids of Tiananmen Square in 1989.

I have another image of him in the Prime Minister's office of the Old Parliament House one Saturday morning, where I'd gone to do an interview about something or other. Tie undone at the neck, feet up on the desk and smoking a cigar the size of a zucchini, he was alternately chatting and listening intently on the phone. Every so often he would solemnly scribble a note. I asked one of the minders who he was talking to. A Cabinet minister, a captain of industry, the President of the United States? It turned out to be his mate Roy Higgins, the jockey, with tips for Flemington and Randwick that afternoon.

Like so many, many people I am grateful that I met Bob Hawke, and I hold his memory warmly. I'll leave the political judgements to others. But, head and shoulders, he was the greatest Prime Minister of my time, and probably all time.

Mike Carlton is a journalist.

John Hewson

Bob was the highly intelligent, educated, larrikin who made Prime Minister. He brought our country out of the recession of the early 1980s united by his Accord, and then led a genuine reform agenda through to the early 1990s. He redefined Labor, and to some extent our nation. He was certainly the best Labor leader since WWII, and arguably our best Prime Minister since then. He understood people and had a fine sense of our national interest. He was a Great Australian.

Probably the first time I ever heard of Bob Hawke was from a comment by my father, in the 1960s. Dad didn't talk much at home about politics, indeed not about anything much at all but, on one of my evenings spent in our small tight garage, while my dad washed his car, which he did almost every day, he mentioned that I should watch that smart, young, union bloke, Hawke—apparently a Rhodes Scholar, to boot—even though Dad would have had no idea what would have made a Rhodes Scholar, given his qualifications and employ as a fitter and turner.

I only came to recognise Bob's political significance in the early to mid-70s. He first loomed large on my radar when I was working for the Reserve Bank of Australia, having returned from the International Monetary Fund and graduate studies in the US, attending a 'We Was Robbed' lunchtime rally in the Sydney Domain in the election campaign of 1975 that followed Whitlam's dismissal. Bob could certainly work a crowd, even though that message then was doomed to fail.

When I joined Treasurer Lynch's staff in 1976, I soon recognised Hawke as a significant, formidable, and increasing political force to be reckoned with, through his role as ACTU President, and especially with the National Wage Cases, on his entrance to Parliament in 1980, and as a mounting threat to, and inevitable replacement for, Hayden as Opposition leader.

I vividly remember the day that Bob assumed the leadership of the Opposition—it was a day that defined Bob's fate, assured his place in our history, and ended the Fraser government. Malcolm had been advised, indeed I believe that there had been a Cabinet determination, that if the ALP ditched Hayden for Hawke, Malcolm should delay the election for about a year. It was expected that by then the world economy would have pulled out of the early 1980s recession, which would have seen us in recovery with about a six-month lag, plus it would have given Malcolm and his ministers a year to 'destroy' Hawke in the Parliament, where it was widely expected that he would have been a 'hopeless performer'. Malcolm thought he knew better—'I can beat Hawke'—a fateful call.

Hawke essentially won in 1983 on his popularity, and the feeling that it was time to give someone else a go. The electorate had tired of Fraser, who had fallen well short of its expectations. Hawke went on to win, and again, beating Peacock twice (in 1984 and 1990) and Howard once in 1987.

But Bob's legacy is not just these electoral wins, or the tag as Labor's longest serving Prime Minister, but the way he ran government, provided national leadership, and for what he achieved in policy terms.

In personal terms, Bob wore his life on his sleeve—all the ups and downs, the excessive drinking, women, marriage pressures and the breakdown, kids, their drugs, whatever. In a sense, we all lived the highs and lows with Bob. His larrikinism dominated all of this, as did the America's Cup win, and so on. People related to Bob, and he understood, and related to, them.

I must admit my embarrassment in the role I apparently played in his downfall. I am told, and it is today widely acknowledged, that it was Bob's inability to respond effectively to my Fightback! package that provided Keating with the issue to replace him as Prime Minister. What can I say? Keating did, and I lost.

We may not learn from history, but we should never let it be rewritten. Bob Hawke's achievements should be recognised and recorded. I recall the enormous momentum that the Fraser government had built, on the back of the report of the Campbell Committee, to deliver financial sector reform. The snowball had been set rolling by Fraser, but Hawke's contribution was to deliver it—bank deregulation, licensing foreign banks, and floating our dollar. (Bob told me, personally, soon after the decision, that he had had to drag some ministers to that one.) It shouldn't be forgotten how significant these achievements were, given that the ALP still had 'bank nationalisation' in its official policy platform when it won the 1983 election.

Bob's contributions spread across most areas of economic and social policy. Again, although it had been the Fraser government's agenda to spread financial sector reform to the goods market and to infrastructure, Hawke did it, and pretty much without the accusation that he had sold out to the Liberals.

He started the process to reduce tariffs, the inevitable move to enterprise wage bargaining, to reform of the tax system, and to start to privatise government assets (such as the Commonwealth Bank), as well as to initiate the drive to what was called 'micro-economic, structural reform'. Moreover, he initiated APEC, introduced the Family Assistance Scheme, along with pension reform, and many others.

I was fortunate to share many memorable and enjoyable occasions with Bob, both within and beyond politics. There is, of course, the now famous photo hanging on the wall of the Parliamentary Press Gallery that recorded the two of us comparing 'knives'. There was also the most memorable time when we lead a collection of remaining veterans to Gallipoli to commemorate the 75th anniversary of that fateful, but nationally defining, landing. This was very early on in my time as leader, but I was impressed by Bob's (and Hazel's) warmth and graciousness—I was never made to feel his lesser. His spirit on that occasion was genuinely bipartisan as, indeed, it was as we worked together behind the scenes to reach agreement to extend the term of Parliament to four years—an opportunity Keating never took up, on assuming the leadership.

We also shared many sporting experiences and events. At one golf game, at Palm Meadows, Queensland, I think, Bob was teamed with Greg Norman, and I with Ian Baker-Finch. Bob's tee-shot on the first was a 'shocker', a duck hook into the crowd, indeed wounding a member of the public gallery. Bob immediately strutted to the front of the tee shouting out 'Jesus Christ!' He then resumed his composure, claimed a 'Mulligans', and moved on with his game—no penalty, of course.

At the end of the round he was greeted by the local Labor member, very concerned at the reaction of some of his constituents, who had feared that Bob was a 'blasphemer'. However, Bob was quick to both deny and to reassure when he announced that, 'No, I am certainly not a blasphemer—I had just hit a shitty shot and was appealing for Divine Intervention!'

On another occasion, an AFL Grand Final Breakfast at the North Melbourne Club, in terms of the custom, Bob and I were expected to make a few remarks. Following Bob, virtually as he sat down, I asked him to join me at the lectern to assist me with my remarks. Without thinking, he arrived just as I said—'Knock Knock'. 'Who's there?' he responded. 'Paul,' I said. 'Paul who?' he said. I couldn't resist it, 'So you've forgotten him already!' Bob was a little surprised but I doubted that he was at all embarrassed.

At most sporting events that we attended together, Bob would always choose his moment, and always before the cameras, to say 'I'll bet you a hundred bucks' that the team he favoured would win, or that he would beat me. This happened several times, but that was usually the end of it. Bob was notorious for never paying out on such wagers. But, on one occasion, I pursued him and, under my threat of calling a media event if he didn't pay up, a member of his office arrived with the payout, but also with the firm statement that 'this might be the first, but it would certainly be the last.'

In our latter years, post-politics, Bob and I did a number of significant business functions together across the country. He was always paid more than me, as it should have been. His usual joust was, in saying how much he admired me, that he could 'never forgive me for giving our nation John Howard'. 'If only,' he said, 'you had put the GST in the bottom drawer, as I advised repeatedly, and pulled it out after the election, you would have won, and Howard would never have become Prime Minister!'

Of course, he was right, in that sense that, yes, I would have defeated Keating. But, in my political naivety, I believed that politicians should 'tell the whole truth, and nothing but the truth'. And, much to my disadvantage, I still do!

Please remember Bob, for what he was, for what he achieved, and for what he tried to do in our national interest. He contributed much, more than most—he was a Great Australian. It was an honour for me to have known him, even as political opponents.

Dr John Hewson was leader of the Liberal Party, and of the Coalition in Opposition, 1990–94.

Marjorie Johnston

Bob the everyman

Bob was a sportsman—a great cricketer and a keen tennis player. He loved to get out on the tennis court at Royal Avenue with his friends and watch when Sue and I and our boyfriends had a hit. He had the critic's eye. I was a good, but not great, teenage player, but in doubles I had trouble on the baseline. I will never forget Bob taking me aside after watching me lose a point and say in his direct way, 'You could be quite good if you only ran for the ball. Don't be lazy.' It's advice I often think about today when I'm not trying hard enough—and I can still hear him say it.

Sue's boyfriend and mine were good friends in Beaumaris, and they organised a 'fathers and sons' cricket match at the Beamauris High School oval one weekend over summer in the late 1970s. As students we were all cricket mad. It was the era of the Chappell brothers, and the Windies tours. Two girls played on each of the teams—I was on the 'sons' side. I had to face the bowling of Bob Hawke and was very nervous. He sent the ball flying down and I stepped out and smashed it for a four. I think I'm the only female to have hit a four off the bowling of Bob Hawke—and I only wish I'd been able to hit a six!

Bob the historian

It was just fantastic to listen in on the times when Bob was talking about an aspect of Australian history and, in one particular case, it was R J Menzies, Australia's longest serving Prime Minister. There was nothing Bob didn't know or understand about the Menzies era—he had grown up in it.

But the best part was to see a group of his children's friends gathered around, hanging on his every word. I wish I'd had a tape recorder, as his insights were gold for the budding history student.

We would sit around Bob, who was in his favourite lounge chair, and listen to him run us through all the years of the Menzies-era opposition moments, including his soundings on Dr Evatt and Gough Whitlam as the key leaders back then. His knowledge was both wide and deep, and his ability to make connections with current times was astounding.

Bob the scholar

I was lucky enough to visit Bob's family home when Sue and I were on a uni vacation in Perth. Sue showed me the desk in the sleep-out where he had studied when he was younger. Mrs Hawke, Bob's mother, still had some of Bob's school books on the shelf. Sue said to me, 'This is where Dad studied and worked so hard over his books.' As a student and as someone interested in the background story of great Australians, I have always felt very lucky to have seen what was, effectively, a time capsule. It made a huge impression on me and helped me understand, having seen something very personal in Bob's boyhood, the drive and intelligence of the man, but also the loving support of his family and their ambition for their son.

Mike Rann

I first met Bob Hawke in 1978 when I was working for South Australia's Premier Don Dunstan and Bob was National President of the ALP. At that time, in totally different ways—with Gough Whitlam now off the political scene—Bob and Don were perhaps the two most charismatic leaders in Australian Labor politics. By this stage, of course, Hawke had been a national figure for almost a decade as President of the ACTU. He was also a force of nature. He'd walk into the front bar of any pub, pick up a billiards cue, take on all comers, and win. It was the same with poker. In fact, it was pretty much the same with everything and, as we know, he could down a beer faster than anyone in the world . . . and had the Guinness World Record to prove it!

Every Saturday morning, after consultation with racing identities around the country, Bob would phone mates, like Mick Young, swapping tips for the afternoon gallops at Flemington, Randwick or Morphettville. MPs and trade union leaders who received his tips would talk admiringly of Hawkie's luck—the punter with the golden touch.

For Bob Hawke, however, these years in the late seventies were amongst the wildest of times, and none wilder or potentially more dangerous than his appearance at the 1979 ALP National Conference in Adelaide and his public brawl with Bill Hayden. It wasn't pretty. It was ugly, and alcohol-fuelled, and commentators started to write off Bob's chances of reaching what had always seemed his destiny: to become Prime Minister of Australia.

By this stage, that destiny had been talked about for decades, ever since Bob was a small boy, at least in the eyes of his loving parents, Ellie and Clem. Bob was born in the small South Australian community of Bordertown, in the district of Tatiara—the local Aboriginal word for 'good country'—275 kilometres east of Adelaide, close to where the Overland train crosses the Victorian border. Clem was the local Congregationalist minister but politics as well as God were always present in the manse on Farquhar Street. Clem had, for a brief time in his early twenties, been General Secretary of the South Australian branch of the ALP. Clem's brother Bert was the Labor MP for Burra Burra in the State's mid-north, before moving to Perth to be elected to the Western Australian Parliament, eventually becoming leader of the party for more than fifteen years, including six as premier in the 1950s. Right from the start Ellie believed her son was heading for greatness, and she was particularly influential with him, if you don't include her advocacy for the Women's Christian Temperance Union.

In 1987, as a backbencher, I was asked to accompany Clem, the gentlest, most humble man, to the unveiling of his son's bronze bust on Woolshed Street in Bordertown. I will always remember that journey. For hours in the car Clem told me stories of Bob's childhood in Bordertown and then at Maitland on South Australia's Yorke Peninsula, and of his teenage years in Perth, and studies at UWA and Oxford.

As I wrote to Blanche last week, listening to Clem was to hear the most loving psalm from a proud father about his son. Bob himself said of his dad: 'He passed on to me the fundamental beliefs I have, and that is: we are in this world not just to advance our own interests, but we owe an obligation to our fellow human beings.' Bob particularly abhorred racism and fought it wherever it raised its ugly head, and again quoted his father who taught him: 'If you believe in the Fatherhood of God then you must also believe in the Brotherhood of Man.' Blanche said that Bob would today have added, and 'the Sisterhood of Women.'

The prediction that his political career had flamed out at the 1979 ALP Conference proved short-lived. Bob gave up the grog in 1980 and stayed off it after he was elected as the Member for Wills, and then through the period that he was a shadow minister, leader and Prime Minister. I worked on a number of elections for Bob, particularly in Canberra on his marginal seat strategy in 1987, where Labor came from behind to win a third term, beating John Howard. I have never seen anyone better on the campaign trail. His connection with Australians young and old, men and women, country and city, and from every background and race, was visceral and tactile. His campaigning never, ever stopped. For the almost thirty years that followed the end of his prime ministership, Bob would come to Labor campaign launches around the country and show our candidates and MP's what real campaigning was all about. He was always there for us, all of us. It is fitting that his last public act, the day before he died, was to write and sign an endorsement of Bill Shorten and Labor.

These days, unfortunately, we live in times when so many 'leaders', including some in Australia in recent years, seek to further their own interests by dividing people, pitting them against each other. In contrast, Bob sought to bring disparate Australians together in the national interest. Again, there has never been anyone better at doing so.

The dismissal of Gough Whitlam by the Governor-General in 1975 bitterly divided Australians, and for many that bitterness soured the Fraser years. In his 1983 victory Bob Hawke promised to bring Australians together. Soon after, as Prime Minister, Bob convened the National Economic Summit on the floor of the House of Representatives of what is now known as Old Parliament House. It was extraordinary to watch: the leaders of big business broke bread with trade union leaders, often for the first time, and in some cases forged lifelong friendships. Together, they and the other participants at the Summit put aside sectional, partisan and even state interests, and agreed on a program of economic recovery that demanded both effort and sacrifice. Out of this process came the Accord, the prices and incomes compact with the trade unions. Only Hawke could have brought that off. He demonstrated that 'consensus' wasn't a code word for weakness, and he earned the authority to stand up to unions and business when it was in the interest of the nation to do so.

A great deal has been said about Bob Hawke's extraordinary popularity with the Australian people, who loved him warts and all. His colourful, 'reformed larrikin', persona added to his authenticity. But it was a two-way relationship. As has been said by others, Aussies loved Hawke because they knew he loved them.

Bob's popularity wasn't an end in itself. Rather than the Whitlam approach to 'crash through or crash', Hawke wanted to win, win again and keep on winning. So his high approval rating was political capital to be paid down. It was about managing political gravity in order to get things done. As a result, his name, character and contribution defines a transformational era in Australian history. The Hawke government was about freeing up the Australian economy, and that flowed on to Paul Keating's compulsory superannuation scheme that now has more than $3 trillion invested in building prosperity and improving the retirement incomes of Australians. These economic reforms were embraced, along with his government's twin pillars of providing greater opportunity and security for Australians, at the core of Labor's credentials.

The achievements of the Hawke government included an embrace of Asia that has been fundamental in underpinning twenty-eight years of continuous economic growth.

Socially, of course, there can be few reforms more fundamental to the Australian way of life than Medicare. Every Australian carries an enduring monument to Bob Hawke in their wallet or purse: their Medicare Card. It is so powerful a symbol of security for the health of Australians, young and old, that no subsequent government dares to tear it up.

The reform agenda was across the board. In education it led to a massive increase in young people completing their schooling and going to university, and the biggest ever roll-out of childcare places. In the environment, the Hawke government saved the Franklin River rainforests in Tasmania, protected the Daintree in Queensland and Kakadu in the Northern Territory. In Aboriginal Affairs, it handed ownership of Uluru back to the traditional owners.

In international affairs, the Hawke government was about our country stepping up and projecting our identity, character and values to the world. We became a bigger, more confident Australia under Bob Hawke's leadership. It was his government that demonstrated that our new economic relationship with China could coexist with our fundamental security partnership with the United States.

A decade ago, when Kevin Rudd was Prime Minister, we gave Bob life membership of the ALP. It had only been presented to two others before: to Gough and Margaret Whitlam. In his acceptance speech, Bob talked about his hard fought but successful campaign to save Antarctica from mining. However, he said his proudest achievement was his campaign to end Apartheid in South Africa. It was Bob Hawke who defied Margaret Thatcher and led the Commonwealth of Nations in applying sanctions that finally broke the Apartheid regime. In this cause he had a hinterland. As President of the ACTU he had applied the bans that prevented racially selected teams from competing in Australia. This history was the reason why Nelson Mandela singled out Bob for thanks as a key figure in bringing about the end of Apartheid.

When I think of Bob Hawke there are enduring images. They are of Bob looking lovingly at his elderly dad. Of seeing him in 2003 coming out the door of the Westminster Parliament with Bill Clinton, Tony Blair and Nelson Mandela. They had been at the 100th anniversary of the Rhodes Scholarship, and at the dinner the night before he had been challenged to equal or better his world record more than fifty years before, of downing a yard of ale in the same glass, in just eleven seconds. I asked him how he did it. He said, 'It's all in the gullet mate, you don't drink it, you pour it down.' I asked how it went and he replied, 'I didn't break my record but I gave it a bloody nudge.'

Another image is of Bob and Blanche dancing at Sasha and my wedding in 2006. They were easily the best couple on the dance floor and Bob, wearing a long coat, was twirling Blanche around with his tails flying, our Fred Astaire and Ginger Rogers.

And in 2008 there was a dinner at Bob and Blanche's

house on Sydney Harbour where, in a night of reconciliation, Bob and Paul Keating shared stories, shared history. There were great yarns about Ronald Reagan and the Queen; about the goings on at Andropov's funeral; impersonations good and bad; campaign war stories; a recitation of Dickens by the British actress Miriam Margolyes; and even a proposal of marriage by a visiting French Count.

I am not religious, and neither was Bob, nor Gough. Whitlam was asked, 'but what if you find you were wrong, what will you say to God if you meet him?' His reply was instantaneous: 'I will treat him as an equal.' So, if there is a heaven, I'd like to think that they've now got a larrikin up there, still carousing, chatting up the angels, or puffing on a giant cigar, a beer in hand while reading the form guide . . . still campaigning, still winning, and still getting things done.

Tribute to Bob Hawke—Memorial Service, Australia House, Friday 7 June 2019

Some additional memories and thoughts about Bob

I was very supportive of the Hawke Centre in Adelaide, which does great work, but it would not have been a success without Bob's constant attention and involvement. I remember him phoning me very late one night to ask for a few million for his International Centre for Muslim and Non-Muslim Understanding. He had also phoned Julia Gillard. Two phone calls and it was funded!

Peter Watson, a friend of mine from uni days in New Zealand who has lived in Washington for decades, worked for George Bush Senior and sat in (silently) on calls between Bob and Bush. He said they got on brilliantly, with Bush greatly respecting Bob, but said it was hard to type up the notes because the jokes they both told were so filthy. Peter would have to collaborate creatively the next day with the Australian ambassador to reach an agreement on an acceptable text to put into the system.*

The Hon. Mike Rann AC is former Premier of South Australia.

Malcolm Brown

As president of ACTU, Bob attended the Coffs Harbour Cup Race Meeting. On meeting him in the Committee Room, and thinking that he was more at home in Melbourne, I remarked, 'Aren't you a bit out of your territory today?'

Quick as a flash, his reply was, 'Australia is my territory!' and I was well and truly put in my place.

Stephen FitzGerald

I got off the early flight from Canberra, and as I headed to the exit I heard a familiar voice call out: 'Hey Fitzy, d'ya wanna share a cab to the city?'

---

* See anecdote by Peter Watson on page 243.

'Sure,' I said, always glad to see him.

It was the late 1970s, and Bob was still at the ACTU, and President of the ALP. As we got into the cab, he started to tell me about his previous day. Early flight to Perth, meetings, long lunch with drinks, more meetings, pub at around 5 p.m. for a few hours' drinks on union matters, back to the airport, drinks at the airline club lounge and a delayed 'red-eye special' flight to Melbourne boarded after 1 a.m., and more drinks and minimal sleep on that most exhausting of all domestic flights in Australia.

He asked about China, and said he'd recently been in Tokyo, where he'd met Cabinet ministers and senior corporate people, and amongst other things had discussed China. He then proceeded to give me an analysis of Japanese thinking on China, of astonishing clarity and recall given his preceding twenty-four hours. Illustrated with verbatim quotes from his conversations, and elaborated with historical context on both Japan and China. With, for good measure, his own interpretation of China's likely path now that Mao was gone.

It was one of those rare and unexpected moments when you can see into a complex and layered mind and discover something you hadn't seen before. It was not Bob on a podium. It was Bob stream-of-consciousness. But what a stream! He would never have claimed to be an expert on Asia, but here he was, with a reading of Japan and China worthy of the best of experts. His intellectual side on sparkling display.

I've told the story often, against prevailing images of Hawke the politician, mediator, larrikin, or whatever other larger-than-life aspect of his trajectory was currently on view (not that I didn't love them too, or most of them). And I thought of it often when he was Prime Minister. He introduced the term 'enmeshment' as the objective of our relations with Asia. And he had the perfect combination to take on the challenge of engaging with China at the highest level. He had the intellect, the interest, the statecraft, and—and I can vouch for this—he liked, really liked, Chinese people. Oh, that we could have such combination in just one leader today!

Stephen FitzGerald is a former diplomat, and Australian Ambassador to China, 1973–76.

Luke Harrison Vardanega

I grew up in Sandringham when Bob and Hazel lived over on Royal Avenue. As kids, we knew that they were special but didn't know why. Hazel was popular amongst the local mums, including with our mum who had stopped to talk to her once at the local shops. The Hawkes lived rather palatially and had a tennis court. Everyone in the neighbourhood knew the house.

One summer day, Hazel came across our local gang playing street tennis and she offered us the use of their court. She was so lovely, and around we went and started playing. Some time later, a chauffeur-driven car arrived, and Bob poured himself out of the back seat. He was completely pickled—even as kids we knew the signs. When he spotted us on the tennis court he went apoplectic, yelling at us to get off his property. We scarpered up the road and heard Bob shout, 'Next time fucking well ask!'

When we got home we told our parents. My dad thought it was a huge joke. He was a journalist for *The Age* and seemed to know a lot about Bob. My mum was disgusted at the language. She kept asking, 'He said what?' and we had to repeat his words but using the word 'effing'. Mum was shaking her head and saying, 'You know he won Father of the Year?!'

A few weeks later, Hazel spotted us playing street tennis again and re-offered the use of their tennis court. She told us not to worry about Bob and said he had just been in a bad mood. We were a bit hesitant but it was an offer too good to refuse so we went around and started playing.

An hour or so later, the chauffeur-driven car turned up and out rolled Bob. He appeared drunk again. When he spotted us, we thought he was going to have a heart attack, he looked so furious. We didn't wait to be told, and ran away as fast as we could. Bob's shout followed us up the street, 'Next time fucking well ask!'

We never went back to the house and I don't recall ever seeing Hazel again. But many years later I met Prime Minister Bob Hawke at a Parliament House function and told him the story. Would you believe it, he remembered the incidents, and even corrected me as to some of the details, and said that Hazel had told him off for it. According to him, Hazel had not told him until later that she had given us permission. More likely, in his intoxicated state he had not remembered.

Tony Blair

My first memory of Bob was actually through my father, who had been a lecturer at Adelaide University in the 1950s and had met Bob then—something of which my Dad was inordinately proud! I remember him saying—this is back in the 1970s when I became politically active—that Bob was a great model for a Left politician and trade unionist, combining instinct for the people with a high-grade intellect and common sense.

Then in 1982 I met him, shortly before he took over from Bill Hayden, and though I was a complete nobody at the time, and had just managed to get a meeting through Kim Beazley, he gave his time, great insights and inspiration. Later on, I got to know him well and as I went up the political ladder, he was one of the people I looked up to and consciously took as a guide. I consider that he would have been a giant in anyone's politics and it was Australia's good fortune he was born Down Under.

Tony Blair is former Prime Minister of the United Kingdom, and Executive Chair of the Tony Blair Institute for Global Change.

Barry Donovan

In the late 1970s Hawke, then ACTU President, was considering his future. Most supporters wanted him to continue as an outstanding union advocate, while some backers wanted him in Canberra.

At a Friday session at the John Curtin Hotel in Carlton, Bob asked me privately what I thought about his options. As a journalist, I'd covered his roles as an ACTU advocate and as President from 1970–79. I said, 'Bob, you should now go as far as you think you can go.'

He nodded and said 'okay' . . .

Hawke, of course, was an astonishing combination of talents: Oxford graduate, an ACTU advocate and president but one whose down-to-earth attitude earned him national respect and affection.

With Hawke as ACTU President in the early 1970s, business contacts were made that foreshadowed the employer–union Accord that was to be a feature of the Hawke's government ten years later.

Lionel Revelman and his family owned the Bourke's retail store in Melbourne and saw the value of going into partnership with a body that then had 1.2 million blue-collar members.

By chance, I bumped into Revelman late one day in Lygon Street and asked him how the ACTU deal would turn out. He said: 'There are only two definite things in life—taxes and death.'

Lionel was on his way to play tennis with Bob that night. They had played one set and Lionel was preparing to serve, when, to Bob's shock, his friend collapsed and died. It was a terrible event, one that stayed with Bob for the rest of his life.*

Excerpted from an article that first appeared in the Herald Sun.

Katrin Ogilvy

Bob and Hazel Hawke came to visit Caulfield Hospital (Rehabilitation and Aged Care) in the late 1970s/early 1980s. I worked in medical administration and showed them around some of the wards, the physio and occupational therapy departments, and the sheltered workshop. I remember well how Bob was so relaxed and interested in the people he greeted. Even the most withdrawn and grumpy felt a connection with him. And naturally, Hazel showed the same warmth and interest in everyone too.

Helen Polley

I was living in West Coburg, the electorate of Wills, when I first meet Bob Hawke. Before my father died and Bob was even elected to Parliament, my father told me he thought

* I remember the friendship, beyond business, between Lionel and Dad and our families. Dad broke the news to us, sobbing, 'He died in my arms . . .' He was devastated, subdued for weeks, and remained saddened by Lionel's early death for a long time.

Bob Hawke would one day be Prime Minister. So, can you image how excited I was to volunteer on Bob's campaign when he won Wills for the first time?

Many years later, on my return to live in Tasmania, I was elected as a proxy delegate to the National Labor Conference in Canberra, and I was invited to the Right Caucus—my first experience of party activities at such a conference. There I was surrounded by all the Labor luminaries and who came up to speak to me? Bob Hawke! I have never forgotten how he listened to me. He was so engaging. He had the ability to make everyone that he met feel equally as important.

We met on many other occasions over the decades and he never failed to engage in the art of conversation, and always had the ability to leave you feeling equal. It is an important skill, and one that few politicians have today. Bob Hawke was a great communicator, larrikin and Australian. It's well documented his outstanding contribution to Australia's economy, his humanitarian leadership, and his vision for a fairer and more equal society. But it was the man himself who inspired so many to be better Australians and to take on leadership roles.

David J F Gray

In 1981, as a 25-year-old ALP candidate for the very marginal Liberal-held seat of Syndal in the Victorian Parliament, I was very keen to have the recently elected MHR for Wills, Bob

Hawke, assist in my campaign. The Opposition leader, Bill Hayden, had formally opened my campaign rooms and I'd got good local coverage, but I knew that if Bob came to assist me my campaign would be greatly enhanced.

I was very excited when he agreed to come to Syndal and do a couple of shopping centre walks with me and give a speech in a local school hall. He arrived in a business-like mood, obviously keen to get on with it as he had a very busy schedule. He was in great demand with ALP candidates across Victoria, as we were trying to end twenty-seven years of Liberal–National Party government.

I nervously greeted him and engaged in some brief pleasantries, and then Bob asked me a technical economic question about the Syndal electorate. I had no idea of the answer, and he let me know in no uncertain terms that it wasn't good enough—as the candidate for a very winnable marginal seat that Labor had to win to form government, it was my obligation and responsibility to be completely on top of the facts, figures and issues. He was right, of course, and it was a lesson learnt for me. He didn't hold a grudge, and the rest of the day went off extremely well.

I was successful in winning Syndal in April 1982 and was fully immersed in being part of the Cain government—the first Labor administration in Victoria since Cain's father was premier in the mid-1950s.

Bob replaced Bill Hayden as Opposition leader in early February 1983, just as Prime Minister Fraser was announcing a federal election date. In the lead up to these events, the issue of the proposal by the Tasmanian government to dam the Franklin River had become a major controversy and a looming issue in the federal election. Bob had made it clear that if Labor won, it would stop the dam. As a committed conservationist, I had already resolved to visit the proposed site of the dam and to join the blockade which Bob Brown and the Tasmanian Wilderness Society had commenced. I had the backing of my constituents and Premier John Cain. My resolve was strengthened by Bob Hawke's promise, and as I was being arrested I took comfort in knowing that he was likely to become Prime Minister soon and that he would deliver on his commitment.

My next personal encounter with Bob was after he had become Prime Minister. He once again agreed to visit Syndal to deliver a major speech in a large school hall that held around 800 people. The hall was packed out and I had the honour, as chair of the meeting and as the sitting local state member, of introducing him. He had been speaking for about five minutes when a small group of noisy 'Right to Lifers' began disrupting his speech. No matter how hard he tried, and despite the obvious displeasure of the bulk of the audience, they were bent on stopping him.

At this point I walked to the podium, and declared that as the chair of the meeting I was exercising my common law powers to direct the police officers to eject the protestors unless they immediately desisted their interruptions. After the offenders had been removed, Bob was able to continue his speech without further trouble, and he spent a considerable time afterwards mixing with audience members. He afterwards gave me a wink and said words to the effect, 'well done, young man'. I felt that my earlier failure when he was last in my electorate had been expunged!

I lost my seat in 1985 and went back to the law. In 1988, I won a scholarship to study Chinese (Mandarin) at the Beijing Language Institute for two years. On 4 June 1989, I was in Beijing when the Tiananmen massacre occurred. In those days there was no internet, and the worried relatives of Australians in China at that time were frantically trying to get information about their loved ones. Among those worried relatives was my mother, Beverley Gray. As it happened, Bob was attending a function at the progress hall in the small central Victorian town of Maldon where my mother lives. My mother managed to buttonhole Bob to ask him for any information about my safety and whereabouts, as she'd not been able to get any information. My mother vividly remembers Bob calming her down, telling her that he remembered me and would do what he could to find out where I was and to let her know. She was subsequently advised that I was safe. To this day, she has very warm memories of the way Bob listened to her and reassured her, and I in turn have always been grateful to him for doing so.

I last saw Bob in 2004 at a function to mark the 100th anniversary of the first federal Labor government. I reminded him of his support for me when I was a state MP, and his reassuring my mother in 1989, and thanked him for what he had done for the country. I have fond memories, and, despite some reservations, think he was a great Prime Minister and a very interesting human being.

Chris Hayes

Much has been said of Bob Hawke so far and much more is yet to be said, but he certainly was a man who believed in Australia, and I think it's fair to say that Australia believed in him. He was a true son of the labour movement, but I believe, beyond that, he was probably Australia's greatest agent of change. There is no doubt that our nation will be forever in his debt, I think, for the magnitude of change that occurred under his leadership as such—not only the structural reform of our economy but also our outlook as a nation.

As a young union official at the time, I was in awe of Bob Hawke's passion and determination that championed the lives of working men and women. I remember how he inspired us in his capacity as President of the ACTU. Even then, he was a household name—he was as well known as any public official in the land.

I remember him being at the forefront of major industrial disputes. He was a skilled negotiator, a fantastic advocate in the Industrial Relations Commission. But, above all, what I remember about him in those days is the way he sought consensus. He was universally respected—whether it was employers, employee representatives, government or elsewhere, this man commanded their respect.

My earliest recollection of him was his ability to persuade strong and powerful unions to moderate their industrial positions to ensure that workers in some of the weaker sectors of our economy were not left behind. No doubt that had some bearing on his thinking after he came to government in 1983, about the Prices and Incomes Accord—the idea of a social wage. He genuinely cared for all workers.

Most of us know him as Australia's longest serving Labor Prime Minister. He will be forever remembered for his work in transforming the framework, particularly the economic framework, of this country. He and Paul Keating were such a formidable duo. It wasn't that they did this by strength; they did it by encouraging people with the argument that we can be better. He deregulated the financial sector. He floated the Australian dollar. He opened up our economy to the world. He caused us to be a more confident nation, and certainly a more outward looking country.

However, it's not just these great achievements in the economy that he will be remembered for. He was also an avid believer in the environment, and he knew wholeheartedly the importance of increasing the government's focus on environment protection. To this end, he pushed for the protection of Antarctica.

He led a UN taskforce at a time when international interests were keen to have mining of some description in Antarctica, and sympathetic states such as the UK and the US certainly thought there was scope to have regulated mining in Antarctica. Hawke sought international cooperation. It wasn't that he opposed mining there—he went one step beyond. He wanted to get a blanket prohibition on mining in the Antarctic, and, after securing the support of the French, he then systematically found allies in other international arenas and he established exactly that. His effort in Antarctica not only prevented mining; it brought the focus of scientific research, which is now so critical to our understanding of climate change itself.

He also fought on many other fronts: protection of our natural environment here at home, the prevention of the damming of the Franklin River, protection for the Lemonthyme and Southern Forests in Tasmania, and the Daintree Rainforest in Queensland; and the banning of uranium mining in Jabiluka and Kakadu's Coronation Hill. He pursued these on the basis that he saw their World Heritage value and these parts of our environment deserved to be protected. He didn't do this to get a vote. He did this in the genuine belief that, for future generations, the natural beauty of our country needed to be preserved. 'The essence of power is the knowledge that what you do is going to have an effect, not just an immediate but perhaps a lifelong effect, on the happiness and wellbeing of millions of people . . .'

Bob Hawke's investment in education and in universal healthcare are a stark reminder that he worked not only for Australia—he worked for every Australian. At the start of Bob Hawke's prime ministership in 1983, only three out of ten kids completed high school—three out of ten! By the time he left the prime ministership, it was eight out of ten. He set us on the path of becoming a smarter nation. The benefits that flowed from that were improvements in tertiary education, HECS, et cetera. Really, getting more young Australians to finish high school did materially affect where we are now.

Through his more persuasive efforts, he convinced significant elements of the trade union movement in this country that looking after workers wasn't just about awards and pay rates but also included looking after the dignity of people in their retirement. In 1983, very few blue-collar workers enjoyed retirement benefits. Through his efforts we saw the birth of universal superannuation, one of the greatest advances for workers in generations.

He had an unshakable belief in our nation's potential. He thought that we could be a better nation, and in his government he set about achieving that. He had a very down-to-earth manner about him. He was a genuine personality, and Australians followed him over the eight years of his prime ministership.

One of the other things that I do remember vividly is how moved he was following the massacre at Tiananmen

Square. He felt that so personally, and it was right after that, that he let thousands of Chinese students who were studying remain in this country. It also showed his great depth of humanitarian spirit. But for many, the efforts of Bob Hawke also led to our nation becoming a more inclusive and open country. We are now certainly the net beneficiaries of the extent of immigration that has occurred in our land. But we have also seen the great depth of humanitarian spirit that did flow from those efforts, particularly as a result of the massacre in Tiananmen Square.

Before I leave his humanitarian aspects, what I think has also got to be seen as an enduring legacy of Bob Hawke is his work to end Apartheid in South Africa and his efforts to free Nelson Mandela. It was his selflessness and forward thinking that really reinvigorated the Australian spirit—namely, we can make a difference for the better in our world.

Following our defeat in 2013 and as we moved into 2014, as the Chief Opposition Whip, I thought that it would be beneficial if we had a function where we got Caucus members—and also, importantly, their staff—together. It wasn't to put Band-Aids on things, but I think we did need to reinvigorate our party at that stage. And we thought: who would we get who would inspire the notion of Labor and get us back fighting for reform, fighting for change—those things that Labor's best known for? We actually got Bob Hawke to come, and it wasn't difficult. He asked me, 'What do you want me to do?' and I said: 'If you could, just speak to the dinner for maybe ten to fifteen minutes. Just give people a bit of a rev-up.' He said, 'Ten to fifteen minutes?' 'Yes, Bob, that'd be marvellous.'

Fifty-five minutes later—meanwhile, the entrees and everything else were getting cold—everyone was still spellbound by this bloke. He had taken us through every major Labor initiative. He said, 'This is where we need to go for the future.' And then he actually broke into the song 'Solidarity Forever'. Most of us could at least hum along with the chorus, but Bob knew every verse. He had such a great night.

Jill Saunders, who was Bob's PA and who worked with him in Parliament House and who was working with him as a former prime minister—this was getting late in the night—said to me: 'Look, I've got to go. I'm going back to my motel. He's now your responsibility.'

We were going to be sitting the next day, so everyone was peeling off and leaving. It got down to where there were only about three or four of us left. One of them was me, of course, because I had the responsibility to get him back to where we had to go. There was Bob and my wife, Bernadette, who was trying to encourage him out because they were turning the lights off in the Press Club. One of the waitress's friends said, 'Mr Hawke, it's her birthday today, she's turning twenty-three.' That changed everything. He had this young woman come over. He put his arm around her. Then he sang to her, and this went on and on. By the way, we had to have another drink while all of this was occurring, of course.

When we left, the lights were going out. There were only about three of us left walking out of the Press Club. Fortunately, I had a car waiting that only had to go 100 metres up the road to Hotel Realm. I got him up there and got him to his room.

A couple of weeks before his death, I got a call from Craig Emerson. He said that Bob's been having a few discussions with Blanche about what might happen after. As long as I've known Bob, despite the fact that his father was a religious minister, I don't think Bob really thought there was another God-head other than Bob—that's probably putting it inappropriately. Anyway, I thought he was a lifelong committed atheist.*

Craig suggested to me that he'd just like to have a talk to someone, and asked if I knew anyone who could go and sit with him and have a talk. He said: 'There are a few things. It's got to be someone who has some Labor leaning.' I said, 'Okay, we can do that.' And then he said, 'But someone who is sympathetic to trade unions.' So that

---

* Dad was never a committed atheist—he simply lost faith, firstly in the Church as an institution, and then in any certainty of belief in God. So although he no longer identified as Christian, he fiercely maintained a belief in the progressive values of the Congregational Church in which he'd been raised, and in its primary value of caring for our fellow humans. He was unconcerned about the God part by the time I came along, but was open and respectful about any and all forms of faith that motivated people towards caring positively about others.

narrowed the field a little. Anyway, I had a talk to Bishop Terry Brady in Sydney. I had known that Bishop Brady's father was an official in the Building Workers' Industrial Union. I was told by Craig that Blanche had agreed that it sounds like I had the right bloke, so Terry went over to see Bob on a very warm autumn afternoon. Terry sat in the sun while Bob spoke to him. I think Bob probably did most of the speaking while enjoying his large cigar. Bishop Terry told me, 'I sort of sat downwind of this cigar, soaking in the aroma.' He said, 'I'm not sure who got the most out of all of that.' I'm not sure where their spiritual discussion went, but I certainly know that Bishop Terry got a heck of a lot out of his meeting with Bob that afternoon.

It is a privilege to have been a part of the labour movement. I worked with Bob Hawke through his time at the ACTU and I've seen what he achieved in this place when he was able to continue to care for Australian working families in such a material way by making the changes that have enabled what we currently have. He has put us on the path for advancement. He has changed the way we think about ourselves. This man has made a difference for the better in our country. To Blanche and to his children I offer my sincere condolences. To Bob Hawke: may you rest in peace.

Edited excerpt of condolence motion, House of Representatives, 3 July 2019.

Chris Hayes is federal Member for Fowler, and Chief Opposition Whip.

Christine Anthony

Who would ever think how much my life would change after coming to Australia? My family and I migrated from London in 1982—two kids, husband, and mother-in-law, arriving in Sydney in August. After a few months I finally found a job as a house mother/cleaner at the New College Randwick, working alongside five other cleaners.

After a few months, the college decided to lay off two cleaners. After meetings and much debate, I was approached by the Miscellaneous Workers Union to become a union delegate representative to help regain the jobs of the two sacked cleaners. Being raised in the East End of London, I was familiar with the great work unions have done. I was happy to take on this task, and happily satisfied after just a few days, when the two cleaners regained their positions.

After moving out west to Penrith to begin life in our own house, in 1983 I took lessons in how to make stained-glass. There I met John Papa, the teacher, an ALP member who belonged to the local branch, which I then joined. At the same time, I began work on the campaign for one of my favourite, most charismatic and down-to-earth politicians, the one and only Bob Hawke, who everyone loved. And what a great moment for everyone, when Bob was elected Prime Minister of Australia and went on to lead till 1991.

After moving to Caloundra in Queensland in 1989, I became an active member of the Currimundi Branch, now the Caloundra Branch. I put my hand up for the state election in 2001. As risky as it was, I decided to run as a state candidate in a staunch Liberal seat. My campaign manager, Mick Graham, was full of great knowledge and wisdom, particularly when it came to politics and all things related to Bob Hawke. Mick had previously worked closely with Bob, and had many fascinating stories of this great man, and he arranged for Bob to do a meet-and-greet for my campaign at a working man's pub at Beerwah.

It was an honour for us all to meet Bob, and along with followers and friends, it was great to see Bob receiving the same greetings that he always did, everywhere he went.

My photo was taken at the pub, and it included Bob, Blanche, the federal ALP candidate for Fisher, Ray O'Donnell, my daughter Bonnita Anthony, and myself. I was humbled by the presence of the great man, and his appearance was one of the highlights of my campaign. I will always be grateful to Bob and Blanche for making the effort for me.

My first election was a fantastic experience that took place a few weeks after this photo was taken. I have always been convinced that Bob's presence made a great contribution to my campaign. Unfortunately, I did not win, but the experience was worth every moment.

John Bertrand AO

September 14th, 1983, Newport Rhode Island, USA. First race for the America's Cup. Best of seven races, first to win four. The Americans had never been beaten since before the US Civil War. One hundred and thirty-two years of American domination!

We, the *Australia II* team, had successfully beaten off all challengers (the Brits, French, Canadians, Italians) to now have the right to race against Dennis Connor and his US Defender *Liberty*.

Bob Hawke and Paul Keating were in town for this first race. Presumably they had stolen away from an international monetary conference in Washington!

The might of America's dominance was on show. US Naval Coast Guard ships in the harbour, a US Navy battleship stationed offshore. Helicopters overhead.

We were just about to leave the dock. 0900 +/- 5 minutes. Our Boxing Kangaroo battle flag was about to be hoisted, our battle hymn 'Down Under' by Men at Work, to be played over our loud speakers as we prepared to leave the dock to do battle at noon.

Bob came down to our boat, the *Australia II.* I was in the stern of the boat behind the steering wheel. I greeted our new Prime Minister. 'Ah, welcome Prime Minister.'

'Call me Bob,' he said. 'John, what are you going to do?'

How do you answer a question like that? All the years of dedicated work, preparation, training and now about to take on the might of the USA. So I simply said, 'Well Bob, we'll give it our best shot.'

'Bullshit. Destroy the bastards!'

He nailed it. How good was that! Typical of the great man. He understood—he got it.

Several years ago, as chairman of the Sport Australia Hall of Fame, I and the Hon. Rod Kemp, director of the Hall of Fame, had the great honour of inviting both Bob Hawke and John Howard to become co-patrons.

Bob said, 'If he's in, I'm in!'

Well, to have these two old warriors together was quite something. I believe it was the first time they had been involved together for a common cause such as this.

The first meeting was fantastic. Bob picked me up in his chauffeured limo, and off we went to Mr Howard's office. On meeting they kind of circled around each other, then the common language of sport quickly clicked in.

John asked me when the Sport Australia Hall of Fame had started. I said 1986. Bob corrected me—1985! I asked how he knew. Bob said: 'I read the briefing paper. But apologies, I'm a bit slow this morning, I've been up all night playing baccarat with my Chinese mates at the casino, so I'm a little slow. We won though!'

That was the start of an incredible sporting partnership between two of our greatest prime ministers. The way they interacted at our various exclusive functions was both memorable and awe-inspiring. Wisdom and humour.

John Bowan

In November 1983, as Prime Minister Hawke's International Relations adviser, I accompanied him to New Delhi for the first Commonwealth Heads of Government Meeting of his prime ministership. As leader of Australia, Bob found himself sitting next to Sir Lester Bird, Deputy Prime Minister of Antigua. Bird was a very tall figure, who had been a long jumper of international class and a good cricketer. I sat behind Bob.

At one point in proceedings, Mrs Indira Gandhi, the Indian Prime Minister and chair of the meeting, announced that there was an important issue for the leaders to discuss that was not on the agenda. She gave the floor to Sir Shridath 'Sonny' Ramphal, the Commonwealth Secretary-General. A draft resolution was circulated that subjected the United States military intervention in Grenada, which had taken place the previous month, to vigorous criticism. This resolution was clearly not popular with the majority of Caribbean delegations, including Antigua. They opposed the overthrow of the democratically elected government of Grenada and so did not fundamentally object to the US intervention, which was heavily criticised in the draft resolution.

Ramphal spoke strongly in support of the resolution, as did Forbes Burnham, the president of Guyana. Mrs Gandhi called for speakers against the resolution. Having been taken completely by surprise, none of the Caribbean leaders took the floor, and Mrs Gandhi suggested tentatively that the resolution could therefore be taken as approved. An angry rumble of protest broke out at this point, including from Sir Lester Bird. Bob leaned towards him. 'No, you were just lengthening your run, weren't you?' he said. It would be difficult to come up with a more appropriate, friendly expression to a fellow-countryman of fast bowlers Andy Roberts and Curtly Ambrose. The draft resolution was decisively rejected. Bob's friendly expression of understanding for Lester Bird contributed to that outcome. Brilliant diplomacy by Bob.

Rod Cameron

Early in his prime ministership, Bob and I were alone together, waiting for the arrival of one of his advisors. After some small talk, he asked me if I could answer a serious question, one that I was not to take as vainglorious. Sensing a trap from a mind as sharp as steel, I reluctantly agreed. He asked me why I thought he was so popular.

Perhaps foolishly, I took him seriously and embarked on a serious answer. I told him that the common response would be that he was a real Australian who could relate to people at all levels. But, I said, it was more complex than this—that he combined two key character traits not usually found in men, particularly men in politics. That is, he was literally strong—often to a fault, sometimes unnecessarily aggressive—but undeniably strong. However, and this was the unusual part, he combined this with a compassionate and emotional side. And that with this combination, he suited exactly the national mood at the time—that is, someone strong enough to knock heads together, but also someone understanding and emotionally intelligent enough to find compromise as an empathetic conciliator.

It might have been a trick played by the morning light filtering through the windows at Old Parliament House, but I think I noticed a slight twinkle in Bob's eye as he said matter-of-factly that he thought I was very perceptive.

Rod Cameron was the ALP's pollster and strategist, 1972–92.

Professor John Langmore AM

On Sunday 6 March 1983, the day after the election, Bob Hawke as the Prime Minister-elect had to focus on the exchange rate. In the last week of the election campaign Andrew Peacock (who became leader of the Coalition after the election) had claimed that if Labor won, it would have to devalue the Australian dollar.

John Stone, Secretary of the Treasury, asked to see Bob on Sunday morning, when he presented a memo arguing that the Coalition had been squandering money in the last months of government, with the result that the incoming government faced what he described as a 'devastating deficit'.

When I returned home from church there was a phone message from Paul Keating's secretary telling me to come to a meeting with Treasury officials that afternoon in the basement of the Canberra Lakeside Hotel. At this meeting, rather than giving Paul the normal comprehensive briefing book which all departments are expected to present to their incoming ministers, the officials passed over the same memo that had been given to Bob that morning. The memo said nothing about the economic policies Bob and Paul had been advocating during the election campaign; it argued only that the highest priority was to cut public expenditure. The officials argued that the Fraser government had left Labor with a projected budget deficit for 1983/84 of $9.6 billion, and reducing that should be the new government's preoccupation.

After the meeting we went up to Bob's suite.* When we arrived, Bob was resting on the couch, exhausted by the campaign and the previous evening's victory celebrations. Everyone agreed that a devaluation was necessary.

---

* I remember when Dad came back up to the suite—we were all sitting around together, digesting the momentous change that had occurred, and were excited about what may now happen in the country. Dad came in, looking anything but celebratory. When we asked him why so grim, he replied along the lines of: 'The bastards lied about the deficit. We have an enormous problem on our hands.' The next days were a blur of urgent meetings. Welcome to the realities of governing.

The economic strategy Bob and Paul had been advocating during the election campaign was for growth of Commonwealth spending on health and education services and infrastructure investment to support economic expansion. This would swiftly begin the process of reducing unemployment, which was over 11 per cent. Inflation would be constrained by the Accord, which Bob and Ralph Willis had negotiated with the ACTU and which had been adopted at the Labor National Conference in 1982.

The meeting with Bob decided that we should talk informally with Mr R Johnston, Governor of the Reserve Bank, as early as possible next morning, and meet again after the financial market closed for the day.

Bob decided to go straight to Kirribilli House, the Prime Minister's official residence in Sydney. Paul and I joined the VIP flight to Mascot and the convoy of Commonwealth cars which drove us to Kirribilli. Bob and Hazel were welcomed by the staff and we started the meeting immediately.*

* Those few hours were an introduction to some of the personal 'behind the scenes' aspects of Dad now being PM (although he was, I think, to be officially sworn in the next day). Convoys of Commonwealth cars, a dedicated RAAF plane, deferential 'servants' in black and white uniforms opening doors and serving dinner, bells to press for a cup of tea—it was as if we had gone down the rabbit hole and landed in a parallel universe. Having grown up around a diversity of people, but in an ethos best expressed in the back bar, wage cases struggling to obtain a rise in the minimum wage, hoary old unionists, and the Vietnam Moratorium marches—it was a bit of a shock, to say the least.

Over time, Mum and Dad modernised what they could, especially in relations to staff, who were 'servants' no more. See note after Gordon Mair's piece, page 190.

Mr Johnston had recommended to Paul devaluing by 10 per cent. This was quickly agreed, and a statement was drafted for release next morning. Paul rang John Howard, who was still nominal Treasurer until Labor was sworn in. Then we went in for dinner.

Though this was a celebratory meal, conversation was desultory. Everyone was deeply weary. As we stood to leave Graham Freudenberg said a few words. 'Bob, the people of Australia have elected you to the most powerful position in the country. This is the highest honour you can receive and gives you enormous responsibilities. We know that you are committed to using these great opportunities to improve the wellbeing of all Australians. We know that you will seek to make Australia a country where there is work for all who want it; where disputes are peacefully resolved; where rights are respected, and social justice is the goal. We will do our utmost to support you in reaching for these demanding goals. I am reminded of Pope Leo the Tenth, who on being elected to the Papacy said, "God has called us to the Papacy. Now let us enjoy it!"'

Most of the guests then disbursed, but Bob said to me, 'Come and we will talk about the Summit'. While he had been chairing the National Economic Policy Committee in 1981 and '82, we had talked about holding an economic summit and that had become part of the plan for government. It was to be a clear expression of Bob's vision for building a national, consensual, economic strategy. So we went to the sitting room and talked about and planned for the Summit for three hours.

In the middle of the evening Bob said he wanted a cup of tea, so told me to ring the bell and ask for it to be brought in. I pushed the only button I could see, and immediately two security guards rushed in! I should have pulled a cord, and on doing so, tea and cake were quickly supplied.

About midnight Bob was ready to go to bed so I said I had better leave. 'Where are you going to stay?' he asked. I hadn't given that a thought. So, he generously said, 'You should stay here', and I was shown to an elegant bedroom upstairs. I woke at first light, incredulous at what had happened, dressed and went downstairs to sit on the veranda and watch the sun come up over the harbour.

After breakfast we flew back to Canberra for Bob's media conference to explain the devaluation. When we reached Canberra, Bob went straight to the media conference and I met with Sir Geoffrey Yeend, Secretary of the Prime Minister's Department, to discuss the plans for the Summit.

During the next six weeks I reported to Bob on most days about progress with preparations, and we discussed the planning issues. An interdepartmental group prepared a major background report. The Summit was held in the House of Representatives chamber from 11–14 April. It appointed a representative committee chaired by Bob to draft a communique, and this was supported by all but one participant, Joh Bjelke-Petersen.

After the Summit Bob sent letters of thanks to those who had been involved in the organisation. On mine he had handwritten: 'You should be especially happy with the Summit's success.'

Anne Summers

Advancing the status of women in Australia: Bob Hawke's legacy

It was February 1983 and I was one of the media pack accompanying the newly-minted leader of the Opposition as he did a street walk in a mall in the central business district of Brisbane. The federal election campaign was in full swing and Bob Hawke was attracting devoted crowds wherever he went. On this day, a middle-aged man, who appeared to be a migrant of European extraction, approached him and pumped Hawke's hand effusively. Hawke looked at him intently and asked: 'Haven't we met before?'

'You would not remember me, Mr Hawke,' the man replied.

'Give me a moment.'

He needed less than that. 'I know,' Hawke declared triumphantly. 'It's George, isn't it? I met you in Melbourne!'

The man could not contain his pleasure, or his amazement, at being remembered by this great man. 'That was more than twenty years ago, Mr Hawke!'

For we in the travelling press it was just one of many examples we would witness during that campaign of Bob Hawke's extraordinary ability to connect with ordinary people, to remember their names and where they'd met and to appear utterly sincere in his enjoyment at seeing them again.

I watched in awe and admiration. I had known Bob Hawke for about twenty years, since his days as ACTU advocate, and as a journalist I'd tracked his seemingly inevitable progress to the prime ministership of Australia. Not all of his colleagues shared Hawke's belief that he was the best—no, the only—person for that job but they had nevertheless decided to install him as their leader the very day that Malcolm Fraser called the election. For we journalists it was a riveting story: the imperious and unpopular Fraser being stalked and then decisively beaten by the charismatic man of the people.

The Hawke government was going to be a hell of a story. I had no idea then that before the year was over, I would leave the Press Gallery to become part of that government. Doing so gave me unique insights into the man and the way he governed—especially into the way in which women's policy, the area that I was hired to run, was so integral to his social and economic policy. I was disappointed that none of the obituaries at the time of his death mentioned this important contribution, and of those who spoke at his memorial service at the Sydney Opera House on 14 June, only Bill Kelty, Secretary of the ACTU while Hawke was Prime Minister, mentioned Hawke's record on women. But he gave no details, so I decided to put on record some of the remarkable and, in many ways, revolutionary changes for women in Australia that took place under Bob Hawke's stewardship.

There were many reforms, large and small, that benefitted women enacted during the Hawke years, but I will concentrate on just three.

I was appointed to run the Office of the Status of Women in the Department of the Prime Minister and Cabinet in December 1983, a position I occupied for about three years and where I was charged with developing, or promoting, the policies that were the bedrock for these reforms.

The three I want to concentrate on were landmark achievements because they each achieved a significant expansion of women's opportunities to participate in the world outside the home: the *Sex Discrimination Act 1984*, the *Affirmative Action (Equal Opportunity for Women in Employment) Act 1986*, and a massive increase in spending on childcare.

Many of these reforms for women had been developed, and shepherded through Caucus, by Senator Susan Ryan, who would become the first Labor woman Cabinet minister when Hawke appointed her Minister for Education and Youth Affairs and Minister Assisting the Prime Minister on the Status of Women. But there was considerable political opposition to all these reforms including, when it came to childcare and affirmative action laws, from within Hawke's own Cabinet. As Ryan herself would be the first to acknowledge, without the strong endorsement of the Prime Minister they would not have happened.

Hawke was not just presiding from on high on these issues, as I discovered when a number of Cabinet submissions relating to them were returned from the PMO (Prime Minister's Office) with little annotations in the margins. They were mostly notes of encouragement to me! Written by the Prime Minister himself. Wow! I thought to myself, these are worth keeping. I stuck them in a personal folder in my filing cabinet, intending to take them home eventually to place among my papers.

That was until a senior officer from the department came to me and asked if I had any returned cab-subs. Sure, I readily admitted, as I did not think I had done anything wrong. I was quickly disabused of the idea that confidential Cabinet documents could be housed anywhere other than the archives where they would be preserved for thirty years before being made public. And, no, for the same reasons, I could not make photocopies of Hawke's notes to me. Every Cabinet submission was numbered and tracked. Which was how they had known where to look for those that had mysteriously disappeared after being sent back from the PMO.

The Sex Discrimination Act changed Australia in a fundamental way. For the first time there was federal protection against discrimination on the grounds of sex (what is now more often referred to as gender), marital status and the condition of pregnancy in employment, and in the provision of a range of goods and services. In practice, this meant that it was now against the law to treat women differently, to deny them employment because they were pregnant, for instance. Or because they were married.

This law was the very first in the world to outlaw sexual harassment. (This was back in the days when Australia was still a world leader in social reforms including, importantly, in the area of women's policy.)

The Liberals opposed this law. They did not want equality for women. It is almost impossible today to explain the hysterical reaction from those on the Right who claimed this legislation would destroy the family and turn women into either raging sex maniacs (working alongside men!) or desexed creatures robbed of their femininity by having to labour in offices or factories.

The opposition to policies designed to enable women to participate in employment and education revealed the fundamental fault-lines in Australia then when it came to pursuing women's equality. Or, as we described it back then, improving the status of women.

One of the most fiercely contested economic views at the time was that married women were taking jobs that rightly belonged to teenage boys. Such talk, of course, ignored the fact that the labour market was even more highly segmented by gender than it is today and there is no way that a teenage boy was in competition for a job with a married woman. But the argument revealed the prejudices of the time. And the determination of some that women should remain within the home. How else to explain the savage opposition, from within the bureaucracy, within Cabinet and from many in society, to the proposal to vastly expand the provision of childcare?

When I was unable to get support from the bureaucracy to expand childcare I undertook the highly unorthodox step of negotiating directly with Hawke's senior personal staff. Normally, public servants did not thwart process by working directly with political staff but I was not a conventional public servant. I did not care about my 'career'. All I wanted was to advance policies of benefit to women. Fortunately, there was an election looming (held on 1 December 1984) and Hawke and his staff were receptive to a big women's policy announcement. I met very early one morning with a Hawke senior staffer at the motel where he stayed while he was in Canberra, and we went over the policy costings that I had drawn up with the secret assistance of two sympathetic staffers from the Office of the Status of Women.

At the time, there were just 46,000 government-subsidised childcare places in the whole of Australia. We knew that for women to have access to education and to employment, they needed childcare. The Whitlam government had established the principle of federal government-subsidised care, but there had been virtually no expansion of places under the Fraser government (1975–83).

We proposed to Hawke, and he agreed, to double the number of places and to adopt a formula that would lead to a rapid expansion of places over the next four years. When Hawke delivered his election campaign policy speech, the biggest single budgetary commitment was for 20,000 new childcare places. This would ultimately be the first tranche of the planned expansion.

Similarly, Hawke took head-on the opposition to the affirmative action legislation. These laws were designed to complement the Sex Discrimination Act by requiring employers to report on the numbers of women they employed, and their seniority and their pay. This was intended to spur increased female recruitment but was, of course, opposed by those who thought women's place was—still!—in the home. To signify his strong support for this law, Hawke took the highly unusual step of introducing the bill in the House of Representatives. Normally, prime ministers do not introduce legislation.

He had also given his strong personal support to a pilot program we had run with more than twenty of Australia's largest companies, as well as three higher education institutions, to test the proposed laws (to demonstrate that they would not end civilisation as we knew it). Hawke agreed to write to the CEOs of each of these companies asking them to participate. It was an invitation that only one CEO—ironically enough his close friend Sir Peter Abeles who ran Ansett Airlines and TNT transport company—initially declined. I had to go and meet with Sir Peter and reinforce the PM's invitation with some additional persuasion. He came on board.

There was initially a lot of scepticism from many people, especially women, about whether Hawke would be an ally. He was, after all, a renowned womaniser, a larrikin, a man's man and not someone who you'd automatically assume would support feminist issues.

I was reminded of this side of him when I travelled to Kirribilli House, the Prime Minister's official Sydney residence, in January 1984, just weeks after I had started in the job. I had been asked to help Hazel Hawke draft a speech to deliver to the National Press Club on Australia Day.

The staff had directed me to go round the front of the house to where Hazel was waiting on a verandah that overlooked the glories of Sydney Harbour and the Opera House. I was, of course, wearing the regalia of the femocrat: beige suit, silk blouse and low-heeled pumps. As I trod carefully over the grass, I heard an unmistakable voice: 'G'day Anne!'

I had not seen him. Or, rather, I had not recognised the little guy in front of me wearing nothing but the tiniest of red Speedos, his nut-brown body daubed in white zinc. I do not remember but he probably had a transistor radio pressed to his ear as well. He might be the Prime Minister, but Bob Hawke was still his larrikin self; he loved the sun and he loved the punt. Fortunately for us he was also a strong and sincere ally for women, and without his support we would be worse off today than we are.

Bob Hawke understood the political arguments for equality. He could see the economic justice in advancing women's opportunities. (He'd supported equal pay for women when he was at the ACTU.) And he also understood the philosophical basis of our arguments. He had read Simone de Beauvoir's *The Second Sex*.

Bob Hawke's support for advancing the status of women was not grudging or half-hearted. He agreed with our proposals (or let us know when he did not) because they made sense. They were consistent with Labor's advocacy of a 'fair go' for all Australians. Including women. It is both a shame and a tragedy, for the country as well as for women themselves, that there is no longer a government in Canberra that even understands this, let alone is prepared to assume responsibility for ensuring that *all* Australians are provided with the opportunities to participate equally in our national project.

Sean Hutton

Coming to Australia from Scotland in 1983 in my early twenties I clearly remember the sense of optimism in the air, a feeling of an unashamed 'can do' attitude where anything was possible, which was in stark contrast to the country of my departure. Bob Hawke had been newly elected Prime Minister, and the country and I were ready to start a new chapter in our lives. In this year I remember him cheering along with the nation at winning the America's Cup and feeling I had found a new home.

In 2015 I had the opportunity to paint Bob Hawke's portrait and recount these memories to him. [Sean's painting is reproduced in the photo section.] During this process I could express my gratitude to him and to this country that has given me so much. He was extremely gracious and generous with his time, allowing me to visit on many occasions. He also attended, as guest of honour, the opening of the Mosman Art Prize, where the painting had been selected as a finalist.

Looking back, arriving as a young migrant, building a successful business and then being able to paint Bob Hawke's portrait, I feel incredibly fortunate to be part of the legacy and vision that he helped create for Australia.

Graham Evans

There were many facets to Bob Hawke. His contribution to Australian political life through four election victories and the substantial policy achievements, supported by an outstanding group of ministers, is one facet. The reforms of the Hawke government are an enduring legacy.

But another is the Bob Hawke that many Australians felt they knew and identified with, despite his well-documented flaws. He shared with them many of the same passions and interests. One of these was sport, and in terms of his own participation, the most important was cricket.

Bob was a first-grade player in both Perth and Canberra, and was 12th man for Oxford, while a Rhodes Scholar. He remained a close friend of the Oxford captain and later English cricketing great, Colin Cowdrey. Bob had a good eye for small ball sports, and in cricket brought a high level of self-confidence to the batting crease. He carried these attributes over to tennis, leading to a number of doubles contests with Chinese Vice Premier Wan Li, and later to golf.

Among the urgent tasks Bob gave me after he appointed me as his first chief of staff was to arrange the reinstatement of the Prime Minister's XI matches against visiting international cricket teams. It was only a slightly lesser priority than the 1983 National Economic Summit, but harder to organise! Bob felt this had been an excellent initiative of former Liberal Prime Minister Bob Menzies, and regretted it had fallen into abeyance under his successors.

The matches recommenced in 1984, with the support of the Australian Cricket Board and the ACT Cricket Association. Apart from the opportunities these matches provided for aspiring young Australian cricketers, the funds generated have been central to the growth of cricket in the ACT, and the development of Manuka as a venue.

The Prime Minister's XI for the 1984 clash with the high-performing West Indies side was chosen by Bob and the Australian Chairman of Selectors, Laurie Sawle, an old friend from their Perth cricket days. The Prime Minister's XI team included some well-known players, including Kim Hughes, Greg Chappell and Dennis Lillee, and some aspiring ones, and there was a keen debate on who these should be.

Bob exercised his authority to insist on the selection of the young Tasmanian David Boon, who subsequently scored 134 and was named Man of the Match in a winning team. The innings launched David's distinguished career, and it was an occasion that was fondly remembered in later years.

Perhaps Bob's best-known personal involvement with cricket was the smashing of his glasses, while batting in a 1984 game against the Press Gallery, on the eve of the federal election in that year. Less well known was that Bob was only batting at the time because he had instructed one staff member to run out another, who he felt was batting too slowly.

But a significant diplomatic event had already taken place earlier that day. The newly appointed UK high commissioner, Sir John Leahy, presented his credentials to the Australian Prime Minister at Kingston Oval, formally attired for the occasion, while Bob was wearing a grubby pair of cricket creams. A prepared speech by the high commissioner on the importance of the UK–Australian relations was cut short by a peremptory interjection from Bob, 'I know all that stuff', at which point the credentials were shoved into the pocket of his cricket creams. The credentials were rescued from there later in the day, when Bob was forced to retire from the playing field, and prior to a close win by his office.

Bob's love of sport (horse racing was his other major sporting interest) was a genuine one, not an affectation for the sake of political advantage, something quickly spotted by most Australians. In the case of cricket, Bob's commentaries on live cricket for the ABC, and his willingness to skol a beer at Test matches, continued to endear him to the Australian public for many years*—as well as his continuing thoughtful engagement in public policy.

Graham Evans was Bob Hawke's chief of staff, 1983–86.

Ross Garnaut

Bob Hawke made his first official visit to the three Northeast Asian countries in February 1984. He explained his objectives

* If there are any gaping absences in this book, one of them is more stories from cricketers. *Mea culpa*. We attempted, with great assistance, to fill this gap but were hindered by the fact that most of the Australian cricket world was in the UK preoccupied, of course, with the World Cup and then The Ashes while we were collating. I know that there are many stories from cricketers who played with or encountered Dad in various capacities, and it would not be too hard to write a whole book about Dad and cricket—but maybe that's for someone else, as I figure that three books about my parents must be approaching saturation point!

in a press conference in Canberra before his departure. There were big changes going on in the three countries, he said, that would create great advantages for Australia. We would do well if we made a major effort to understand the countries and the changes that were going on, to get close to them, and 'enmesh' our economy with those of our Northeast Asian neighbours.

Bob spent a lot of time with his staff before the departure and in the plane on the journey, defining our main goals in each country. There was a general objective to show Australians the nature of change in the region and the opportunity that would come from being closely linked to it. This would be made real to Australians by concrete examples of trade advantages that could be secured from having a productive relationship. We would explain to our hosts the advantages to their own people of expanding international trade in areas of importance to Australia. In Japan, we would introduce the idea of long-term easing of restrictions on imports of food, especially beef, that kept prices high and denied Japanese consumers choices available to people in other developed countries. In China, we would focus on persuading leaders that China's own development would be enhanced by using high quality Australian raw materials in the new, expanding steel and wool manufacturing industries. Use high quality Australian iron ore and coal, and the same investments in steel manufacturing would produce more and higher quality products.

Public servants travelling with the Prime Minister, and at the Australian embassies in Tokyo and Beijing, warned that while there was no harm in expressing an interest in the subjects, there should be no expectation of any effects. That was not the way Japanese and Chinese governments did business.

This was the beginning of an historic expansion of Chinese imports and Australian exports of steel-making raw materials that is now, amongst other things, giving us our first budget surplus for over a decade in 2019–20.* There is a big and interesting story there, but I will concentrate on Japanese beef.

Japan came first. Bob Hawke and Yasuhiro Nakasone struck up a warm and personal conversation. 'Call me Yasu, and if you don't mind, I'll call you Bob. We'll have a Yasu Bob relationship.' Bob was encouraged to describe the beef issue in detail. Tight quota restrictions meant only tiny amounts of beef were allowed entry. Because the quotas were allocated by bureaucrats, they tended to be disproportionately given to grain-fed beef that happened to be of primary interest to the US, and not to Australia with its grass-fed product. Given a choice, Japanese consumers could enhance their standard of living by buying much

* Although a surplus has indeed been announced, it is highly contested. If you look at the underspend of much needed money allocated for the NDIS, for example, and other underspends, it is not a true surplus achieved by good and just financial management.

more of whatever type of beef they preferred. 'Let's agree,' said Bob, 'on gradually increasing the quota, eventually by a large amount, and gradually shifting from quotas to tariffs that would fall over time so that consumers and not bureaucrats decide what type of beef would be bought from the supermarket.'

Yasu thought that was a great idea. 'Yes, we'll do it.'

'No doubt it will be a challenge to implement what we have just agreed,' said Bob. 'If we run into any roadblocks, can we get in touch with each other to remove the block?'

'Yes,' agreed Yasu. 'If there is any problem, you just call me and we'll sort it out. We'll have a Yasu–Bob hotline.'

As we left the meeting, the senior MITI (Ministry of Trade and Industry) official present came quickly to my side. 'Please make sure that your Prime Minister knows,' he said, 'that our Prime Minister was not authorised to say what he said about beef.'

Bob was to give a press conference for the Australian and Japanese media half an hour after the meeting. A few of the Australian officials present at the meeting huddled with Bob on the way to the press conference. 'Be careful, Prime Minister,' the Australian Deputy Secretary for Trade advised. 'There is no way that the Japanese are going to liberalise beef imports. If you build up hopes, you will be criticised for being unrealistic.'

'What do you think, Ross?' the Prime Minister asked me.

'The Deputy Secretary is right to point to the risk of embarrassment.' I said. 'And MITI has just let me know that they will oppose any change. The safe thing is not to mention beef. That will guarantee no progress. On the other hand, talking publicly about what the Japanese Prime Minister has said creates a chance of change. Just a chance.'

'Well,' Bob said. 'If the downside is some embarrassment for me, and the upside is a chance of a good outcome for Australia, then I'll talk about it.'

'The Prime Minister and I had a very good discussion about beef trade,' our Prime Minister told the press conference. 'We agreed that there would be official discussions leading towards liberalising Japanese imports. If there is a problem in the discussions, we will get on the phone to each other to sort it out.'

MITI said the same things as it had said to me when it had private briefings of the Australian media. The Australian media duly reported that our Prime Minister had unrealistic hopes of progress in the beef trade. An Easter cartoon in the *Sydney Morning Herald* had beef and Chinese steel loads weighing the Prime Minister down.

Nothing important was ever forgotten by Bob. 'How are we going on the beef discussions with Japan?' he would ask at weekly intervals. Official discussions weren't getting anywhere.

After a couple of months Bob said, 'Can you organise that phone call to Yasu.'

I met the Japanese ambassador to set up the call. He was horrified. 'That is not how the Japanese government works,' he said. 'The whole of the Japanese government will be embarrassed. You must talk the Prime Minister out of it.' I explained that Bob had received an invitation from Yasu to take up the matter in a phone call in exactly these circumstances, and Bob was going to do it.

An interpreter and a note-taker from Foreign Affairs were to join me at The Lodge. The ambassador was waiting outside The Lodge in the dark, in the driveway. 'Please stop this call,' he pleaded. 'It will be embarrassing for everyone.'

'I'm afraid that it has all been set up and can't be stopped now,' I explained.

But it didn't happen quite as planned. The interpreter needed to be able to hear both sides of the conversation and speak to both prime ministers, and The Lodge wasn't immediately equipped for the complexity of the exchange. None of those present was a telecommunications whiz, and in 1984 there were no smart phones with easy ways of patching in multiple parties. We heard from the single line that Yasu and his party were having similar challenges in Tokyo. Maybe the bureaucrats would have their ways after all.

But no. After twenty minutes we were ready to go. Yasu and Bob. Very friendly. The Japanese Prime Minister glad to know of our concerns, Yes, he would look into it. It would be fixed.

The rest is history. In mid-1985, Nakasone said in a public statement that Japanese growth in future would be focussed less on export growth and more on satisfying the needs of consumers. Liberalising beef and other food imports would be an important part of that story. Beef import quotas started to expand. In June 1988, Japan signed a new beef access agreement with Australia and the US. Quotas would continue to expand, and be replaced by tariffs that would fall over time. This laid a base for further steps in the Uruguay Round of trade negotiations concluded in 1995. Beef exports to Japan became an important part of the Australian farm economy.

Jan Pieters

It was a dreary winter's evening in January 1984 when I caught the train from Shimokitazawa to central Tokyo—destination: the Emperor Hotel. Bob and Hazel Hawke were on an official visit and I was about to meet them.

I met Sue in Japan in 1983 while we were studying Zen Yoga in the Oki Dojo of Mishima, on the footsteps of Mount Fuji. On a brief visit home to Australia in December 1983, Sue mentioned to Bob and Hazel over dinner that she'd met this Belgian guy she was 'very interested in'. Bob promptly told her that he wants to meet him on his official visit to Japan in a few weeks. It was impossible for Sue to get back to Japan in time for this meeting, so I was about to introduce myself to my future in-laws—on my own. Suffice to say, I was terrified. The highest ranking official I had ever met in my life was the local priest of my parish in Belgium; to now meet a prime minister was daunting.

The winter rain turned into melting snow during my train ride. I forgot my umbrella and the downpour continued when walking from the station to the Emperor Hotel; then the temperature dropped and the walkways became icy. I got soaked, and to make matters worse, I slipped on the driveway of the hotel, fell flat on my face and looked like a wet zombie. Meanwhile, back in Australia, Sue was surely wondering how things were going—not so great really, up to this point.

Konbanwa, watashi wa Jan Pieters desu. Ōsutoraria shushō to no kaigō ni kimashita (Good evening, I am Jan Pieters, and I have come to meet the Prime Minister of Australia). I merely got pointed to the elevator and top floor. The lift was empty—what a relief.

Doors opened and there were Johnny and Graham, two Australian Federal Police. I wondered what they must have thought; they didn't let on. Very friendly and terrific guys, Graham ended up accompanying Hazel to our wedding in Belgium—second best wedding ever, he reckoned.

Then Hazel welcomed me warmly, 'A tad wet I see,' she said, and promptly offered me one of Bob's suits and shirts to change into. A perfect fit! (I have continued to wear Bob's suits for many years.) 'Bob's in the shower and will be ready to meet you soon,' she said, and we chatted a bit. She surely broke the ice for me—an incredible warmth and a mutual friendship that would accompany and nurture me and my family for many years to come.

Off to Bob's study, where he was sitting behind his desk reading Top Secret papers, cigar in one hand, a cup of tea in the other. He had indeed just finished his shower and had a towel loosely wrapped around him. I walked up to him extending my hand, 'Hello Mr Hawke, I am Jan.'

He stood up and, while extending his hand, the towel dropped: 'G'day, I'm Bob.' There was my future father-in-law standing sheer naked in front of his future son-in-law, who was wearing his suit. And he didn't flinch. He sat down again, back to his papers. 'Will be with you in a minute, taking you out for dinner.' Turned out I became the guest of honour at a dinner for all Australian Foreign Affairs staff in Japan. Bob introduced me as his future son-in-law and translator for the night.

What an encounter—and what a giant of a man. I didn't even have to ask his permission to marry his daughter. Bob showed me that night that there is nothing to hide, nothing to be embarrassed about, nothing to fear, to be always open and frank. I have only been able to follow that advice to a fraction of his capacity.

Not long after I met Bob and Hazel, our daughter Sophie was 'Made in Japan' and born in 1985 in Sydney. The last time I saw Bob was during her wedding in 2017 when we both walked her down the aisle. An honour to be at his side.

Bob was the best and it has been a privilege to have him as my father-in-law. I will miss him, but I can only imagine how much more Blanche will miss him. Their love for each other over more than twenty years has always inspired me, has taught me, has benefitted me. To Bob and Blanche—I salute you!

August 2019
Cornus, France

Dr Ric Charlesworth

The 1984 election campaign

In 1984 Bob surprised many by calling an early election, ostensibly to align the House of Reps and the Senate after the double dissolution election of 1983, which would have necessitated a half-Senate election. Bob was at the peak of his powers at the time and very popular in the polls. It was expected that Labor would win easily; however, the long campaign ended with the loss of seats by Labor, and Andrew Peacock did better than expected.

Part of the reason for the government's slip up was the unpopularity of the 'pensioner assets test', which was good public policy but criticised by pensioner groups and the subject of attack by our political opponents. Good public policy would see the very wealthy excluded from a pension entitlement, yet opponents whipped up pensioner sentiment, distorting the reality in much the same way as they did recently when opposing Labor's proposals for franking credits. Suffice to say, pensioners were hostile!

As a newly elected backbencher in a marginal seat, I was keen to have the Prime Minister visit my electorate, and so various possibilities were sought. It turned out that during one of Bob's visits to Perth (WA had warmly supported Labor in 1983, and there were many marginal seats—Bob's WA credentials helped) it was proposed that he would open the new grandstand at the WACA ground which was in the seat of Perth (my seat). This would occur at lunch time during the test match between Australia and the West Indies. I was delighted to be invited, as the local member. After all, the ground was where I had plied my trade as an opening batsman for WA in the 1970s.

The plan seemed perfect, as there would be a good crowd in attendance with media coverage, and Bob was a very keen and genuine 'cricket head'. There was, however, one problem: pensioners loved their cricket, and many, many had time on their hands to attend.

The day arrived and at lunchtime, as the players made their way off the ground, it was announced that the PM would be entering the arena to open the new grandstand. Bernie Prindiville, the past cricket association president, was in attendance—the stand would bear his name. So he, along with Premier Brian Burke, Bob and myself, walked through the gate and onto the field—not to polite and sustained applause, but to loud booing and sounds of general discontent.

I was not much surprised, being aware of the age of the patrons, and having taken the temperature of the electorate over the first weeks of the campaign. Bob did seem surprised, but he had that peculiar megalomania that all who aspire to be PM must have, as well as supreme confidence in his popularity. As we moved towards the microphone he turned to me saying, 'Crikey, you're unpopular here, mate! Maybe it's the way you batted. You should invite me over here more often—I could lift your profile!'

Suffice to say, I was lost for words.

1984 cricket at the MCG against Crusaders

It was early in 1984. March 9th was a Friday, and I was drafted to play cricket for the PM's X1 at the MCG against the Crusaders, a team captained by Robert 'Swan' Richards, former CEO of Gray Nicholls, whose wandering team would go on to play cricket on almost every continent.

The PM's team contained genuine parliamentarians including myself, Barry Cunningham (Deputy Whip), Don Chipp, Michael MacKellar, Ray Groom and Alan Rocher—and, of course, it was led by our cricket-loving PM, Bob. We had a few ring-ins in Bruce Yardley, Max Walker and Ross Edwards to boost our stocks! Swan's team contained Keith Stackpole, Phil O'Meara and Nigel Murch, all first-class players, and Rob Elliott, director of Kookaburra Cricket. They were softened by former pollies Tony Street and Sir Billy Snedden.

This was to be a fun afternoon in which everyone had a bat and bowl, and there was camaraderie and tales from yore told by all. There were many interesting characters playing. The Crusaders knocked up 185, and so after the break Ross Edwards and I set about chasing the target. After losing Ross, Barry Cunningham, Don Chipp and Hawkie we were in a bit of trouble at four wickets down. I had gone well, but after reaching 50 decided it was time to hit one in the air and depart, as was the etiquette for first class players in such matches!

Before I was able to effect this plan, I received, from the PM, the message that I was not to throw away my wicket as the aim was to win the game! Here I was between a rock and a hard place, with the opponents expecting my departure and my boss requiring me to stick around to win the game. I remember Keith Stackpole sledging me for staying—not a new experience for me on the MCG with Stackie! Meanwhile, the whip was making it clear that I should flout the convention as I was indeed a legitimate pollie and ought not be subject to friendly match conventions.

Eventually, when we were close to our target, I retired myself, running 'Bradman-like' from the field, relieving myself from the grip of ambiguity and the displeasure of our opponents. In the end, Bob's team won by about twenty runs and all was sweetness that evening, and the boss was pleased by his backbencher's contribution!

Barrie Cassidy

Bob Hawke's head was buried in papers, his brow furrowed, a pen in one hand, a cigar in the other. It was 11 November 1986. A long flight to Perth. My first day as senior press secretary and, I thought, an ideal opportunity to get to know him better. But we didn't speak. The constant notations went on all the way out west.

Once we'd landed he handed me a pile of crumpled newspapers, which of course I discarded. Only later did a panicked federal policeman explain the Prime Minister had given me a meticulously marked-up form guide: racehorses engaged in Melbourne, Sydney and Brisbane, all of them graded according to weights, track conditions, jockeys, recent form and times.

I had thrown the lot—four hours' work—in the bin. On day one.

I survived and went on to better appreciate the intellectual larrikin that was Bob Hawke—the man as much at ease with world leaders as he was with punters at the races, just as dedicated to forging economic accords as he was to picking winners at the track.

He was persuasive and committed when he needed to be, yet a good listener at the Cabinet table. He was a hard worker and an excellent judge of trends. He was comfortable with people, and they with him. And he had a strong moral compass.

The economic reforms that flowed from the initial Economic Summit and the Accord are well documented. Not so well known were his achievements around education. When Hawke came to office in 1983, Australia had one of the lowest high school retention rates in the developed world. Just 30 per cent completed Year 12. When he left office that number had increased to 70 per cent. You can only imagine the difference that made to this country.

Hawke was also proactive on foreign policy. He was disgusted with Apartheid in South Africa and couldn't abide the timid responses around the world. As head of the ACTU, he was a leader in the protests against the visiting Springboks.

As Prime Minister, he marshalled support at Commonwealth Heads of Government meetings—in the Bahamas in 1985, and in Vancouver in 1987—to put together financial sanctions against South Africa. He secretly flew the international banker Jim Wolfensohn to Vancouver to put the bans in place. Years later, a South African Foreign Minister described that action as the 'dagger that finally killed Apartheid'.

He took the same approach when Cabinet ministers told him that world leaders were intent on mining Antarctica and the momentum was unstoppable. He would have none of that. He flew to Paris and lobbied the French president. He got conservationist Jacques-Yves Cousteau on board. And eighteen months later, the continent was locked up to mining.

But the character trait that most endeared him to me was his total abhorrence of racism in any form. He detested it. No matter how often he was advised to step warily on racism, given the diverse nature of Australia's electorates, he was uncompromising, calling it out whenever he saw it, or any hint of it.

Bob Hawke was the exception to two rules—well, maybe many, but two in particular.

First, he overcame a drinking problem—a serious drinking problem—and went on to be Labor's longest-serving Prime Minister. An old golfing buddy of his, Col Cunningham, said in the recent book *Wednesdays with Bob*: 'They say beer destroys the brain. Bob disproved that theory. He's still got his marbles when he should be a raving lunatic.'

And the second is an exception to a rule once articulated by John Howard: that no politician is popular forever—'That is one of the great ironies of politics.'

Howard may be right, generally. But somehow I reckon Bob Hawke was never more popular than he was in his fading years. That's when people reflected on what once was, and may never be again.

This piece first appeared in The Guardian, *16 May 2019.*

Barrie Cassidy is a political journalist and was host of the ABC's Insiders. *He was senior press secretary to Bob Hawke 1986–91.*

Wendy Dobson

My Dad, Bert Dobson, was one of eight kids growing up in the bush in NSW near Griffith. His family was poor and he joined the Army at eighteen and was a prisoner of war from age nineteen to twenty-two. After surviving Changi, he became so appreciative of the Billy Hughes type support for Australians.

As we grew up he became very successful, and always thanked the Labor philosophy of support for battlers. He loved Bob's 'straight talk and lack of fluff', often espousing the need to hide any visible trappings of privilege that may make others feel less worthy in this life.

He saw Bob as one of us. Work and study hard; however, share the honour and rewards with others less fortunate. He used to say that 'Bob has your back,' thereby influencing the next family generation of Labor supporters for battlers.

Martin Gallagher

December 14, 1986 saw our beloved Prime Minister visit the Central Coast of NSW to open the newly completed Mooney Mooney bridge. The event was timed for the morning, with another duty to be performed later at the Gosford Golf Club. The club had recently completed a major overhaul of its layout and the thought of a hit around the course appealed to the Prime Minister. Before that he unveiled a plaque in the forecourt of the club to mark the opening of the newly revamped course.

After the ceremonies were completed, off to the first tee. I was designated the club's official photographer on the day and got to walk with the great man whilst he continued to 'carve up' the course. On reaching the 9th green, his lordship requested to play a couple more holes. There was only one problem: it would mean butting into the Sunday afternoon husbands and wives competition. At the time, Gosford Golf Club had some vocal Liberal supporters, particularly in the Sunday afternoon set.

'Well who does he think he is, just butting in, and we have to wait for him to play on!' Much consternation, spluttering and raised voices could be heard as Bob merrily went on his way down the 10th without an inkling of the kerfuffle he had caused—although I do suspect that he knew all along and just ignored the protests. It was a delight to see Bob enjoy himself at the expense of the Opposition supporters.

Martin Gallagher is Member 344 (since 1977) of Gosford Golf Club.

Terry Aulich

Back in 1987 I was the chair of the Labor Party's Caucus Legal Committee. Before then, Bob and I had worked together very productively on industrial relations matters when I was a minister in Tasmania and he was President of the ACTU.

When it came to a proposed War Crimes Bill in 1987 there was a feeling that there were an awful lot of war criminals running around in out-of-the-way places in Australia. I thought that had been exaggerated. Bob and I weren't seeing eye to eye and we needed to sort it out before the bill went to Parliament. I was invited to meet him at The Lodge.

Hazel met me at the door and nodded in the direction of the lounge room. I was about to get out my papers with the relevant dot points. You always had dot points when you were debating or briefing Bob. Always no more than ten points, one for each finger, because he had this counter-attack which involved peeling off each point like he was peeling a banana. Any more than ten dot points would have buggered him and led to bad blood.

'What about Werribee?' Bob's voice stopped me in my tracks.

Werribee? I thought, as I entered the room, *We've caught a war criminal in Werribee?*

I walked in and there was the Prime Minister of our great brown land lying on the floor of the lounge, a phone at his ear. Around him were what seemed like acres of racing form guides. He waved me to a seat.

'Take another look at Werribee, Mick,' he said. Obviously this was his betting mate, minister Mick Young, who is now helping Bob clean the bookies up in that great betting ring in the sky. They sorted the races, and his bets were out there in the ether.

'I didn't know they still ran mid-week in Werribee,' I said.

He fixed me with that special eyebrow lift reserved for slow learners. 'And your bloody old man trained horses,' he said, reaching for my papers.

The War Crimes (Amendment) Bill 1987 went through the Parliament exactly as Bob wanted it.

Terry Aulich was Senator for Tasmania 1984–93.

Chris Bastic

I was a friend of the family and one autumn Saturday in 1987 they asked me over to Kirribilli House for a bite of lunch and a catch up, since we hadn't been in contact for a while.

We sat out the back in a sunny spot near where Bob was lying on a banana lounge in his Speedos. He had a small transistor radio and the phone next to him whilst he was studying the racing form for the day's thoroughbred racing.

I certainly wasn't an avid punter; however, having been the mayor of the City of Randwick and a Randwick City councillor for many years I did regularly attend the Royal Randwick Racecourse to mingle with constituents and, more often, as a guest of the Australian Jockey Club.

Also, at the time I was working for the Deputy Prime Minister, The Hon. Lionel Bowen AO, who, like Bob, was an avid punter. So Bob understood that I knew something about the horses and asked whether I had checked out the form for the day's racing.

I advised him that I hadn't; however, Lionel had tipped me a horse that was running at Randwick that day. Bob laughed and looked at the horse's form and said to me: 'no hope'.

He said, 'Did you put any money on it?' and I replied that I didn't have time to go to the TAB; however, I was interested to see how it went.

He said to me that he had picked out a horse that was at long odds, 30–1, and he thought it was the best bet of the day and did I want to back it? I advised him that I didn't have a TAB account and was keen to just see how it went.

Bob straight away said that he would put on a bet for me on his account if I wished. I thought that this was exceptionally generous, and exactly the type of person he was; however, I declined.

So, over the next hour, Hazel had prepared some sandwiches and a pot of tea, which we had on a small table in this beautiful sun trap. (I thought it was amazing that at Kirribilli House, the Prime Minister's residence, Hazel actually made the sandwiches!)

Bob was eating a sandwich on his banana lounge whilst listening to the races when I saw him getting excited, with the race he was listening to coming to a glorious end. Bob's 30–1 horse came in and paid 33–1.

Bob got straight on the phone to a mate. 'I am brilliant, I am brilliant. I just picked that winner in the last in Adelaide.'

The person on the other end said to Bob: 'Yes, that was the one I had tipped to you earlier this morning.'

Bob said back to him: 'You bloody well did not! You did not tip that to me. I studied its form and picked it myself. You did not tip it to me. And I have a witness here to say that I chose the horse.'

And whoever was on the other end of the phone wouldn't have anything of it.

And Bob said: 'Well, if you're so smart then who's going to win the next?'

Anyway, the horse tipped won the next, and Bob was even more cranky because he didn't put any money on it.

And to top it off, the horse that Lionel Bowen tipped also won! So as a bystander I thought the whole thing was just hilarious.

Ben Churcher

In January 1987, Bob made an official visit to Jordan. At the invitation of the excavation director Professor Basil Hennessy, he included a side-trip to the Australian archaeological excavations at Pella in Jordan where work had begun in 1979 under the auspices of the University of Sydney.

For us archaeologists, the visit was very memorable. There was no digging that day and the excitement built as a couple of large military helicopters came into view. Not only were helicopters in the Jordan Valley a rare sight in those tense times, but all of us longed for the view the PM's party were seeing: the Jordan Valley from above.

The visit of Bob and Hazel to our dig house was a bit of a whirl. He was greeted and escorted by Professor Hennessy while we watched on, but the place was also teeming with Jordanian diplomatic and military staff which made it all a bit chaotic. However, Basil walked the Hawkes down to the Byzantine period basilica at the heart of the site to give them a view of where we worked and to show off the beauty of Pella.

Along the way, Bob enquired how we funded the excavation, and on being told of the hand-to-mouth funding made up of small grants from various Australian institutions, he declared in his imitable way: 'That's bloody ridiculous.' But rather than just say it, Bob acted on it, and was able to secure corporate funding for the next couple of years that allowed a team to stay on at Pella after the digging had finished to work through the sizeable backlog of material that had accumulated. Bob also pledged an unending supply of Vegemite, but I'm not sure what ever happened to that pledge!

Fortunately for us, Bob's visit coincided with Australia Day, and as was the custom, we all trooped up to the

Australian ambassador's residence in Amman to celebrate. There we had time to actually speak with Bob, orange juice in his hand, without all the formality of an official visit. With great good humour he tolerated us as we took advantage of the ambassador's alcoholic largess, and he seemed to take great delight in finding out about our experiences so far from home. He even graciously awarded the Pella teams' annual 'drunk and disorderly award', which went to the person who stood out from the crowd during the annual Australia Day bash. Holding the victor's arm in the air, with the famous Bob grin stretched from ear to ear, like all who met him you couldn't help thinking that he was one of us.

The Pella excavations this year celebrated its fortieth anniversary under director Dr Stephen Bourke. It is a many-storied place, but the visit of Bob to Pella remains one of the fondest episodes in the long history of the dig.

Ben Churcher is Field Director of the Australian Expedition to Pella in Jordan for the University of Sydney and the Department of Antiquities, Hashemite Kingdom of Jordan.

Dominic Grenot

In 1987 I was dating a young lady whose father was responsible for Desmond Tutu's trip to Australia after he had won the Nobel Peace Prize. He asked me if I wanted to be Tutu's driver for the week that he was in Sydney. Of course I said yes.

Apart from the big highlight of driving out to the plane on the tarmac at Sydney Airport to collect Mr and Mrs Tutu flanked by ASIO staff, one of my responsibilities for the week was to take the Tutus to Kirribilli House for a meeting with the Prime Minister.

We parked out the front, and then wandered around the back, where Bob was dressed very casually, cigar in mouth, and practising his driving golf swing into a net.

He wandered over, greeted all of us equally, and conversation began before I left with the guys from ASIO. I remember being treated without any difference by Bob, a lesson I took from that day onwards in all my dealings with anyone—politicians or homeless beggars.

Sandra Groom

It was around 1987. I was thirty-eight years old, in the prime of life, a professional, mature, and (I now realise!) an attractive woman. I had taken our son Joshua (then aged ten) and three of his mates to the Royal Easter Show. They were having a ball; I had a challenge keeping track of all four boys, as they were running all over the place, going on rides, wanting show bags, eating ice cream and hot chips.

Suddenly, I was face to face with the Prime Minister of Australia. I literally bumped into him, and his eyes lit up. I could not believe who I was looking at. He was handsome, charming and magnetic. My jaw dropped, and then

With us kids in the backyard of our first house in Melbourne. Dad had just come home from fishing with mates.
(Personal collection)

Oh what a night! With Dad during the early hours of 3 December 1972 at Labor Party headquarters in Melbourne on the morning following Labor's historic win after 23 years in opposition. An enterprising soul had gone down to the loading dock at *The Age* to collect a copy of the first edition straight off the presses.
(Personal collection)

Of all the photos of Dad at the races, this is my favourite. He's already studied the form and is holding a well-thumbed race guide, and is with his best mate Col Cunningham. (Courtesy of the Rhonda Senbergs Collection/State Library of Victoria)

Dad and I wouldn't always fight or play with words. Here we are having a water pistol fight at a picnic circa 1973. (Personal collection)

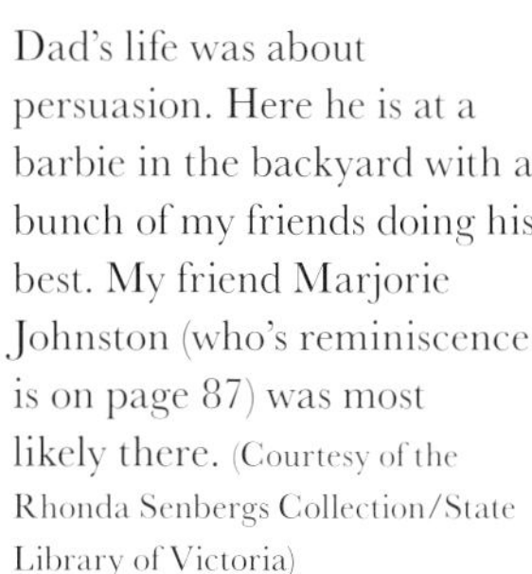

Dad's life was about persuasion. Here he is at a barbie in the backyard with a bunch of my friends doing his best. My friend Marjorie Johnston (who's reminiscence is on page 87) was most likely there. (Courtesy of the Rhonda Senbergs Collection/State Library of Victoria)

Dad never tired of campaigning amongst working people. Here he is on a Sydney building site during the 1983 election knowing that it was more important than ever to bring people together. (Getty Images)

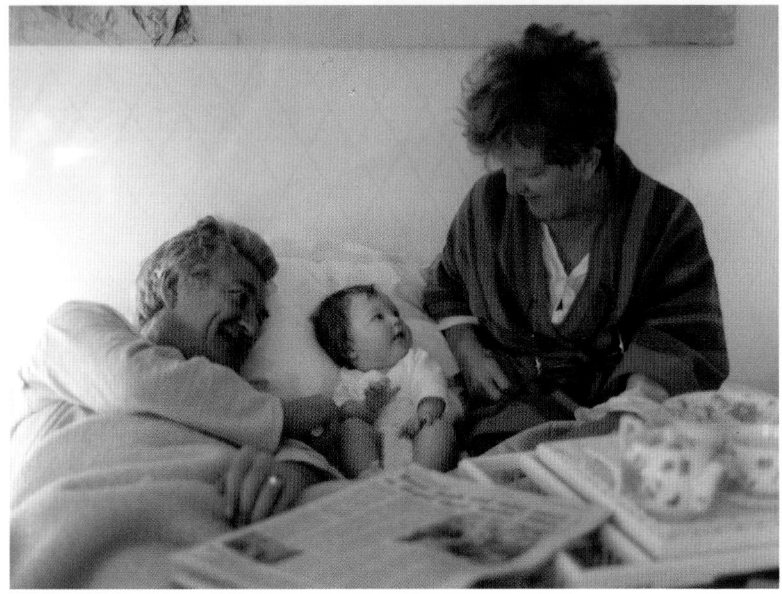

It was a family tradition to pile on Mum and Dad's bed on weekend mornings to read the papers and muck about. That tradition continued in The Lodge. This is mid-1983 and my daughter Sophie is with her Nan and Pop. (Personal collection)

Election night 1987 in Sydney. From left to right Mum, Dad, Sophie, me, my ex-husband Jan and my grandfather Clem Hawke. (Kenneth Stevens/*SMH*)

As a family we loved escaping to the bush on holidays, much as Mum and Dad had done in their earlier years. During this long weekend (I think in 1987) we stayed in the old cabins at Pebbly Beach on the NSW South Coast and played disputatious board games, dozed, read and chatted. Dad, as usual, had work to hand. (Personal collection)

Between engagements. Mum and Day playing with the kids on the lawn at Kirribilli House. (Personal collection)

It might have been Christmas morning at The Lodge, but it was no different to Christmas morning in most family homes across Australia. (Buce Postle/*The Age*)

Dad loved golf partly for the quiet, internal nature of the game. It allowed him time for reflection, and absorption in something other than work.
(James Pozarick/The LIFE images Collection via Getty Images/Getty Images)

Dad at a charity cricket match in 1995. As a first-class cricketer, he'd been a batsman/wicket keeper. (Patrick Riviere/Getty Images)

Dad and Blanche look very relaxed watching the early runners on race day for the Mick Young Scholarship Trust in June 2001. (Matt Turner/Getty Images)

As Dad got older, he mellowed. This photo taken at the 2007 Labor campaign launch, captures the happy older Bob, his warmth and his humour. (Bradley Kanaris/Getty Images)

Dad admired all athletes and was enthusiastic about all sports including, it seems, surfing.
(Peter Carrette Archive/Getty Images)

Dad at the 2010 Labor campaign launch. The old campaigner in him never died.
(Lisa Maree Williams/Getty Images)

Dad and Blanche, playmates at sea with a couple of huge red emperors. Blanche is making a face at the fish. (Personal collection)

You never had to drag Dad to a party, as Anthony Marano and his friends discovered during the Melbourne Spring Racing Carnival in 2008. He certainly never expected to end up at a party with Dad. (See Anthony's reminiscence on page 281). (Courtesy of Anthony Marano)

Dad loved cricket and cricket loved him. He was embraced by Indian supporters during the Australia and India Second Test in 2012. (Ryan Pierse/Getty Images)

Dad celebrating the 30th anniversary of Medicare with Tanya Plibersek, who was Health Minister at the time. Tanya and Dad had a warm personal relationship, as Tanya recalls on page 312. (Personal collection)

Blanche and I love this portrait, as did Dad. Sean Hutton recalls how he came to paint it on page 137. (Courtesy Sean Hutton)

A relaxed Dad working his way through the Sudoku with the inevitable coffee and cigar in hand at the 2014 Woodford Folk Festival. (Megan Slade/Newspix)

Dad loved going to Woodford. This is his final appearance on stage in December 2017. (AAP)

On his beloved balcony, with the well-thumbed dictionary on hand for his cryptic crosswords, this is one of the last photos taken of Dad before he died. Bill Shorten writes of that meeting on page 325. (Getty Images)

Dad's public memorial service on 14 June 2019 in the main hall of the Opera House. Dad had conducted the 'Hallelujah Chorus' with the Sydney Symphony Orchestra on his 80th birthday. Nobody in the hall for the memorial service (including me) knew that the footage would be shown with the Sydney Symphony actually on stage. For all the world, it was as if Dad was there with us. (Mark Metcalfe/Getty Images)

inexplicably, I turned into a 'teenage groupie'. My heart pinged, I sighed, my knees shook, I squealed in delight, I flung myself at him, trying to hug him and shake his hand, and spoke gibberish in my haste to 'get acquainted'. I think I may have tossed my hair. (I'm cringing as I recall this.) And I giggled. All without a shred of shame. And I couldn't have cared less where the four boys in my charge were, either.

It took only a couple of minutes, but the sheer force of his charisma hit me like a brick; it was a palpable thing. I cannot remember what he said, but his smile was enough. I just clung to his hand, trying to prevent him from leaving, but his aides murmured in his ear, and then he said goodbye, and as he walked away, I realised I was CRYING! Yes, CRYING! Then I realised that all four boys were standing, staring, open-mouthed, at what had just happened. Thank God I hadn't mislaid them, after all, in my brief encounter with the PM. That had never happened to me in my life before—or since.

Adrienne Jackson

The Bob Hawke I knew was the Prime Minister of Australia. When I joined his staff early in 1987, he had been PM for four years. The office I joined was crammed into the PM's suite in the Old Parliament House, a small maze of offices, cubby holes and shared spaces filled with dedicated, focussed and cheerful people. We all called Bob 'The Boss'. There was always a palpable surge of energy when the Boss arrived—he bounded up the back stairs or charged through the main door. He was a presence!

The political and specialist advisors were all men. The banter was competitive and partisan over many sporting codes and, of course, horseracing. Bob was paramount in his knowledge of whatever sport was the topic. He could name every winner of every event in the 1956 Melbourne Olympics—or so it seemed to me.

I was the first woman selected for the senior private secretary position for any Australian PM. I had no knowledge of horseracing. I carefully avoided Bob's challenge to give him odds on which topics would come up in question time, saying that I knew better than to bet against him. Bob ran his office the way he ran his Cabinet—implicit trust and empowerment of his staff. Demanding, but not unreasonable; he had two qualities which made his leadership a particular inspiration to me. He was fun—humorous, witty, quick on his feet—and he was a great user of the full vocabulary, both the vernacular and erudite versions.

Bob mastered and assimilated any well-argued brief, barely looked at his script, and always lifted the topic at hand to be fully authoritative and compelling. He knew Parliament was political theatre, and he commanded that space as he did all the other platforms of his prime ministership.

Once, he detoured to the parliamentary office on his way from The Lodge to the airport, after hearing on police radio that I had been attacked by a pit bull terrier (I hadn't but our family dog had) to make sure that I was okay.

When I left the Hawke office two and a half years later, we were ensconced in the new Parliament House. The range of issues on my watch had been huge and momentous—I will not adumbrate (one of his words) them here—but however tough the issues, there was not a single day when I did not look forward to the day ahead, working for Bob Hawke, Prime Minister of Australia.

Three parliamentary reminiscences

My first day in the job

On my first parliamentary sitting day working for Bob, the PM's buzzer sounded for me to take him his Question Time briefing pack. I'd been meticulous, checking all the papers, re-inscribing the Boss's comments or emphasis marks where an earlier brief had been updated, and clearing and annotating anything that needed a political spin. I entered his office, crossed to his desk and gave him the brief. He started looking through it, looked up suddenly and said, 'Bend your back, you bloody fool!' I thought he was speaking to me. I hadn't noticed that the TV was on behind me, sound off, and Australia was bowling in the test match! He flashed his famous eyes up at me and gave me a wry grin.

Visit to New Zealand 1987—parliamentary luncheon

New Zealand has, like Queensland, a unicameral parliament. In the New Zealand psyche, there are brownie points to be had scoring off Australia. Bob set out to employ the charm offensive and, of course, it worked! Speaking at the parliamentary luncheon held in his honour, he told the assembled guests that he might have been born in New Zealand but for the timing. His father had been the minister at the Congregational Church in Upper Hutt near Wellington for a period before moving to South Australia. There was laughter at this, someone called out, and Bob retorted, 'You may have your Upper Hutt, my friend, but be thankful you don't have an upper house!' Brilliant.

April Fools' Day

On April Fools' Day, Clarrie Miller, National Party Member for Wide Bay used my first name to summon his party's leaders, Ian Sinclair and Ralph Hunt, to an urgent meeting in the PM's office. It was, of course, an April Fool's hoax. The Cabinet attendant sent a message into the Cabinet room to let Bob know his visitors had arrived. Bob quickly surmised it was an April Fool's stunt but invited them in to his office for coffee and a chat before returning to the meeting. He then got me to set up a Dorothy Dixer for the afternoon's question time and his answer had both sides of politics chuckling, and Ian Sinclair rose to thank the PM for his hospitality.

It is hardly conceivable to contemplate such overwhelming good humour in politics these days.

Michael Mangos

Bob just loved people, and he just loved us 'wogs'. He was fascinated by our stories, where we had come from, and our love of life. On 4 February 1990, my wife Mary and I got married at the Greek church in East Melbourne. It was a Sunday. Bob was coming back from a Commonwealth Heads of Government Meeting (CHOGM) that morning—I think it was held in New Zealand. I had invited him to the wedding and before he left for CHOGM he said to me: 'Don't tell Mary but I will try to get to the church. I will not be able to stay very long because then I will go to 4 Treasury Place and do some reading for Cabinet the next day.'

Well, not only did Bob turn up to the church, but the wedding was delayed until the church was security cleared (it was pre-9/11, so it didn't take long). The priest then decided to tell Mary that she should re-arrange the wedding procession entrance so that it would look better for Bob! Not only did he stay for the 45-minute wedding service, but he had a photo with everybody who was in attendance. He loved it. He loved the people and they loved him. In the end, we had to tell him to go and do his reading for Cabinet the next day!

•

Bob had an ability to do something that I have never encountered in any other human being I've met: the ability to not powernap but actually have a fifteen- to twenty-minute proper sleep during the day. It makes sense because that is what allowed him to work the long hours that he did. One day in the electorate office in Munro Street, Coburg, Bob was having a twenty-minute nap and I needed to get something from his office. I was reluctant to go into his office and get what I needed until the late Jean Sinclair said to me, 'Go and get what you want from his office. He is fast asleep. You could drop a set of telephone books next to him and he won't hear them.' She was 100 per cent correct. I went in and he was snoring like he was in deep sleep. I got what I wanted and got out of there. Five minutes later, I walked past his office and he was on the phone and back into it!

•

As staff, we loved Bob and he genuinely cared for us. When I think back, he was amazing to us. I was always based in Melbourne and would fly and stay in Canberra during parliamentary sitting weeks and other times when required. Bob was amazing, he never took his personal staff for granted. For instance, he would go out to work dinners and functions in Canberra and then rather than go straight back to The Lodge and get some sleep for a big day the next day, he would come back into the office and see how we were going. I was only a junior researcher running up and back to the Parliament Library (remember: pre-internet) and Bob would want to know how I was going. He would light up a cigar (it was a non-smoking building) and just ask me how I was. Nothing work-related, just inquiring about me. I, like the rest of the staff who were working the night/morning shift, would just tell him to go to The Lodge and get some sleep. But not Bob—he wanted to know how we were going.

•

He was a flirt and a cheeky bastard. The first time my then-girlfriend now-wife Mary met Bob was at the electorate office. He was getting ready to attend a function that night and changing from his normal working suit into his evening black-tie attire. He could not help himself—knowing that Mary would see him, he had to run through part of the electorate office in his jocks. What he didn't realise was that I saw him and questioned him about what the heck he was doing? In normal Hawkie fashion with a big cheeky grin on his face, he said, 'Mate, I was just grabbing my strides!'

•

In the very late 1980s and early 1990s there was a redistribution in the seat of Wills. The seat now took in Windy Hill football ground, which was Essendon Football Club's home ground. I arranged for him to go to the footy, have lunch with his new Wills community members, and watch Essendon v North Melbourne. But all Bob wanted to do was kick back on a Saturday afternoon, have a few bets and listen to the Randwick races. So we came to a compromise. He would attend the footy, attend the lunch, meet as many people as he could, sign as many autographs as he could for the kids, as long as he could have his earpiece in and listen to his beloved nags. The world thought he had the earpiece in listening to Rex Hunt commentating the footy match, when in fact he was having a good day on the punt!

•

I am not sure what Bob was like after his political career, but when I worked for him technology was not his strong suit.* On the morning of Friday 20 December 1991, the day after he was deposed as Prime Minister, he came into his Parliament House office. We were all packing up the office, including the staff who were normally on the front desk looking after incoming phone calls. Bob went into his office to sit behind his desk, and his phone lit up like a Christmas tree. I happened to walk in and he said, 'How the fuck do these things work?' We both looked at each other and just pissed ourselves laughing. Inside, I was thinking, good luck, and welcome back to the real-world, boss!

•

* It didn't improve!

Diplomacy the Johnnie Walker way. Bob's longstanding personal assistant, the late Jean Sinclair, shared a cracker of a story of when Bob was head of the ACTU. It was the Monday before the Melbourne Cup and most of the overseas ambassadors in Canberra were looking for a reason to get to Melbourne the day before the Cup, so that they could justify being in Melbourne for the race itself. A number of high-profile ambassadors had arranged meetings with the head of the ACTU, Bob Hawke, on the Monday afternoon. Bob had been at a long lunch and the ambassadors were now arriving for their one-on-one meetings with him. He was running so late that he essentially had the United Nations waiting for him in his office! These were the days of pre-mobile phones, and 'a runner' had been sent out to find Bob and bring him back to the office. By the time Bob was found and made his way back to the office, he had had a serious liquid lunch and was not in great shape.

However, true to form, Bob reportedly said: 'Jeannie, grab a couple of bottles of Scotch and send all the lads in!' The 'lads' comprised of ambassadors from all around the world, some who would not normally be sitting in the same room. Jean was very concerned that this would be a diplomatic incident, but instead it was a hoot of a night with the 'meeting' going into all hours of the night. Each ambassador was able to get to the Melbourne Cup the next day and send cables back to their respective homelands saying they had spent six to eight hours with the head of the Australian Council of Trade Unions!

•

Bob was always very grateful for the generosity and friendship of my parents, Con and Dorothy Mangos. The Mangos' operated the New Excel Cafe at 347 Elizabeth Street, Melbourne, which was directly opposite ACTU House on the corner of Latrobe and Elizabeth Streets. After moving from Lygon Street Bob was well known to frequent the local watering holes—the Duke of Kent and the Elizabeth Hotel to name but two.

Bob would give it a fair nudge, and then want to drive himself home to Sandringham. On occasions, he could hardly stand; however, he would be determined that he was okay to drive back to Sandringham. The very wise, compassionate and even more determined Dorothy Mangos would escort Bob into the cafe and pump him with black coffees until she was satisfied that he was okay to drive home. Forget the booze-buses, Dorothy Mangos was Bob Hawke's own personal breathalyser machine!

Michael Mangos is friend and former staff member.

Professor the Hon. Stephen Martin

After some persuading, the PM's office agreed that Bob could come to Wollongong for a day at the invitation of myself (I was the Member for Macarthur) and Colin Hollis, the Member for Throsby.

Air Force 1 landed (late) at Albion Park airport, whereby Colin and I met him with great enthusiasm. One lone protester was there with a hastily prepared sign raising concerns about, I think, East Timor. The protester was one Peter Knott, who later became a member of the Parliament himself!

A frenetic day ensued—visiting shopping centres where Bob was mobbed as usual, visiting my old high school whereby a small group of agitated protesters sought to disrupt his speech by banging on the doors and windows of the school assembly hall, and a lunch at the local Italian club. This was followed by a meeting with local trade union officials, and finally a media conference.

Notwithstanding the obvious success of the day with so many positives that could be spoken of and reported, it was Bob's answer to the very first question that has gone down in legend status in the Illawarra.

Reporter: 'Mr Hawke, what is your impression of the Illawarra following your visit?'

Prime Minister Hawke: 'An absolutely beautiful part of the country, BUT that lake [Lake Illawarra]—boy does it pong!'

The next day, the local newspaper, *The Illawarra Mercury*, had a front page that led: PM SAYS LAKE PONGS!

Thank you, Mr Hawke, for enhancing the tourism prospects of our region!

As a footnote, Bob's comments actually got some long-overdue reaction from the state government, and plans were subsequently enacted that kept the mouth of the lake permanently open to the tidal influences of the sea. No more pong!

Ross Free

Bob as PM was leading a spontaneous singalong in the corridor outside the old Parliament's House of Representatives chamber following the final adjournment at 1.33 a.m. on 3 June 1988.* The party raged for some time and strong refreshments were consumed by many (but not Bob). He was in good voice and completely occupied in leading the singing. There were many renditions of 'Solidarity Forever', 'Waltzing Matilda' and 'The Internationale', as well as others that I forget. There was a story of one unnamed reveller who was found in the lift still fast asleep the next morning.

On a more serious note, Bob's reports to the weekly

---

* This refers to the fact that this was the last time Parliament would meet in Old Parliament House. For all its inadequacies, many people were inordinately fond of the place, not least because it kept politics 'human'—people of all parties and ranks and jobs would constantly bump into each other going from A to B, and it fostered genuine friendships and quasi non-partisan 'we're all in this together' feelings across MPs, staff, journos et al. Many a problem or deal was resolved fairly simply by wandering to each other's rooms, or at the bar.

The structure of the new Parliament House, whilst magnificent in many ways, and with superb detailing, tends to have the opposite effect. People are separated, bunkered, and are much more likely to be looking only to their own. It doesn't take a genius to note the sharp decline in camaraderie across party lines!

meetings of Caucus were well known for their comprehensiveness—some unkind souls may at times have even considered them overly lengthy.

On one occasion, Bob was overseas and Deputy PM Lionel Bowen delivered the report as acting PM. My recollection is that it went rather like this: 'I talked to the PM last night. I can report that he is well. I can also report that the country remains in good hands. Are there any questions?'

Lionel's report was received by thunderous acclamation.

Ross Free was an MP 1980–1996.

Anonymous

I most vividly remember, with joy, Bob Hawke's decision in 1989 to plant a billion trees in Australia.* I had become aware of the greenhouse effect in the early 1970s, so this decision made a lot of sense to me. In the following years I noticed the large number of trees appearing along newly constructed highways outside of Sydney. Had Mr Hawke's successors continued in this vein, instead of removing trees, Australia, and the world, would be a much safer and healthier place ecologically.

---

* This was upon the relaunch of Landcare, which Mum and Dad worked hard to support. Mum sometimes said she figured she'd planted thousands herself at gatherings around the country. Landcare recently celebrated its thirtieth anniversary, and has grown into an organisation that works with farmers, councils, community groups and others to care for and improve our environment.

Peter Harris

My favourite Bob Hawke story is about my younger daughter, Stephanie. Almost all of her life she has been known as Polly. Here is why.

In the office, my job as senior private secretary (SPS) was focused on Parliament, Question Time, ministerial standards and the Cabinet work program. I had another role in progressing micro-economic reform, but we called that my night job. And I shared that with Craig Emerson and Rod Sims.

Because of the nature of the SPS job I would often get calls at home at odd hours (given Bob's prodigious appetite for work) about some briefing paper he had up at The Lodge or some idea he had for this week in Question Time. It was pre-mobile phones, so the phone in our lounge room would ring and I had to get there first because my younger daughter loved a chat with her grandmother, and even though she was only three or maybe four years old at the time, she was very quick off the mark to grab the phone and refuse to give it up. STD charges were high back then.

On this Sunday afternoon, I was working in the yard and didn't hear the phone. Neither did my wife. So when I passed by the lounge room and saw Stephanie on the phone singing 'Miss Polly had a dolly that was sick, sick, sick' to her grandmother, I thought I'll have to go rescue that, but went in to wash up first. A few minutes later I'm back, the song is still on continuous repeat from the three-year-old, but I extract the phone expecting to speak to my wife's mother who regularly called on Sundays.

But it was the Prime Minister.

He didn't blow up, and he hadn't hung up on what I gathered was at least five minutes of trying to reason with a very persistent three-year-old. He just said something to the effect of 'she does go on a bit'.

During the week, I sometimes had to pick the girls up from after-school care or day care (I had the family car due to my late hours, and my wife had a job too of course so couldn't always collect them before the 5.30 deadline), and I would put them in the corner office where the PM's visitors wait. After 6 p.m., it was usually unoccupied and it had a TV, so it was good as a holding pen for little girls.

The Prime Minister came down the corridor looking for someone, and observed the little girls (Polly and her older sister) sitting quietly in the big armchairs watching the TV. He comes around to my office and he says something like, 'I see Miss Polly is in residence tonight.' Smiles.

She is still today known in our family as Miss Polly.

It's not the story of Hawke the leader or the reformer or the nation-builder. I'm sure you will have lots of them. Just about patience, and understanding that people have lives outside the big show, and creating a bond inside the tight little group that his office was. No one ever questioned why there were little girls occasionally parked in the orange room. And what might have been an embarrassing episode became part of our family.

Brendon Murley

My most profound memory of Bob Hawke was his response after the Tiananmen Square massacre. His unilateral decision to allow the Chinese students to stay was just the right thing to do. Then when he was told by a public servant that he couldn't, Bob's response was 'Well I've just done it.' He responded humanely with what was needed and right, and figured out how to make it happen later. I was proud—proud to be Australian, proud that he was my Prime Minister. I haven't had that feeling often. That's the memory that will always stay with me.

Rod Sims

Bob was great to work for—full of energy, interested in all issues, and so easy to engage with. While many, many stories can be told about Bob, my abiding memory, and gratitude, comes from some key lessons that I took from him.

Bob was stunningly well organised in his thinking, and in his work organisation. First, Bob would get on top of issues in great detail as they came his way, and deal with them. He would not defer issues.

For example, as a deputy secretary in the Department of Prime Minister and Cabinet, and as his economic adviser, I was often in Cabinet or Cabinet Committee meetings. Bob knew each Cabinet paper in more detail than all other ministers, usually more than the minister sponsoring the paper. Having got completely on top of each issue that came before Cabinet, at later press conferences he would then have complete recall of why the government had acted a particular way.

He was the same with other decisions. Deal with it when it comes to you. Read, discuss, and do not let it go until the right decision was made. Take as long as was needed. He then handed all papers back, and his desk had nothing on it. By giving his full attention to the issue at hand, and not deferring and accumulating issues, he freed his mind to focus fully on what next came his way. His thinking was always clear, in large part because it was uncluttered.

I try hard to emulate all this as best I can: deal with an issue as it arrives, in detail, once, and then dispose of the papers. These days this also means an empty email inbox.

Second, Bob was a master at chairing meetings. What were the key issues that had to be settled? Do not let the conversation get side-tracked on peripheral issues. Allow all views, but provided they were on point. Test views, get to a decision, invariably the right one.

Bob would also calibrate his thinking by who was giving

what view. He knew the strengths and weaknesses of his ministers, when he should give weight to their opinions, and when not.

Bob was an amazing individual. Extremely smart, outstandingly wise, and stunningly well organised. He was in a class of his own.

Rod Sims is currently the Chair of the ACCC.

Bill Bowtell

From the beginning of the Hawke government, I was a senior policy adviser, firstly to the Health Minister and then to the Deputy Prime Minister. The pace of change and events in the Hawke government was always breathtakingly fast but accelerated even more when elections came around.

After the great victory in 1983, things had gone into reverse at the 1984 election with a worrying swing against the ALP, which nevertheless was returned to office. But when the 1987 general election was called for Saturday 11 July, there was no margin for error and every expectation that the result would be very close. Since the 1975 election, the Liberals had held all five Tasmanian seats in the House of Representatives. After over four years in government, few commentators expected that the Hawke ALP government could defeat the incumbent Liberal MPs in any of the five Tasmanian seats.

I came from Hobart, and kept a close eye on local political developments. In 1987, my old Tasmania University friend, Duncan Kerr, had been preselected by the ALP for the Hobart-based seat of Denison. Duncan would be up against Michael Hodgman MP, the long-time, ebullient and very well-known Liberal member. Michael's hold on the seat seemed unshakeable. But I was very happy to move back to Hobart to do what I could for Duncan's campaign. Once I arrived, it became clear that Duncan had put together a very good campaign strategy and team. It became clear to us that, despite all expectations, Duncan was doing more than well enough to bring off an upset victory against Michael Hodgman.

In the final weeks of an election campaign, prime ministers have to make a choice about whether to spend their valuable campaigning time in seats held by their party, or those held by their opponents—that is, whether to play offence or defence. Duncan believed that a visit by Bob was the sure way to seal the deal, and to win the election for Labor. The challenge was to convince Bob to visit Hobart to support Duncan in those critical countdown days to the election. No one at campaign headquarters in Canberra thought that Denison was even a remotely likely victory for the ALP. Their advice to Bob was not to travel to Tasmania but rather to spend time in ALP seats elsewhere that were at serious risk of falling to the Liberals. We argued that a visit by Bob might be the difference between victory and defeat.

To our great relief, Bob accepted the logic of our case, overruled the doubters and cheerfully accepted the risk of spending some of the last few precious campaign days in Hobart, in pursuit of what seemed to be an extremely unlikely prize. Bob duly arrived in Hobart on one of the last days of the 1987 campaign.

Accompanied by a large media contingent, Bob and Duncan set off on a hectic tour of Hobart's southern suburbs. The final stop of the day was at the suburban Taroona Bowls Club, where a tournament was being held. The members greeted Bob enthusiastically. Seeing the Prime Minister, the players on the bowling green invited him to join them. The aim of lawn bowls is to place the bowl as close as possible to the jack. It is not an easy thing to do at any time, let alone in front of the national media and a club full of excited members (and voters). In my superstitious campaign mind, the consequences for the Denison campaign of playing a botched shot on national television were very troubling. A lousy shot would have been a very bad omen.

Of course, no such doubts troubled Bob, who did not hesitate to accept the invitation, stepped onto the green and took the proffered bowl. In front of the packed galleries of members and the media, Bob smiled broadly, waved to the crowd, assessed the state and length of the green and the weight of the bowl. Pausing for effect and suspense, Bob swung back his arm and despatched the bowl. It came to rest just clipping the jack. It was the perfect shot.

The clubhouse erupted in waves of applause and laughter. Bob's bowl had become the metaphor for the Denison campaign. Bob Hawke's qualities as a competitive sportsman, crowd-pleasing entertainer and consummate politician came together in one unforgettable moment. Clearly, it had never occurred to Bob that he could ever bowl a bad ball. Bob beamed, raised his arms in a victory salute, and then embraced the soon-to-be new Member for Denison.

Bill Bowtell AO served in the Hawke–Keating government as senior private secretary (1983–87) to the Minister for Health, senior adviser (1987–91) to the Deputy Prime Minister, and as senior political adviser (1994–96) to Prime Minister Paul Keating.

Bob Brown

Bob Hawke was the environmental prime minister of Australia. His legacy includes Landcare and the listing of Queensland's Daintree Wet Tropics, Shark Bay in Western Australia, Uluru–Kata Tjuta in the Northern Territory, the Gondwana rainforests of the New South Wales–Queensland border region, and large extensions to both the Northern Territory's Kakadu and the Tasmanian Wilderness World Heritage Areas.

The latter was in contention in 1989 after the 'Whispering Bulldozer', Tasmanian Liberal Premier Robin Gray, lost office to Labor's Michael Field and myself leading the five Greens holding the balance of power. We Greens negotiated the expansion of the Tasmanian Wilderness World

Heritage Area by more than 600,000 hectares to include such iconic wilderness as the Walls of Jerusalem, Central Plateau, Denison River Valley. At the end, Field had had enough and called a press conference to announce the outcome. I did not go.

Instead, I was on the phone to Hawke's office arguing that the eastern end of Macquarie Harbour—some 40,000 hectares—should also be included. Hawke agreed so that the most magnificent part of the harbour, including Kelly Basin, the mouth of the Gordon River and the convict ruins on Sarah Island, is, these days, a natural delight, free of otherwise inevitable industrial fish farming, for hundreds of thousands of people catching cruises out of Strahan.

After taking over leadership of the Labor Party before the election in 1983, Bob Hawke committed to saving the Franklin River. The Wilderness Society's peaceful blockade of Premier Gray's dam works threatening the river had seen thousands of people come to Strahan and more than 500 go to Risdon Jail. In Melbourne, at a rally of 15,000 people, Hazel Hawke famously put on 'No Dams' earrings and Bob made an ironclad commitment to stop the dam. On election night, 5 March 1983, he made just one specific commitment: the dam would not go ahead but those affected would be duly compensated. He carried through with both promises.

One recent US outdoors company put the Franklin at the top of the world's ten most desirable whitewater rafting adventures. Had Hawke and Labor not won that election the river would now, instead, be a series of dead impoundments.

Hawke's following masterstroke for the environment was to replace Barry Cohen, his first Minister for the Environment, with Graham Richardson. Never before or since has such a powerful figure on the political landscape of Australia held this portfolio.

Richardson told environmentalists that if he was going to take action he needed to 'hear the crowd roar'. So the late 1980s and early 1990s were perhaps the greatest period of public involvement and environmental advance in Australia. This was not without contention. Richardson faced a jeering anti-environmental mob at Ravenshoe in northern Queensland on the way to the Hawke government having the rainforests given World Heritage status and protection.

In Tasmania, Richardson, working with Hawke's office, made repeated visits to back that 1989 extension of the Tasmania Wilderness World Heritage Area against mounting opposition from loggers and miners and the state government. They stopped the polluting Wesley Vale pulp mill project after a huge campaign led by farmers' daughter Christine Milne.

Of course, Hawke did not please us all the time. He backed uranium mining and flirted with Ronald Reagan's proposal to test MX missiles over the Pacific Ocean. He backed off on a treaty with Australia's First Nations when the proposal came under fire from WA Labor Premier Brian Burke.*

A Hawke masterstroke was to accept the proposal of the Australian Conservation Society's Phillip Toyne and the Farmers Federation's Rick Farley to set up Landcare. This became a beacon of global interest in government-funded repair of rural lands and rivers. That Landcare and general environment spending has been gutted in recent years highlights the loss of vision in Canberra since the great environmental innovation era which Hawke ushered in.

Key to Hawke's environmental success was his listening ear. He knew the Australian public was keen on protecting nature and he made himself open to direct liaison with environmental leaders. He was a tough negotiator but he and his staff opened an ear to the environment.

Richardson was the first Minister for the Environment to alert Cabinet to the onrush of climate change. Decades later, at the twenty-fifth anniversary of the saving of the Franklin in Hobart in 2008, Hawke lambasted the Coalition's lack of concern for the heating planet: 'And as you look at the arguments and the positions of political parties today you see a complete replication of what we experienced back there in 1983. The conservatives: they never change, they never learn. What was their argument back then? You can't

---

* There is comment elsewhere about the failure of this treaty. See Simon Balderstone's piece on page 256 and my comment on page 344.

do this, it will cost jobs. It will cost economic growth. You can't do it, you mustn't do it.'

Hawke did it and, were he Prime Minister in 2019, I reckon the very unpopular Adani coal mine proposal would be headed for the bin.

Hawke initiated the movement, with Paul Keating in the fray, and was joined by the French government in leading the world, against Bush administration misgivings, to formulating the Madrid Protocol which protects Antarctica from mining industrialisation.

Perhaps the Southern Aurora, visible across southern Tasmania the night he died, was nature's accolade for the life of a natural champion.

First published in The Guardian, *17 May 2019.*

Gordon Mair

When I was interviewed by Bob and Hazel in Old Parliament House for the job of house manager at The Lodge, Bob turned to Hazel and said, 'Do you think we will need an interpreter?'*

I replied, 'No, Prime Minister. I understand you perfectly.'

'You're in!' he exclaimed.

It was the beginning of the most exciting period of my life.

---

* Gordon is Scottish.

SPH

Happy days

When Mum and Dad moved into The Lodge, they inherited 'the way things had been done'. Guests, family, everyone, were greeted at the front door by a butler in a morning suit, tails and all, with a bit of an *Upstairs, Downstairs* vibe. It was also an odd building in which to make a family home, whilst retaining standards and capacity to fulfil The Lodge's role as official residence and reception house for meetings, visitors and official guests. Talking about it after a few months living there, Mum and Dad felt 'it isn't very Australian, or at all *us*.' To which Dad added, 'And I don't like being buttled.'

Mum liaised with the relevant parts of the public service, and a plan was drawn up for modern management Aussie-style—professional and personable, efficient yet relaxed. Actual job descriptions were written and advertised. Gordon Mair, who had years of experience in hospitality in Scotland and Australia, was appointed to the role of manager, and others came on board. Over the years, The Lodge did its official job splendidly, whilst becoming a happy, almost extended family-like place behind the scenes. Gordon's wife Jean filled a later vacancy, and our kids, theirs and various others could often be found racing around the place, inside and out. Mum hung a tyre swing from one of the bigger trees, installed a sandpit, made sure there were toys around, and together with the 'official' gardeners threw herself into the garden in her 'spare' time.

Respect and kindliness became the norm, and bonds and friendships formed that lasted long beyond leaving office. In many ways this was a respite from life before and after—our family was growing as grandchildren kept being born, and it was easier to see more of Dad than ever before as he tended to work from home on weekends and pop home for meals sometimes during the week. Mum and Dad were thriving, both busy and focused and happy, sharing a partnership again. Happy days.

Tjerk Dusseldorp

In the year prior to Bob entering politics proper, I met him in my capacity as the first executive director of the Evatt Foundation, when he was still President of the ACTU.

I'd gone to see Bob to ask him what he thought the Evatt Foundation should do to gain the necessary bipartisan support (Fraser was the PM at that time).

I'd been referred to Bob by Dick Kirby, who I had only recently met as he was then the president of the Evatt Foundation. Dick had already told me of their fond regard for each other, which had grown during the time they had met and jostled at robust sessions of the Conciliation and Arbitration Commission.

I used to quip that I had 'two dicks and a bob' in my life, as the other dick was my father, Dick Dusseldorp, of Lend Lease.

It turned out that my dad and Bob also had a fond regard for each other—one famously forged by a long night of drinking, with my father coming out much the worse for wear.

Bob's idea for a 'start up' project for the Evatt Foundation was the genesis of what was to become Work Skill Australia, which he launched at its first national finals event at the newly opened Exhibition Centre in Melbourne's Docklands. Bob was also on hand seven years later when Australia hosted the '88 Youth Skill Olympics, a feature event of the Bicentennial Celebrations in the newly opened Exhibition Centre in Sydney's Darling Harbour.

At the midpoint of this period, I received a phone call at home one evening. 'Arrr, it's Bob here. I want you to come to Canberra and work with me as the head of the Office of Youth Affairs.' My immediate reaction was to say, 'Listen Robert (another friend of mine) you don't fool me with that fake Hawke accent. Bugger off!' And I hung up.

The phone immediately rang again. A furious Prime Minister said in my hot red ear, 'Now listen! I'm asking you to come to Canberra because I'm making "youth" my first priority this year. Get down here as soon as you can and we'll talk about it.' And then he hung up.

A year later, as I was leaving Canberra to return to my family and work in Sydney, I went to see him at The Lodge where he was sunbaking by the pool. He was expecting my visit, of course, and expressed concern that I was leaving because I had felt let down.

I was flabbergasted by this insight as I had thought he had let me down, but only up to a point. The Canberra jungle had not been as rewarding as I'd hoped, and that was hardly Bob's fault.

I last saw Bob in his Sydney office towards the end of last year. He knew I'd come to pay my respects. I wanted to thank him for the opportunity he'd given me thirty years earlier, and all his support along the way. He'd have none of it. 'Listen Derrek,' he said—he could never pronounce my Dutch Christian name, Tjerk—'I've had a fantastic life, and it's time to let go. The last thirty years have been the best, I've got Paul to thank for getting me out of Canberra!'

I realised then that I'd always had more than a fond regard for Bob.

Rob Jolly

The context of this story is that the Cain government was elected in Victoria in 1982 after twenty-seven years in the political wilderness. The incoming Labor government had inherited a ballooning deficit and, in 1983, was looking for tax measures to boost the government's budget position. One of the revenue measures relied on by the Victorian government was the Pipeline Licence Fee. This was a fee paid by

Esso–BHP on the pipelines in Bass Strait that were used to extract oil and gas from the floor of the ocean.

The Pipeline Licence Fee was established under the *Pipelines Act 1967 (Vic)* and initially was set at $35 per kilometre of pipeline. In 1981 the Liberal Thompson government increased the licence fee to $10,000 per kilometre. This was a catalyst for the joint venture arm of Esso–BHP (Hematite Petroleum) to seek a ruling from the High Court as to whether the Victorian government had the constitutional power to collect this revenue. Essentially the challenge was based on the view that the licence fee was an excise duty and that the Victorian government, under the Australian Constitution, did not have the power to impose excise duty. In August 1983, the High Court found in favour of Hematite Petroleum.

This was a significant financial setback for Victoria, as around $50 million revenue was taken from the Victorian budget as a result of the High Court decision. This was a complete surprise to the Victorian government as the strong legal advice received by government was that Hematite Petroleum would not win this case. Following the High Court decision, and after consultation with Premier John Cain, I gave Bob a call asking for the Australian government to compensate Victoria for the loss of revenue. In the Victorian government's view, the principle was clear. The High Court decision had reduced Victoria's underlying revenue base. As the state's revenue base was the foundation for Victoria receiving financial grants from the Commonwealth Grants Commission, it was critical that the Victorian government was compensated for the reduction in its revenue base. The reduction in Victoria's long-term revenue base and potential compensation from the Australian government was the focus of my phone conversations with Bob.

The phone calls to Bob as Prime Minister took place during the closing hours of Parliament in Victoria. The purpose of the calls was to arrange a meeting with the Prime Minister and the federal Treasurer, Paul Keating, to deal with Victoria's revenue loss. After several phone calls, the Prime Minister and the Treasurer agreed to meet with me and the head of the Victorian Department of Management and Budget, Peter Sheehan, the next day in Canberra at 8.30 a.m. The problem was that the Victorian Parliament was sitting and the time was around 11 p.m. This meant that all commercial flights to Canberra from Melbourne were finished for the night. It was back to Bob to find a solution to this dilemma.

I rang Bob and explained our dilemma. He told me that he would contact 'Peter' to find out whether he could find a way for us to get to Canberra for an 8.30 meeting the next morning. The 'Peter' Bob referred to was Sir Peter Abeles, a long-time friend of Bob's. Soon after speaking to Bob, I was contacted by Peter Abeles' office saying that he would arrange for a Learjet to be flown from Sydney to Melbourne to fly Peter Sheehan and myself to Canberra.

Once we were notified, we headed to Essendon airport to catch the Learjet to Canberra. The plane duly arrived at Essendon airport sometime around 1 a.m. We boarded hastily and took off, landing in Canberra a bit after 2 a.m. A great flight in quick time.

We thanked the pilot and headed to our Canberra hotel. After a few hours' sleep, we met with Bob and Paul on time at 8.30 a.m. As you can imagine, Paul was a bit reluctant to hand Victoria any money, but Bob was more sympathetic with Victoria's position. An interesting discussion took place on the pros and cons of Victoria getting compensation for the loss of the Pipeline Licence Fee. In the event, we finished on a positive note and the Victorian coffers were better off by several million dollars.

This episode highlighted a number of Bob's great characteristics—his focus on fairness, his capacity for finding a solution to a perplexing problem and, finally, his ability to produce a result that was accepted by all the parties involved.

Peter Lubans

I lived in Canberra for twenty years and saw lots of politicians come and go but Bob was a delight to watch.

I drove past The Lodge on a daily basis and rarely saw anyone at the front gates, which were normally closed. Then one day to my surprise, there was Bob, leaning on the gate post, arms crossed over his chest, legs crossed, and wearing a pair of Australian Rugby League shorts! He was casually watching the traffic go by as if he was an average Aussie in his average suburban backyard!

Bob was not average.

Anonymous

During the 1980s, I was employed as a drug and alcohol counsellor at the Mount Druitt Polyclinic. Mount Druitt was, and remains, a primarily working-class suburb with high unemployment, large families with many children, many public housing estates, and a high rate of social issues e.g. crime, substance use, domestic violence, poverty, a lack of housing, and so on. The area was socially disadvantaged with a growing adolescent population needing guidance, alternatives to antisocial behaviour (including substance use), support to overcome established life problems, encouragement to be proud of themselves and their suburb, and 'more to do' e.g. leisure and sporting centres.

Being in my twenties, with lots of enthusiasm and a 'can do' attitude, I set a goal to improve the above reality and to specifically address the issue of substance use amongst adolescents in Mount Druitt. As the area was still quite new, it was relatively easy to identify and network the primary 'movers and shakers' within this community. It was with the support of these identified people that a committee was established to prioritise this issue. This community-based committee and associated movement became known as Drugs and Young People-Outwest (DYPO).

The National Campaign Against Drug Abuse had been launched under the direction and support of Bob Hawke and the governing Labor Party in 1985. This assisted DYPO in gaining momentum, media attention and support for this issue in the western suburbs of Sydney.

When forming the concept of DYPO, I was aware of the importance of finding a high-profile individual who could become associated with the movement and its ideals. I needed someone who was perceived as genuine, honest, down-to-earth, understanding of the demographics of Mount Druitt, and who would be accepted by its population. A person who spoke in simple yet inspiring language, who could identify with the challenges of the western suburbs yet also recognised the strengths of the area and its people. If this individual also had some knowledge of the issues around substance use and addiction, that would be ideal.

With the brashness of youth and an innocent naivety as to the protocols around contacting the Prime Minister of Australia, I wrote Bob Hawke a letter asking him to be the patron of DYPO. He was the real, human, emotional yet strong, motivated, educated and inspiring individual the movement needed. I had also always personally admired him for being the unique individual he was—complete in his imperfections, and proudly himself. I sent my letter to Bob Hawke in the hope that he would get it and maybe even respond. I never totally believed that he would (or could) accept such an offer.

I next remember being formally summoned to attend a meeting at the Parramatta offices of the NSW Department of Health. I was very apprehensive in attending this meeting, as I did not know who I was meeting with or why. I feared that I would be severely reprimanded (or terminated) for writing a letter directly to the Prime Minister and ignoring government protocol.

On arrival at the scheduled meeting, I was ushered into a room with three male representatives from the federal government. They asked me about DYPO, its history, my motivation for writing to the Prime Minister, what I expected from him as a patron, and why I did not go through the normal government channels to approach him. They also made it very clear to me that the meeting we were having was not common or within protocol. They stated however that 'Mr Hawke makes his own rules', and that he was considering becoming the patron of DYPO. This made me smile. ('Good onya Bob,' I thought.)

Towards the end of this meeting, these representatives pointed out to me that DYPO would get no preferential treatment in any way from the federal or state government should Mr Hawke become its patron. They also stated that I could in no way ask for preferential funding, extra resources or support if Mr Hawke accepted the offer. All I could do was to say that Mr Hawke was the patron of

DYPO. I accepted these conditions without hesitation. The representatives then left, advising me that I would receive an answer within a fortnight.

I next received a formal letter from Bob Hawke, dated 23 October 1986, accepting the co-patronage of DYPO. I remain extremely excited, pleased and proud to have received this letter. I know that he would have pondered his decision to accept the DYPO patronage. The fact that he concluded that the DYPO movement was a worthy enough cause to be associated with his name, status and reputation continues to humble me.

His patronage gave the DYPO movement further recognition and credibility. It also made the people of Mount Druitt proud, for the Prime Minister of Australia Mr Bob Hawke (the 'lovable larrikin' they all admired) had symbolically joined them, to make their suburb a better place for adolescents and their families.

I never met or talked to Bob Hawke in person; however, his letter remains one of my proudest treasures. He had the guts to be himself, even though 'himself' produced many highs and lows for him and those who loved him. His journey was real and thus magnificent.

Stephen Mills

As Prime Minister, Bob Hawke served five years in the Old Parliament House and three in the new. He was delighted to be the incumbent who made the historic transition from the old to the new.

Some mornings, arriving from The Lodge, he would be dropped off at the front steps of Old Parliament House. He'd spring up the stairs, deliver some doorstop wisdom to the journos, and dazzle the families and school tours inside King's Hall with a burst of high-voltage prime ministerial charisma. Reaching the office, he would stride through the general office and down the staff corridor, greeting us all. Such energy and access couldn't happen in the new Parliament House; it seemed sterile and corporate by comparison.

Most people only saw the public Bob Hawke, campaigning in shopping malls and spruiking his message on TV. We had the privilege and joy of seeing the other half of the political leader, hard at work behind his desk. Cigar in hand, Hawke was intellectually disciplined, focussed and energetic—reading, quizzing a group of ministers or advisers, or meeting with a foreign leader.

Hawke had less regard for the parliamentary side of the job than most prime ministers. Unlike Gough Whitlam or Paul Keating, he had not spent a lifetime as a parliamentarian, mastering the procedures, building his political program and strutting his stuff in question time. He had risen outside Parliament, had exercised more real power in the trade union movement, and had generated more media attention than most elected MPs.

But when it came to convening the Summit—a major 1983 election campaign promise—he moved immediately to open the doors of the House of Representatives for the purpose. He issued invitations to nearly 100 men and women—trade union leaders, business CEOs, leaders of churches and welfare groups, along with federal, state and local government leaders—to come to Canberra as delegates, and to participate in an unprecedented discussion about the nation's economic, industrial, fiscal and investment future.

Hawke's opening speech as chairman of the Summit was his first as Prime Minister in the Reps chamber. In his speech, Hawke's sense of identification with his predecessor John Curtin was deep and emotional. The Summit did achieve consensus, despite it being the first time that many of the business titans had met real trade unionists, and vice versa. It cemented the Labor–union Accord as the centrepiece of the nation's economic policy for the 1980s, delivering wage restraint in a very Hawke-style negotiated trade-off for increased social spending. And it laid the foundations, economic and electoral, of the most successful and effective Labor reform governments that we have seen.

This is an edited excerpt of an article originally published in June 2019 on the Museum of Australian Democracy's website.

Dr Stephen Mills was Bob Hawke's speechwriter, 1986–91.

Jack Newton OAM

I was honoured to get to know Bob Hawke so well over forty years. I played snooker at his house in Melbourne, I played golf with him on a number of occasions, and we became relatively close on all fronts. When he became Prime Minister in 1983 I decided to ask him if he would be patron of my Jack Newton Celebrity Classic, and then later when I set up my Junior Golf Foundation in 1986, both of which he agreed to.

He was the perfect patron to escalate the value of the event, particularly when he wandered on stage, grabbed the microphone, and contributed an outstanding rendition of 'Waltzing Matilda' with about seven verses. He rattled everybody in the room; we all stood up and applauded him. We will now all sing in honour of Bob each year! I hope we do him proud. I am sure he will be listening!

Not long after Bob became Prime Minister, I was flattened by an aircraft (Cess 210) on the tarmac at Kingsford Smith airport. I ended up in nearby Prince of Wales hospital. The damage was serious—the propeller had gone down through my right eye, my right arm and across my stomach. I was in intensive care for two months under the care of Dr Jim Neild, Professor Fred Hollows and Dr Michael Baldwin. Bob Hawke came to see me in intensive care, and this gave me a good 'kick'.

Bob was an extremely intelligent man. He was always forthcoming in his opinion as a Rhodes Scholar, but was never insolent in what he had to say. I admired the way he could always manage to include himself, no matter what the conversation, especially with a beer and cigar in hand. He was not only a great Prime Minister but also a wonderful man with a big heart. I'll miss him, but will always remember the great memories. RIP.

Llyr Otto

I met Bob when I was a fourteen-year-old participant in the public speaking competition Youth Speaks for Australia. The speech we were to give was about being Prime Minister of Australia. Bob was there as a visiting dignitary, and he told me that I could do anything I set my mind to in life, and that I should aim to be the first red-headed female prime minister!

My path lead me elsewhere, and Julia Gillard took that title, but Bob's words inspired and motivated me. I was an awkward black girl from an abusive home where my father told me that I was useless and, like all women, I would amount to nothing. Yet this jolly man who shook my hand and looked me straight in the eye told me different.

Now, over forty years later, I have spent my life aiming for my dreams, and whilst I did not become prime minister, I have had a very busy and productive life where I remembered Bob's words: I could do anything if I set my mind to it. I am an accomplished nurse with a Bachelor's and two Masters' degrees, and my own business. This one encounter when I was fourteen years old shaped my life, and I will always remember him for this.

Mark Riesel

In the early 1980s, when I was in my early twenties, I decided to sell candles to the picnic-going public at the Concert in the Domain series in Sydney. At one of these concerts I learnt that Prime Minister Bob Hawke would be arriving, so when I saw the limo arrive onto the lawn backstage I hot-footed it there.

Bob got out of his limo, dressed immaculately in his suit, and I approached in T-shirt and shorts and announced: 'Ah g'day Bob! Wanna support free enterprise and buy a candle?'

His reply was instant and unmistakable: 'I do enough to support free enterprise!' followed by a 30-second speech.

My response? 'Ah, so you wanna buy a candle?'

Bob patted his suit pockets, which were empty, and frustratedly turned to his entourage, who handed him the few dollars.

'Thank you, Bob. Can you autograph the label on one of the candles?'

Bob obliged.

About fifteen years later as I left Jack Cowin's office after watering the plants, I headed down the corridor to catch the lift back down. Bob's office was just along the corridor. Blanche and Bob got in the lift at the same time, both immaculately dressed. I was in my The Plant Man company uniform. Bob immediately struck up a conversation like a good old mate, even though he would not have known me from Adam.

The thing that struck me both times was his accessibility, warmth, sincerity, and his natural engagement with people.

Leon Saunders

In the mid-1980s, when the Cold War was still on, I was a script writer on *A Country Practice.* In response to recent surveys revealing that an alarming proportion of young people were so fearful of a nuclear war that they couldn't see the point in getting married and having children, we plotted an episode to address the issue. It involved a young Wandin Valley High student who has become suicidal because of the recurring nightmares he's been having about the destruction of the world as we know it. His schoolmates rally round him, and come up with the idea of staging an anti-nuke rock concert to raise awareness of the issue. But they'll need to have a high-profile public figure as guest-of-honour.

We racked our brains at the plotting session. Who could it be? A rock star perhaps? A famous writer; a politician, maybe? How about the Prime Minister? But who would you get to play Bob Hawke? More brain racking, until a light went on upstairs, and I said, 'Why don't we ask the man himself?' And the rest, as they say, is history. The only time a sitting Prime Minister of Australia has appeared in a television soapie.

We staged the concert at a showground near Richmond. Bob was flown into Richmond airbase, and driven to the location in a white limo, Aussie flag flying. He delivered the script I'd written, from memory, word-for-word, in which he promised the kids of Wandin Valley he would do everything in his power to prevent the possibility of nuclear war.

I was introduced to him at the end of the shoot. He shook my hand and said, 'It was a great speech. I couldn't have written a better one myself, and I can't offer you a greater compliment than that.'

You might say humility was never Bob's strong suit. But his occasional lack of it gave me one of the proudest moments of my life. And the script, 'Listen to the Children', went on to win a Media Peace Award from the United Nations Association in 1986.

Thanks Bob, for being one of the great leaders of my lifetime.

Jeni Simpson

I didn't know Bob personally; however, I did knew Sue and Jan Pieters-Hawke.

I remember the friends they gathered at Kirribilli House in Sydney before the birth of their first child, Sophie, and how all those I spoke with had a great respect for Bob and Hazel Hawke. How Bob was there in the capacity of father to Sue and future grandfather of the forthcoming baby; he never pulled rank on anyone there—he was their equal. That, to me, is a wonderful man—someone who can put aside the public persona and be the father. I found it very gratifying that my friends all thought the world of Bob Hawke from their experiences with him at that time.

SPH

Magical days

Mum and Dad loved the peace and water and sunlight at Kirribilli House, the PM's Sydney residence. We lived nearby, which was a bonus, so as well as visiting them in Canberra, we spent a lot of time with them at Kirribilli. Staff, friends of family, and whoever else was around mingled there. My daughter (who, in the piece above, was about to be born) has fond memories of all the kids and cousins rolling down the grass slopes, then being all put in the bath together by Mum 'to wash off the itchy grass'.

Weekends there had a familiar pattern: Dad would be sitting in the sun or the lounge, working his way through several briefcases full of briefings, interspersed on Saturday with form guides and calls with the racing fraternity. (Not many sisters at that time!) He had a ferocious capacity for concentration, so never seemed bothered by the goings-on, and would sit amongst us rather than in the study unless he had meetings. As the kids grew in number and activity, they would often go to him, or he would look up fondly or briefly do something with them. He seemed so happy at these times—working away, surrounded by family—it is one of my enduring memories of him.

Kirribilli House would also have to be one of the best places in the world to watch New Year's Eve fireworks. We'd often have a small party of family and friends, watching, wonderstruck as plumes of colour exploded above us and the ash drifted slowly to the water below. Magical days.

The Hon. *Jason* Clare MP

I grew up watching Bob on TV. He was the man with the funny voice and the big wavy hair. The man so often with the tears in his eyes. And the man with the lairy jacket on the day we won the America's Cup.

As I grew up, I saw a different Bob Hawke. I realised that he was the man who gave my mum the green card she used to pull out whenever we went to the doctors. And he was the man responsible for a lot more kids from working-class suburbs finishing high school. In 1983, only about three in ten kids finished high school in Australia. By the end of that decade, more than 70 per cent did. I was part of that 70 per cent.

I only met Bob in the last few years of his life. Meeting your heroes can be a scary thing. But not Bob. He was very kind to me. He was always very generous with his time and with his advice. He was also very funny. He used to tell a lot of jokes. And he always asked about my wife, Louise. He used to remind me that the age gap between Louise and me was the same as him and Blanche.

We also talked about death. He always seemed very much at peace with it, whenever it came. I remember telling him that maybe that was because he knew that even after he was gone, so much of him and what he did would live on. And I think he knew that.

There are a lot of us who yearn for another Bob Hawke. I can understand that. But people like Bob are like Halley's Comet. They don't come around that often.

I miss him terribly. But instead of mourning what we have lost, or hoping, somewhat vainly, for some kind of political reincarnation, maybe we should just take a look around and be grateful for everything he has left us.

He is the green card in your pocket. He is the superannuation you will retire with. He is the architect of so much of what is Australia today. His invisible fingerprints are all around us. And we are a better country for it.

Catia Malaquias

I migrated to Perth, Western Australia, with my family, at the age of thirteen. It was February 1986, the same year that Australia became legally independent from the United

Kingdom, and the year that *Crocodile Dundee* became a worldwide hit.

Only three years earlier, *Australia II*, the yacht owned by Alan Bond, had won the America's Cup for the Royal Perth Yacht Club, and WA-raised Bob Hawke became Australia's Prime Minister, a position he held until 1991.

Within a few weeks of arriving, I had enrolled at Bob Hawke's old high school, Perth Modern School, and eventually I would study law at the University of Western Australia, like he did.

When Bob Hawke passed away in mid 2019, those memories rushed back. It's hard to describe how it felt as a child, to arrive from grey old Europe in winter, into this modern, prosperous metropolis, glistening in the dry summer heat, but I remember being told at the time that I'd just moved to the world's most isolated capital city. And yet, I was sure that I had landed at the very centre of the world.

It wasn't until much later that I understood the detail of how Bob Hawke transformed this nation and the enormous legacy he left as a Prime Minister, but what was palpable to me back then, as a child, was the mood of those times, unapologetic in their optimism and embracing promise and progressive social values.

Today, as the parent of three children, including one with disabilities, and as an advocate for human rights and inclusive education, I have come to recognise Bob Hawke as much more than the larger than life prime minister of my childhood. He was also the bold architect of some of our most significant reforms, especially when it comes to our responsibility to our society's most marginalised.

Next year, my eldest daughter, Laura, will start high school at Perth's new Bob Hawke College Subiaco, when it opens its doors in 2020. [Catia's daughter's story is on page 330.] I have been involved in the Principal's Advisory Group, and the words 'extraordinary together' have guided us in our work, capturing both the school's inclusive ethos and the values of difference and diversity.

Bob Hawke was indeed extraordinary, and so was his legacy; from Medicare to education as well as workplace, superannuation and progressive tax reforms, environmental protections and anti-discrimination laws among other things, he left our country a fairer place.

Bob Hawke has inspired me and I hope that his memory will inspire my children and a whole new generation, including the students who will pass through the doors of Bob Hawke College, to be the best that we can be as unique individuals and as a community of people who are connected and collectively responsible, to each other, to our nation and to the world beyond it.

Kim Beazley

Bob's friends are legion and his admirers even more. He was so much bigger than life at large, and the things which made him attractive, so media vivid—it is impossible to set that aside to get at the deep seriousness of the man. When he needed to be, he was a man of iron discipline. The country he loved and feared for required his concentration, skill and his deep experience. He gave Australia that in government.

He was deeply invested in the history of things, not least in his own historical setting. He eschewed the view, and did not compete for the title, of him being the best Australian Prime Minister. He deferred to John Curtin with the existential challenges the nation faced in his day. It was not a throwaway proposition. He had studied Curtin's actions putting together a fragmented Labor party. Not moving on conscription 'til converting the party. A relationship with unions throughout the war. Preparation for post-war societal change. A willingness to challenge shibboleths when national survival dictated it on foreign or domestic policy.

He was a small boy when Curtin was PM but in Bob's political family his profile loomed large. In the face of Curtin's example Bob wanted to be Australia's best peacetime Prime Minister. A year or two ago I discussed with Bob what he thought prepared him for office. I expected him to say years of advocacy for the ACTU in the National Wage Case and years of union leadership. This background endeared him to millions of Australians, giving them the idea that he was on their side and he could fix things. Bob acknowledged the value of all that but he said on reflection, another service was most valuable: the then Reserve Bank

Board on which he sat for much of the 1970s. At that point the board, not the Treasury, was at the forefront of national thinking on freeing up the sclerotic regulatory encirclement of the Australian financial sector and broader economy. The bank had studied the dilemma extensively and Bob was across the study. When he took office he was prepared for change often in the face of recalcitrant senior officials in the Treasury. He was arguably the best prepared PM we have had for a period of deep reform.

I said at Bob's memorial service that he manifested British nineteenth century theoretician Walter Bagehot's view of what constituted great prime ministers—'men of common-place opinions and uncommon administrative abilities.' Bob's views were not so commonplace. His personal attributes and values were. He had typically Australian aspirations and affections and values. That helped people trust him. He knew that political stances he took on his reforms and even more broadly on social matters, such as immigration or race, were not necessarily broadly shared. Here his view was not to retreat but to convince. He had boundless, well-founded confidence in his ability to persuade. The basis of that ability was a public perception that he was one of us.

There is no question of his uncommon administrative abilities. He was unsurpassed in his comprehension of the structure of decision-making: who needed to be brought into a decision, what processes a decision needed to transit, how it should be followed up for evaluation. Combined with his deep understanding of Australian history and economy, this was decisive. At Bob's memorial service I talked about how he governed. He was conscious that the process was critical. He faulted the Whitlam government, not for its directions and intentions, but for chaotic decision-making processes. I left one component out of my list in the eulogy and will add it in here. This was his view of the public service.

Firstly, he wanted his ministers to be effective. He had a superb office, an engine of reform, but its functions did not include micromanaging ministers and suppressing them in daily messaging. He told ministers: 'You know the policy, you know your resources, you proceed. I will interfere when you invite me in or to resolve matters where a policy issue crosses portfolios. My reputation will rise or fall on the quality of my ministers' performance.' He meant that. He took great delight in ministers' successes.

He did, however, want disciplined decision-making from ministers. Here his regard for them intersected with his regard for the public service. The latter were crucial to a well thought through, implementable decision. I remember, a week or two into office, Bob calling the ministry together. Those who had been Opposition frontbenchers were giving their Opposition advisors chief of staff roles. He told us to set them aside. Appoint them advisors but not the managers of business. He told us to ask our departmental heads for an up and coming public servant for chief and two public service liaison officers. He was determined that what we said and did was efficiently staffed.

Then there was Cabinet. For Bob, Cabinet was above all. Cabinet, for him, was what made the government cohere. That point was driven into me when I had successfully nagged Bob into taking the Cabinet to sea. It was the Navy's seventy-fifth birthday. We were put on the biggest ship, HMAS *Stalwart*, joining it at Garden Island in Sydney. A Cabinet table had to be put aboard. A photo exists of a cheerful Bob at that table. That was taken before the *Stalwart* passed through Sydney Heads. Then, as the boat rocked in the open ocean, the table moved, threatening to pin Bob to the bulkhead. It moved throughout the entire Cabinet meeting, which was completed despite a repeated prime ministerial cry of 'F . . . this' as he fought the table off. Afterwards, he was not happy with me: 'You know Cabinet is the heart of our government. We cannot have the Cabinet table running away and killing a couple of us on the way through.'

Peter Walsh, no fan of Bob's, told me that only two ministers read every submission: himself and Bob. On Sunday afternoon, Bob would have his senior advisors around for tennis and then go through every submission. That knowledge was clear whenever your submission came up. He was across your flaws even if you weren't. The big decisions of government drew Cabinet even more into focus. Tax reform, communications reform, for example, would produce large submissions. They would be set a week out from the Cabinet meeting in the Cabinet room. A roll of ministers was presided over by a public servant. They would mark off each attendant and time. You would not want to appear neglectful.

Bob was available to his ministers, particularly if you were worried about a submission but also more generally.

Bob's working days, particularly when Parliament was in town, often ran to eighteen hours. A minister could see him but not guarantee the time. When I was Defence Minister, my time was often around midnight and the last of the day. This was because I was one of the few ministers like Bob who smoked cigars. End of day, time to light up. We would, and what would follow would be very productive for me. Every now and then Bob would go on the wagon but would insist I light up. Then he would ask for a puff—more frequently, 'til he took over. I tired of this unhealthy exchange of bodily fluids. I then responded to his invitation by lighting two cigars in my mouth at the same time. 'You bastard,' he said as he took one and the nonsense ended.

Bob's big agenda was domestic reform. Secondarily, it was foreign policy, with large initiatives, as he pushed the frozen boundaries of the Cold War. The eminent person's initiative on South Africa was one. The Antarctic Treaty to ban mining, numerous arms control initiatives like the South Pacific Nuclear Free Zone. The creation of APEC, the Cambodian Peace Initiative, and many more. He was deeply engaged with his Foreign ministers.

He was interested in Defence but not so forward-leaning. He supported reform and privatisation in the Defence industry. He was interested in the Defence White Paper. I remember meeting him at a Perth hotel during Australia's America's Cup defence to brief him on it. I waited for him below when a bus drew up with seventy sprightly older women on board. 'How nice of you to meet us, Mr Beazley,' they said. 'Oh no, I am waiting for Mr Hawke,' I replied. 'Can we wait too?' 'Sure,' says I. They descended on him cuddling and kissing him robustly. I separated him, him reluctant, after twenty minutes and briefed him there sitting around the pool on the top floor. He was distracted.

He could be intrigued by the big Defence items. There was a fraught Cabinet debate on source selection for the Collins submarine. The German offer was bid from Newcastle, expected to win, and NSW ministers were keen. Bob expected that too, as did I. However, I took the Royal Australian Navy's preference for the Swedish submarine to be built in Adelaide to Cabinet. The debate was long 'til Bob ended it. 'Okay, it's what the Navy wants which counts. They have to sail it. We must go along with them.' Duly passed, then Bob said to me, 'I will go with Oscar (programme director Admiral Oscar Hughes) to Adelaide to announce it. You will go to Newcastle to explain it!'

Once I had to go with Chief of Navy, Admiral Mike Hudson, to debate with Finance Minister Peter Walsh over whether the new frigates should have a 76mm or a 5-inch gun, Bob presiding. In the end, Peter gave way and said, 'Well, Defence has a global budget so they can make the savings for their preferred more costly option.' Bob was intrigued by the admiral. Guns over, he suggested with movements afoot like the new Armed Forces Federation the admiral might like to think of a broader environment of discussion in the Navy. The alarmed admiral drew himself up to say, 'Prime Minister, in the Navy, we defend democracy, we don't practise it.' Bob referred to that frequently for some time afterwards.

Bob was conscious that we pushed Cold War limits but he did not want to offend the allies. He was cautious that the terms of the South Pacific Nuclear-Free Zone should not be perceived as pushing the South Pacific nations in the New Zealand direction of bans on nuclear ship visits. He was anxious after the White Paper was tabled. I should visit our Southeast Asian friends and allies and convince them of our continued military commitments. He was annoyed by the New Zealand stance but was anxious we sustain the defence relationship even if we had to purge the intelligence component of it of US-sourced material.

He was aware that the MX missile testing issue had damaged America's views on us. After urging me to stick with the policy, he decided it would open lines of debate in Australia that called into question our policy supporting ship visits, and more importantly the US/Australian joint facilities in Australia. He convinced Secretary of State George

Schultz, a deep personal friend, to pull the proposed test. Having succeeded, whilst Bob was visiting Washington, he didn't take a backward step. He was irrepressible. He suggested to President Reagan at their meeting that Reagan's Strategic Defence Initiative (Star Wars) was destabilising the peace-preserving stasis of mutual deterrence in the global nuclear balance. Australia kept out of it.

The essence of the thing was Bob always having an eye to what could be sustained in the party and movement. He accepted, like Curtin, that they were a legitimate part of the Australian political debate. As with Cabinet, he would operate through them, not against them or by sidelining them. When a submission of mine to the Security Committee leaked which suggested, given US/UK escort of Australian ships in the Gulf, that we were morally obliged to help, he was supportive. I suggested, given the mine threat, we should deploy RAN clearance divers. The most practical contribution during the Iran–Iraq War. He insisted before putting it to Cabinet and Caucus that I should visit the secretary of the Seaman's Union to elicit his views. The latter was not pleased to see me. 'Security issues are a matter for you, not me,' he very reasonably said. That was good enough for Bob, and he supported it through the two bodies.

Bob was intrigued by the US/Australian joint facilities. He was conscious of their value and aware of the party position of Australian full knowledge of and concurrence with their operation. We extended the treaties, and Bob closely monitored negotiations that saw mutual agreement on massively increasing the Australian presence at Pine Gap and Nurrungar. He then put more on the public record than had been the case to that point, with a supportive speech in Parliament.

Bob's point of reference on party priorities was Curtin's engagement of the unions and party federal conference in ending Labor opposition for conscription for overseas service. That had been a focus of Gough Whitlam's view on Curtin and the US alliance also. Using the machinery, not circumventing it, was Bob's view across all issues. When he removed me from Defence, 'You have been working for yourself to this point; now you must work more broadly,' he said to a disappointed me when in his abbreviated last term he made me Transport and Communications Minister. He told me the portfolio issues would be central to his next phase of micro-economic reform. 'Your first job is to get this (the reforms) through the Caucus and the union movement to a successful outcome at a federal conference of the ALP.' A minefield, but it was done.

Bob was fascinated by the potential of peak organisations to drive his agenda. The unions, of course, but also the employer groups—Indigenous, environmental and rural groups, multicultural, arts, sporting, social and religious groups. For him, they were the transmission belts of change to the community. Not all or even most of them were Labor supporters, but they were vital parts of the Australian community—so he loved them and many, despite themselves, requited it. He built trust in his agenda. For him, the overwhelming calculation was his love for his country and our people.

He never forgot who he was fighting for. He once said: 'The essence of power is the knowledge that what you do is going to have an effect, not just an immediate but perhaps a lifelong effect, on the happiness and wellbeing of millions of people, and so I think the essence of power is to be conscious of what it can mean for others.'

I am indebted for that quote to a WA businessman, Charlie Bontempo, who was deeply impressed by it. I don't believe we shall see Bob's like again in politics in my lifetime. Now, as was said of Abraham Lincoln by his Defense Secretary, 'He belongs to the ages.'

Where is he now? Bob set great store by his pastor father Clem's saying, 'If you believe in the fatherhood of God, you must believe in the brotherhood of man.' We talked of this in our last conversation. I believe, as I said in my eulogy, that he is in the arms of a loving God. He believed he would live in the hearts or at least the minds of those who knew him. Then, when we are all gone: in the history books and stories of future generations. There he will reside while ever his nation abides.

Corrie Furner

I worked for Sue Pieters-Hawke in the late 1980s* and found that Bob was exactly like you saw him on TV. I used to drive into Kirribilli House so that Sophie and Ben, Bob and Hazel's grandchildren, could spend time with them, have a swim. I would take them in my partner Brooke O'Mahoney's 1976 Toyota Corona. Security would diligently check under the car using a bomb detection mirror!

My first and most memorable moment with Bob was seeing him laying back on a deck chair at Kirribilli House, budgie smugglers and brown as a berry, transistor radio in hand listening to the horse races. I also remember my partner Brooke, nineteen and studying a Bachelor of Business at the University of Technology Sydney, chatting with Bob on a number of occasions about the state of the economy.

Richard Flood

I am a long-time member of the Professional Golfers Association of Australia and was the head professional at The Lakes Golf Club in Sydney and that's where I had the honour

* At that time I was running a couple of things (Mum's office, and a Qigong clinic and school with Chinese Qigong masters) mostly from home, but the kids were still young and work was more than fulltime! Corrie saved my sanity and our family's wellbeing by being an amazing and flexible 'nanny' and companion to the kids. She even took them on holidays once to her home town in regional NSW.

of meeting our Prime Minister. This all came about when a good friend of the PM called and asked if I could assist. The brief was simple: make him look good. Well, there was some pain and suffering, but to his credit he stuck at it.

The voice

He would usually ring just before dinner on a Sunday to say that he was okay for our early start on the Monday. Then one week he told me he would be away, so I wasn't expecting a call at any time. At around 10 a.m. that Sunday morning, the phone rang when I was in another room. My young son answered the phone, 'Hello?', and the caller said, 'G'day mate, is your dad home?'

My son told the caller, 'I will get him for you', and, with the phone in hand, he sang out to me: 'Hey Dad, there is a man on the phone with a funny voice who wants to talk to you!'

Straight away, I thought, *My God, it's the PM. What am I going to say*? I just said, 'You are back early!' and we arranged to meet the next morning, all good.

My boy did get to meet the Prime Minister soon after that, and we took a nice photo of them.

Lost in the moment

We were on the golf course playing our last hole for the morning and after three good shots on this par 5, he was putting for a birdie. He then called the four minders who were with us and we directed them into position behind him to form an instant gallery—and would you believe it, he goes and makes the putt!

We all clap and cheer. Even the PM lifts his putter in the air and goes into his characteristic laughter. It was a very important birdie—I think it was his first—and with all the excitement going on we were lost in the moment, especially the PM. Eventually, he asked his main minder the time of his first appointment. The PM then turned to me and asked if I had time for more playing. I said, 'Okay with me!' He then had his main man ring and advise the company that were expecting him that the PM had been delayed. Could you imagine a red carpet laid out, with the company's managing director and staff waiting for the PM to arrive? While he plays golf!

The Bob Hawke I knew was a good person and loved his golf, as he did most sports. I was happy that he was our PM back then as he made you feel special and so many liked him. I also enjoyed coaching and golfing with Mrs Hazel Hawke who always enjoyed her outings. My memories, coaching and golfing with the Prime Minister, will always stay with me.

Richard Flood is a golf professional and member of PGA Australia.

Gareth Evans

As Bob was always himself the first to acknowledge, he wasn't *perfect*. He was famously sheepish (not that Hazel and the kids gave him much choice in the matter) about being designated in his ACTU days as 'Father of the Year'. To drink with him, as I often did, along with the trade union crowd at the John Curtin Hotel in his pre-political boyo days, was to appreciate that he was an unusual anatomical and sartorial combination of short arms and deep pockets.

To play tennis with him, as I often did at his home at Sandringham in the early days, was to learn that his eyes, when it came to line-calls, saw things differently from other mortals. And to play golf with him, as I often did on cold early mornings in Canberra when he was Prime Minister, was to learn quickly that he had a different understanding than the rest of us of the basic laws of arithmetic.

But if Bob wasn't perfect, *gee he was good.* Bob Hawke at his best was as good as it gets for an Australian Prime Minister, and I suspect for a Prime Minister just about anywhere else in the world. For nearly a decade, through four successive election victories, he had a remarkable hold over both his colleagues and his country, leading a government that is almost universally still judged—including on the other side of politics—as the Australian gold standard. And he had and maintained that hold for at least four good reasons.

First, there was his great capacity to craft a grand political narrative. From the outset we had what any successful government needs: a clear philosophy and sense of policy direction, in our case built around the themes of very dry, pro-competitive economic policy; very warm and moist social policy, with the dry economic discipline accompanied by delivery—through health, education and superannuation policies—of a very compensatory 'social wage'; and liberal internationalist foreign policy—essentially the Third Way model subsequently embraced by Tony Blair and Gordon Brown.* Bob Hawke was a leader who led.

Second, there was Bob's legendary ability to connect with people at all social levels, and to make others warm to him, both privately and publicly. Partly, this was a function of his manifestly exuberant pride in and affection for all things Australian. Partly, in the Australia of the 1980s, it was his uncontrived blokiness: his obvious ability to empathise with anyone preoccupied with sport, sex, having a beer, having a punt, or making a buck.

And less blokey types, including among his colleagues, could relate to his obvious intelligence. On absolutely no subject was Bob anyone's dummy, notwithstanding his almost complete lack of interest in less carnal pursuits such as art, music, literature, philosophy or history (despite punishing his Cabinet colleagues for some months with anecdotes from a biography someone had thrust upon him of the first British Prime Minister, Sir Robert Walpole!).

Not the least of Bob's attractiveness to people, even those (like Margaret Thatcher) who didn't share all his beliefs, was the obvious genuineness of the beliefs he held. The

---

* A contestable assertion, but . . .

tears he shed in the Australian Parliament for the victims of the Tiananmen massacre forty years ago were as genuine as those ever shed anywhere by anyone in public life. He had a total and absolute abhorrence of racism in any shape or form, which made him a formidable advocate, in the Commonwealth and around the world, for the downfall of South Africa's Apartheid. And he was, ahead of his time, an equally passionate environmentalist, leading the global charge to make Antarctica a mining-free wilderness park in perpetuity.

One of the more intriguing features of Hawke's personality, which again made people warm to him, was his grace in victory. His battles were usually fought with no holds barred—with snarling invective almost always preferred to the verbal rapier—but once won, were usually followed by great generosity to the losers (the only exception I can remember being the hard Left of the Victorian State Labor Party, for whom he retained a visceral lifelong distaste). Malcolm Fraser was an early beneficiary of that instinct, as were a number of Cabinet and ministry colleagues (including me in my Attorney-General days) who fell out of favour from time to time. And all this was equally matched with grace in defeat, as we saw with the Caucus ballot that finally ended his long political reign.

Bob's grace toward his opponents, which seemed invariably to be reciprocated, is exemplified in his 1994 memoir in what he says about the British Prime Minister with whom his battles, particularly over South Africa, were legendary: 'I have a certain admiration for Margaret Thatcher. There is so much of her philosophical approach to domestic and international politics that I cannot share, but she is a formidable and remarkable person—applied, committed, dogged, dogmatic, determined and certainly courageous.'

The third reason why Bob's reign lasted as long as it did was that he operated in a genuinely collegiate manner. His Cabinets operated overwhelmingly on the basis of argument rather than authority. The Prime Minister may have been first among equals, but only just. Everything was contestable, and contested. We argued everything out, often very fiercely, and didn't just succumb passively to the exercise of leadership authority. The language used around the Cabinet table was sometimes more redolent of the schoolyard than 10 Downing Street. But it reflected the intensity of the views held, and everyone's willingness to fight for their corner.

When it came to cheerfully obscene language, around the Cabinet table or anywhere else out of public earshot, Bob had rivals in Paul Keating and some of the rest of us, but no real equal. I remember an occasion back in the mid-1980s at the ALP national executive when, having been quoted in the media as telling the last executive meeting that we would 'shit it in' at the next election, and having suffered a deluge of wowserish public complaints thereafter, his oral language at this meeting was actually a model of decorum. But the urge to compensate in writing was overwhelming, and at one stage—after a particularly dull and plodding half-hour—he passed me a note which read as follows.

> Have you read McGooligan, the 19th century poet, I offer the following with no undue deference to him:
>
> Do you enjoy the mental stimulation,
> Or is it intellectual masturbation,
> From your attendance at this meeting
> Which, thank Christ, is very fleeting?
> If the size of their minds reflects their organs of sex
> And you applied De Minimis Non Curat Lex,
> Then if you rated their chance of getting a fuck
> They'd get what they deserve—no bloody luck.

Bob's collegial and consultative instincts extended to the way in which he worked with ministers on their individual portfolios: so long as we weren't screwing up, or deviating too far from the government's collective storyline, he let us get on with the job and make our own running in the media and Parliament as we saw fit.

Bob's collegiality was certainly genuine and instinctive, but it was reinforced by the character of the government he led. He operated on the clear understanding that unilateral captain's calls would never fly, not least because he had a Cabinet around him that was neither timorous nor deferential. We demonstrated that early on in the life of the government, with a spectacular assault on three centuries of established Anglo-Saxon Cabinet tradition.

Although Bob was famously punctilious about starting meetings on time (and famously regular in lambasting Paul Keating for his indifference to that constraint), one way he kept his record intact was by regularly rescheduling Cabinet meetings at the last minute when he found himself with something more urgent to do. On the day in question Cabinet had been called then postponed in the morning, then called and postponed again in the afternoon, and finally called again for 6.15 p.m. We were all milling around the ante-room when the message came through that the Prime Minister was busy again and had now cancelled it, although as before there was no obvious crisis running of a kind that would make this understandable.

About six of us then said, more or less in unison, let's go ahead and have the bloody thing anyway, which we duly proceeded to do, with the result that Bob rather sheepishly joined us about twenty minutes later. The rebellion did not extend to dealing with any particularly contentious item in the boss's absence, but the point was made—and accepted. Neither Bob nor Paul—who followed his example in this respect—always loved the reality of Cabinet peer group pressure. But both of them accepted they were running a Cabinet, not a presidential, system.

The fourth and remaining major key to Bob's success as Prime Minister was the personal and institutional discipline he brought to the role. If never quite a candidate for Mount Athos, his lifestyle became almost ascetic, certainly by comparison with the exuberance of his larrikin days at university and with the trade union movement. And he led his ministerial colleagues by example, working long hours, thoroughly reading his briefs, and maintaining a disciplined diary.

Bob was determined to avoid the manifest dysfunction of Gough Whitlam's wonderfully exuberant but very short-lived government eight years earlier and, from the outset, important ground rules were laid down and observed about Cabinet–outer ministry, ministry–Caucus, executive–public service and ministerial office relations. Good Cabinet process, including prior consultation with all relevant portfolios and interests, was rigorously followed; as I have already mentioned, free debate was not only allowed but encouraged (not that it could really ever have been suppressed, given the ministers round the table); and outcomes were practically never stitched up in advance (albeit not, in many cases, for want of trying).

The Hawke Cabinet was, throughout, very much a team of rivals, a highly-strung collective of very capable, forceful personalities. That we managed to work together as we did, for as long as we did, and achieve as much as we did, owes almost everything to the quality of the leadership we had. The government was brilliantly led, and the country was brilliantly led. I suspect that it will be a long time before we see Bob's like again.

Gareth Evans was Attorney-General, Minister for Resources and Energy, Minister for Transport and Communications and Foreign Minister in the Hawke governments 1983–91. He has been chancellor of The Australian National University since 2010.

SPH

Dad, music and th'arts

Dad didn't show a heightened interest in any of these publicly, but he always loved music. There was a lot of it in our household—Mum playing the piano, our music lessons and practice, classical music LPs were often on the record player, and as we grew up, all of us began to play our music. Social justice music often featured—Dad had been given a couple of American LPs of union-based and social justice music, and I reckon we knew all the words off by heart.

Mum and Dad talked in reverential tones of having attended a Paul Robeson concert in their early Melbourne days, and of him singing 'Joe Hill', which was virtually a hymn in our home. Music was one crucial way I learned much of the history of social justice, labour and civil rights movements around the world.

The Beatles were played, of course, a bit of The Rolling Stones, and *The Woodstock Album* was another—Country Joe and

The Fish's 'I-Feel-Like-I'm-Fixin'-To-Die' rag was probably THE song of the anti-Vietnam War movement, and great to sing REALLY loud. We all liked Simon and Garfunkel, and I remember this crazy cavalcade of Mokes, old VW Bugs and Commonwealth cars with family and friends on its way to the Moorabbin footy ground once in the late 1970s when, for some reason (probably another of the regular death threats), we had cops and protection around. The crowd was enormous, Simon and Garfunkel flew in by chopper, and it was all a bit surreal. I was sitting next to Dad, and I remember having a premonitory chill while they were singing 'Bridge Over Troubled Water'. I rested my arm against Dad's, and looked at him—he glanced at me with a smile, and I could see he was feeling it too.

He also had a penchant for Beethoven, and for Neil Diamond, who would feature along with the labour and union classics in the hearty singalongs, usually with Mum at the piano, that often ensued when there were guests with us (which, as you'll realise by now, was often).

In Canberra, I remember Paul excitedly calling Dad once, saying he'd just gotten these fabulous new speakers and that Dad 'had to come around and listen'. When Dad came home I asked him how it was, and he put on his so-so face. Paul loved Wagner, while Dad had reservations—'Wasn't he a fucking Nazi!?' he asked of nobody in particular.

We talked with Dad in advance about his public memorial, and when I asked him what music he would most like, he looked almost shyly at me and said, 'The 4th of the 9th?' He was referring, of course, to Beethoven's famous symphony, and its last movement, the fourth, often called 'Ode To Joy', which is exactly what it sounds like. He was being shy because he knew that it was a massively complex piece of music to stage. When the time came, we all tried, but the logistical challenge at short notice proved too much. But he had been thrilled to conduct Handel's 'Hallelujah Chorus' a few years previously, so that was a great substitute. [There is an image of Dad conducting in the photo section.] Together with Beethoven's 'Emperor', I will always fondly associate those three great pieces of music with Dad. We listened to them together occasionally during his last year or so.

He appreciated other artforms, sciences—you name it—without knowing any more than the average Joe or Josephine about them. He was forever fascinated by any sort of accomplishment that stood beyond the average, not only in sports and the arts, but in anything. He was not parochial in his tastes, and always proud of Australian achievements in any field.

Sandy Hollway

As the Prime Minister's chief of staff, I came to work every day with a spring in my step. It was a joy as well as a privilege to work for Bob Hawke.

He would often like to start the day with nine holes of golf at Royal Canberra, hitting off around 6 a.m. and phoning ahead to the staff at The Lodge as we came down the ninth fairway to have the bacon and eggs ready for us on return. I recall on one occasion passing another couple of early morning players who glanced at me, and one saying to the other, 'Nice work if you can get it!'

Quite right.

•

When Bob died, I was very pleased that the commentaries looked beyond the over-simplified likeable larrikin image to the huge accomplishments of his government. But, for me, there is another thing which needs to be recorded, namely Bob's extraordinary conscientiousness, diligence and discipline in his day-to-day responsibilities. He was a dedicated reader of the endless flow of policy advice and other documents, always sharply focused in discussions, an attentive and critical listener, a person with ideas who provided intellectual as well as political leadership, and much respected by his public servants and staff. In other words, he held himself to the highest standards of work and therefore, by example, held us to the highest standards as well.

Mind you, this was balanced with other interests. I have a particular image in my mind of the sitting room in The Lodge one Saturday, a pile of Cabinet submissions sitting on the couch, and Bob working carefully through them but with the occasional glance at the television which was, of course, tuned to the races.

•

The Prime Minister's office in Bob Hawke's time was the best example one could find of the kind of egalitarianism that is such an essential part of any well-functioning Australian workplace. It doesn't mean that everybody's job is as important as everyone else's, but it does mean that if anybody, wherever they stand in the hierarchy, does their job to a standard of excellence, they are deserving of absolutely the same level of respect as even the most senior person. There wasn't an office celebration, birthday party or farewell he missed, and he was unfailingly relaxed, friendly and encouraging with all his staff.

•

One considerable strength of the 'Hawke method' of governing was recognising the distinction between policy and politics. Naturally, any successful government needs ultimately to bring the two into alignment. But Bob believed that throwing onto the table simultaneously a confused mishmash of the policy and the political considerations involved in any issue was unlikely to produce clear thinking. He wanted first to understand an issue on its merits, and the pros and cons of the various policy options, before overlaying the political considerations. At least then, if one adopted the second or third best option because political realities ruled out the first, one was doing so with eyes wide open.

•

Most of us who worked for Bob Hawke heard his frequent admonition: 'You've got to get your timeframes right.' He meant by this that while there were indeed issues needing a positive result in time for the six o'clock news, there were also issues on which success could only emerge in months or years. He believed that it was a recipe for failure to position an issue wrongly in this spectrum, but that getting it right was a key to governing effectively for the long-term.

It is far too glib to say that the 24-hour news cycle makes such an approach impossible these days. I don't have the slightest doubt that Bob would have stuck with it and turned the new media opportunities to advantage in prosecuting his long-term vision for Australia.

•

It didn't happen often but occasionally the Prime Minister could lose his patience, with amusing results.

On parliamentary sitting days it was his habit to sit quietly and uninterrupted from 12 p.m. to 2 p.m. digesting the Possible Parliamentary Questions (PPQs) briefing notes from the Department of Prime Minister and Cabinet. These were the department's efforts to anticipate the questions that might be put to the Prime Minister in question time, and to suggest appropriate answers.

One day, however, the Prime Minister called in several of his advisors to say that he didn't fully understand one of these PPQs, and to ask whether any of us did. Various stabs were made at an answer, but none to the Prime Minister's satisfaction as the clock ticked inexorably towards 2 p.m. Then somebody suggested that the PM phone the author of the PPQ, whose name was helpfully given at the bottom of the note.

I picture Mr X (I can't remember the name), a good public servant, just settling in for a sandwich at his desk and a well-earned break, getting a call out of the blue with the arresting opening 'Mr X? This is Bob Hawke.' The Prime Minister proceeded to quiz Mr X about the PPQ, Mr X making a valiant effort to explain the issue. However, the Prime Minister's exasperation was becoming increasingly evident, not assisted by Mr X's unfortunate habit of saying 'you know' at the end of every sentence. As advisors we listened on the speaker phone, anticipating the inevitable explosion. Finally it came: 'No, I don't (expletive deleted) know, that's why I'm (expletive deleted) asking you!'

•

In the lead up to the 1993 election, I was Deputy Secretary in the Department of Prime Minister and Cabinet with responsibility to ensure that whoever won would immediately have all the briefing and support that they needed to set up government. Much of this is tried and tested standard practice across the public service. Nonetheless, I recognised that if John Hewson's Coalition was successful against Paul Keating's Labor, this would be the first party political change of government in ten years. It therefore occurred to me that it would be a good idea to take a closer look at what the department had done in 1983 when Bob Hawke came to power.

I called for the files, which were old-fashioned paper files in those days, and these were duly retrieved from the archives and landed on my desk with a thud. I blew off the dust and started to read.

Before long I struck gold in the form of a record of conversation prepared by Sir Geoffrey Yeend, Secretary of the Department of Prime Minister and Cabinet, and one of the last great Mandarins* of the Australian Public Service (I say that with high respect; we owe a lot to the service that these great traditional public servants gave to Australia).

The document described Yeend's first post-election meeting with Mr Hawke. Perhaps my memory has embellished it after all these years, but my recollection is that the document went along the following lines: *I had an appointment to meet the incoming Prime Minister, Mr Hawke, at the Lakeside*

* This term may be unfamiliar to some but it is the highest accolade one can use for somebody who has spent their life in public service accumulating knowledge, wisdom and an intelligent capacity to contribute to the workings of government for public good (you could say the opposite of *Yes, Minister*!).

Hotel in Canberra at 12 noon on the Sunday following the election. Mr Hawke arrived for our meeting at 2 p.m. (One can imagine that the celebrations had gone on long into the Saturday night.)*

I congratulated him on his victory.

I then raised a number of matters with Mr Hawke.

The document then went on for a couple of pages, summarising what was obviously a solid and useful discussion on various pressing policy and administrative issues. It was not hard to read between the lines that the incoming Prime Minister was finding this well worthwhile, and rapidly warming to Yeend, an impression confirmed by the following delicious exchange worthy of a script from *Yes, Prime Minister*:

I then took the opportunity to note that Mr Hawke had mentioned during the election campaign that his government might abolish the Department of Prime Minister and Cabinet.

Mr Hawke said that this would not be an immediate priority.

Of course, Mr Hawke will have known and respected Geoff Yeend before becoming Prime Minister, and there is no doubt that he had a deep and traditional understanding of the important role of the public service.

Nonetheless, I like to picture the dyed-in-the-wool bureaucrat and the newly minted Prime Minister somewhat warily circling each other at their first encounter, their confidence

* He had actually been 'up and at it' for hours by then, but was late because they were already dealing with the shock deficit crisis—see page 124.

growing that a good partnership could indeed be formed—but with the new Prime Minister leaving just a hint that the department would need to measure up.

It's worth adding that it did indeed measure up, with the start made by Yeend being followed by superb leadership from his successor as secretary, Mike Codd.

Sandy Hollway was chief of staff to the Prime Minister 1988–90, and a senior public servant.

Beverley Turner

I worked with Bob Hawke as one of his close personal protection officers from 1989 to 1991. There were numerous special moments during my time with Bob, but the one I used to tell the new AFP recruits was about the day we escorted Bob to the Adelaide Grand Prix and I was introduced to Johnny Farnham who kissed me on the cheek. I told the recruits that this was the highlight of my career and I have never washed that spot since.

I also mentioned that the biggest disappointment of my career was when we were at the Raiders grand final and my boss, Bob Heggie, told me to get the cars ready whilst he accompanied Bob Hawke to congratulate Mal Meninga, Laurie Daley and Ricky Stuart on their winning the premiership.

I remember escorting Bob early most mornings to the Royal Golf Course in Canberra after a late finish the night before. Bob made a comment in his farewell speech to me that I was a good operator but hopeless in spotting the golf balls for him. I was later told by my colleagues that they always carried a spare ball or two just in case they lost sight of the original one.

We went to many events and I always enjoyed the races and chatting to Tommy Smith and Bart Cummings. This was very special, as my dad, Archie Turner, was a prominent trainer in the Canberra/Queanbeyan region.

An overseas trip to PNG proved to be very eventful in more ways than one. We started at Port Moresby, and the hotel we were staying in was broken into by some raskols who stole money from the reception. Later on, Larry Andrews and I did advances to Rabaul and Madang where the locals followed us around due to an interest in my light-coloured hair. Larry also negotiated to sell me to one of the PNG police for one cow, two pigs and several chooks.

Bob Hawke was always kind and respectful towards all members of the Prime Minister's Squad and treated us like family, which made our job very enjoyable despite the pressures of protecting him in and outside Australia.

Peter Watson

The vignette is set around the phone calls between the PM and President Bush Senior during Operation Desert Shield. The fun backstory to the official narrative of the calls has to do with the 85 per cent call-content never being releasable. As Director of Asian Affairs of the National Security Council at the White House, I was the official notetaker on discussions between the President Bush and the PM. And indeed, while the first minutes did fully canvass all relevant decision-making, once concluded, there ensued a spirited verbal-race to recount the most salacious jokes and stories husbanded since the last call, each out-performing the other. At this point I would smilingly retire my pen, and quietly delight in the sublime bonhomie of these two stunningly remarkable men, likely close to the top of their respective careers.

The Australian ambassador to the US, Michael Cook, would phone me the following morning, with the refrain: 'Ah, Doctor Watson, I have in front of me the *draft* of what *purports* to be a faithful transcript of last night's call between your President and my Prime Minister.' The line would then go quiet for several seconds, before I would reply: 'Well, let's see how close your final draft is to mine this time, Ambassador.' We would then relive the last night's fun between our two principals, concurrently deleting the same sections.

How to explain the truly historical repartee between these two apparently totally dissimilar personalities, of dead-opposite family heredity? Now that really is the fun thing for friends of both to continue to explore.

Narelle Pitt

During the early 1990s I was a senior constable with the NSW Police, attached to Special Branch. One of our many duties was close personal protection of dignitaries and VIP's. I was about thirty-two years of age and would always volunteer to work weekends when Bob and Hazel were in town and staying at Kirribilli House.

Saturday mornings would consist of meeting his federal protection officer and his driver Cookie at the house, and from there we would take Bob, and sometimes Hazel, to the Australian for a round of golf. Then it was off to Randwick for the races, sometimes followed by a Rugby Test at the Sydney Football Stadium, where we would be in the VIP section, right on the centre line, and he was happy to see us all cheering the Wallabies to victory.

From there, we would swing by Sir Peter Abeles', or Frank Lowy's for a quick catch up, and then return Bob to the house for the evening. Before saying goodnight, he would instruct his staff to take us to the kitchen for a gin and tonic, something he would insist on, and we never refused. He would later pop back into the kitchen and encourage us to stay for another, and always took a moment to thank us for giving up our time/family to 'protect' him.

It was an absolute honour and a privilege to be in his company, and as I reflect on that time, I'm pretty sure that

I would have taken a bullet for him. He was such a wonderful man and will be sadly missed.

Robert (Robbie) Rowland

If the Bonnie Doon breeze carried the scent of Cuban cigar smoke, it was a fair bet that Bob Hawke was out on the course. It says a lot about Hawke, and the country he helped shape, that one of the most distinguished political leaders in Australia's history would arrive for a game of golf with no fanfare or security detail. As soon as he emerged from the car, always from the front seat beside the driver, he would greet everyone with a robust, 'G'day mate. How're ya going?'

Bonnie Doon's mix of social strata appealed to him, and he wasn't fussed that some members didn't share his political views. Even though we were close friends, I told Hawke early on: 'I never voted for you, or voted Labor in my life.' But we got on very well. We met soon after Hawke and Blanche's relationship grew in the early 1990s. The couple had found a discreet ground floor apartment in Bellevue Hill. Myself and my wife lived on the top floor and invited Bob and Blanche for coffee, and the friendship developed from there.

His usual tipple at the bar was a bottle of Shiraz, and as its level decreased Bob's exuberance and anecdotal verve increased. His vocabulary could become more boilermakers' union than Oxford Union. Former general manager Stewart

Fenton had a word in Hawke's ear about moderating his language, and by all accounts Hawke took this in good grace.

Bob struck up a strong friendship with golf-mad George Bush Senior, who visited Australia in early 1992, a few weeks after Hawke had been deposed. The 41st US president presented Australia's 23rd prime minister with a long putter bearing the inscription: 'To Bob Hawke from George Bush, 1992'. Bob treasured the putter and practised on the synthetic putting green he'd installed on the roof of the harbourside home they moved to after leaving Bellevue Hill.

In 2003, his clubs were stolen from outside the clubhouse while he was having a post-round drink. They mysteriously turned up at Woolloomooloo police station; it seems the thief had seen the engraving on the putter and decided the clubs were too hot to handle.

In his final years, the club extended Bob the courtesy of a Pro Shop trainee to join him on course. Tyrone Jackson mostly filled this role, and is full of admiration. 'He was always a gentleman, and insisted on buying me a soft drink afterwards,' Tyrone said. 'He never let me buy him one.'

SPH

Dad, cricket and golf

As I'm sure is crystal clear by now, cricket was supreme amongst the many sports Dad loved to play and follow. I grew up surrounded by cricket—on the radio, TV, and in the yard or on court next door where Dad would bowl endlessly to my brother and other kids. (The idea of women playing cricket was unknown to me then, as to most folks, although I occasionally joined in.) There were endless tales of cricket days of yore—his own and Australia's, from both Dad and Mum, who had been hooked many a year earlier. It's a sport that knows and loves its history, which is part of what I enjoy about it. 'Keep a straight bat!', 'Eye must follow the ball!', 'Follow through with your stroke!', 'Head over the ball!'—whether at my brother or the TV, vigorous statements along these lines were just part of my early universe.

Mum occasionally got a phone call from Dad when he was working or socialising, asking her to arrange a meal at home at very short notice. It got to the point where she could ring the butcher and greengrocer at home if they were closed, and they'd pop to their shops and bring a delivery around, so it all flowed smoothly. She became renowned for rustling up a feast from nothing, or feeding late extras at a meal without blinking. One of the more memorable of these events involved the English Test team.

Dad had played cricket whilst at Oxford with the late, great Colin Cowdry, and he became a good friend and part of our family folklore. 'The Poms', as we all called them, were in Australia for an Ashes series, and sure enough, one of those calls came in. For the rest of that very warm day, our yard was filled with the team and some of its entourage. I remember it as being enormous fun. There was a lot of food and beer, and our place was full of more posh accents than I'd ever heard before. I forget the year, but no doubt the on-field rivalry with the rather sunburnt Poms was soon resumed, and I was now able to put faces to names that had previously been 'the enemy' (it's an Ashes thing).

To my amazement, I found that when I tuned into cricket many years later, I'd unconsciously absorbed a lot, including a belated fascination with the game. I've never managed to master all the names of fielding positions though! So in later years Dad and I would sometimes talk about cricket and watch it together. Tests remained his keenest love, like many purists. It seems fitting that the assembly of this book has been regularly interrupted by a magnificent summer of cricket in the UK—and this is also, incidentally, why there are few stories from cricketers in this collection. Most of the Oz cricket world was in England, and all of them preoccupied with the World Cup and the Ashes series. I left my run too late to gather stories from them, and thus the lack. Another book could be written about Dad, cricket and cricketers, but that's for someone else, another time.

As with many cricket nutters, golf was also of interest to Dad. (Theories abound as to why this is so—something about sending and fending small, rock-hard balls gets to people!) As PM, Dad still played and watched cricket whenever he could, but golf featured increasingly as his body aged. He didn't play regularly until he became PM, and then it was perfect for him. He played early in the morning, several times a week. It combined enjoyment with his commitment to be fit and well so that he could give the utmost energy to the job. It was convenient, another outlet for his highly competitive nature, and often a good way to spend quiet time with himself or private time with advisors, friends, and other leaders. (It's amazing how many of them play golf!) He became increasingly fond of it and his handicap went down steadily, I'm told.

After he left Canberra, he continued playing in earnest, mostly in Sydney at Bonnie Doon. Robbie (whose reminiscence is on page 246) was a member of the tightknit blokes' group who played together twice a week for about twenty-five years—the golf and the friendship was one of the big features of Dad's post-Canberra life, even more so as he withdrew to some degree from interaction with most of the outer world. Despite pain and all sorts of obstacles, he kept playing until about a year before his death. Golf also became his favourite obsession on evening TV, and I sat up many an hour with him watching a sport that mystified me as to how it fascinates so many. He was good at explaining things—as long as I didn't distract him at the wrong moment. Some things never changed!

That he could no longer hit the course was another factor in his feeling that he was ready to die. It had been such a source of enjoyment for him, another one gone.

Ken Clifton

My fondest memory was when Bob Hawke was Prime Minister and he had been playing golf at the Lakes course, he arrived back at the Regent and I opened the door of his car. As he was getting out I softly asked, 'How did you hit them?'

He quickly replied, 'Ah Ken, it's got to be my grip.' He showed me his grip. 'I couldn't get the five iron off the ground.'

Looking at his grip, I said, 'You have to bring your right hand a bit more over the top.'

He said, 'I will give it a go next time I play.'

One of his security people came over and quietly said, 'When you are ready, Mr Hawke,' who replied, 'I will just be a minute. Ken and I are working on my golf grip.'

A couple of young guys were walking past, and one of them said, 'G'day Bob!' to which the PM replied: 'And a g'day to you, son!'

It was then that I thought: only in Australia could a hotel commissionaire give the PM advice on his golf grip, and only in Australia would the PM reply to a casual 'G'day!'

Another day, Mr Hawke arrived at the Regent and, after greeting him, I said, 'I have a problem. My son would like your autograph.'

'Leave it with me,' was Mr Hawke's reply.

Later that morning, one of his staff handed me an envelope. My son was very happy with the autographed photo of the PM.

Mr Hawke was a great man and a great PM.

Craig Emerson

From the earliest days of joining Bob Hawke's office in June 1986 as a 31-year-old economic and environmental adviser, to the day I left in November 1990, Bob also appointed me his horseracing adviser and blackjack-playing partner. Bob reasoned that as an economist I must be familiar with statistics and probability theory. He taught me how to analyse the form of horses based on their more recent performances. His preference was for horses that had run fast times and were down in weight from their previous races.

Early on, I dutifully did the form for the Newcastle Cup and picked out a horse named The Brotherhood. I told Bob, we backed it, and it won at the very attractive odds of 15–1. Bob thought he had employed a genius.

Bob had made sure he personally knew a bevy of trainers by sidling up to them at the track on race day, chatting and obtaining their phone numbers. Who was going to refuse direct telephone access to the Prime Minister of Australia?

The afternoon before each race day, my job was to mark up the *Sportsman* form guide by writing the initials of trainers we knew against any runners they had in each race. Bob would do his form analysis on the form guide in the evening and early on race day we would ring the friendly trainers.

When all this science and wizardry was completed, I would phone the tips through to a small number of insiders, including Barrie Cassidy and Grant Nihill, both media advisers to the Prime Minister. I'm sure the information went no further than to these trusted advisers. Well, pretty sure.

After a year or so of taking on these responsibilities, Bob gave me another one: placing his bets for him on the midweek races.

One Wednesday when the midweek races were on, Bob rang one of his favourite trainers who told him that his horse had a very good winning chance, at the long odds of 33–1. Bob was very excited about this and he asked me to put $100 each way for him on that horse. He didn't closely monitor his account, which was a good thing.

But before the race was run, Bob had to go into the Cabinet room for a formal Cabinet meeting and he asked me, 'Mate, would you please slip me a note and tell me what happened in that race.' Well, I listened to the race and to my absolute astonishment the horse won. So I slipped a note into the Cabinet room and at that time a minister was really struggling to convince his colleagues of the merits of the extra spending that was contained in the submission. The notetakers later said: after receiving some sort of note from the office, the Prime Minister abruptly said, 'It'll be right mate, your submission is approved.'

When Cabinet was finished, Bob waltzed into his office and declared, 'Cups of tea all round!' It was a happy day. The whole office was happy. The steno-secretaries were happy. The advisers were happy. The minister was happy—the Cabinet was bewildered but the minister was happy. The CSIRO was happy. The trainer was happy. The jockey was happy. The horse was happy. Everybody was happy. Except me. I wasn't happy. I was pacing around in my own office while these celebrations proceeded. What to do? What to do? You see, I forgot to put the bet on.

As a young economic advisor, I reasoned this through. I could confess—I could lose my job, and make everybody unhappy. Well, why would I inflict such unhappiness on anyone, especially on the Prime Minister of Australia? So I never told Bob. Never. Never. But I'm telling you today, to confess to you, to celebrate Bob's life and the wonderful, inspiring, decent human being he was.

Extracted from the tribute at Bob Hawke's memorial service.

Simon Balderstone

Bob's first speech in federal Parliament

While at my desk one morning in *The Age* bureau of the Parliamentary Press Gallery, I got a phone call from Jean Sinclair, extraordinary senior staffer, adviser and confidante of the newly-elected Member for Wills, Bob Hawke. Jean said Bob wanted me to come up to check the draft of his 'maiden speech' (nowadays a 'first speech'), which he was due to deliver the next day, 26 November 1980, in the House of Representatives.

I had known Bob in Melbourne through my very close friend, the late great Michael Gordon, who was then an industrial relations reporter for *The Age*, and who spent a lot of time with Bob. After Bob won pre-selection in October 1980 (and was appointed Industrial Relations spokesman for the ALP, despite not yet being in Parliament) I was the sole journalist to travel with him throughout an election campaign trip mainly up and down the north Queensland coast: Cairns, Townsville, Mackay.

So I gladly went up to Bob's office and he showed me his draft speech. It was obviously way too long. While being brilliantly quick on his feet, Bob was used to speech-making in forums where there was no formal time limit. I offered some (not many!) suggestions, then suggested I mark up some sections and sentences which were probably 'nice to haves' rather than 'need to haves' as, I pointed out, he would have to shorten the speech considerably to fit it within the time limit—though, of course, he would almost certainly be given a time extension. He was trying to cover too much territory.

'If you try to fit all this in, Bob, you'll sound like the chipmunks, Alvin and Simon,' I said.

'No, I want to say all of it.'

'Well, I'll mark up some bits anyway, and you choose the ones you feel you can drop so you can fit all the most important stuff in without rushing it.'

'Okay.'

Of course, he didn't leave anything out, and, to many people, he sounded like a chipmunk! But, in truth, it didn't really matter, as everyone concentrated on the actual content, which was, as always, substantive, forthright and compelling.

Bob and Indigenous Australians

Bob Hawke, as many have noted, was always vehemently opposed to racism and discrimination of any kind, and with that opposition came a deep commitment to human rights in Australia and abroad, instanced by his leadership in the fight against Apartheid in South Africa.

But, ironically, one of his biggest regrets was not doing more for Indigenous Australians as Prime Minister, particularly in regard to land rights—especially not 'standing up' to the campaign (and the state legislation introduced) against land rights by WA Premier Brian Burke, and mining interests, in 1984. And the following year, a 'nationally preferred model' proposed by Aboriginal Affairs Minister Clyde Holding, even though watered down and approved by federal Cabinet, failed to come to fruition.

His commitment to Indigenous people led to several key government decisions during his prime ministership (including the handover of title of the Uluru–Kata Tjuta National Park to the traditional owners of the area, the Anangu, in 1985) but eventually came at a major loss of personal political capital, and in the end contributed to his removal in

December 1991. And it was to be on his mind right up until the last minute of his prime ministership.

In June 1991, the federal Cabinet had discussed a submission in regard to protection from mining of Coronation Hill, an Aboriginal sacred site (and part of a BHP mining lease), in an area, the Kakadu Conservation Zone, 'excised', pending further consideration, from Stage 3 of Kakadu National Park.

I had been involved in this issue since 1987, when the federal government declared the first part of Stage 3. In mid-1990, I had become Hawke's senior advisor on Indigenous Affairs and Environment, and had been working closely with him in regard to Coronation Hill and consultations regarding it. The Jawoyn, the traditional owners, were overwhelmingly opposed to mining on Guratba, the hill they believed contained the spirit Bula.

The February 1991 draft report of the Inquiry into the Kakadu Conservation Zone by the federal Resource Assessment Commission concluded that mining would be incompatible with the values of the traditional owners; could have a substantial negative social impact on the Jawoyn community; would impact on environmental values adversely but to a limited extent at Coronation Hill; and that the economic worth of the project, although significant on a project scale, would be marginal on a national scale.

The Cabinet decided to protect the Aboriginal sacred site from mining and make it part of the national park.

But the five-hour discussion was very bitter, and the decision momentous, as it had, uniquely, been the Prime Minister's casting vote that had broken a stalemate in the divided Cabinet (this was a convention of the Hawke government Cabinets). In reality, the Prime Minister's view had prevailed against the views of many ministers.

Also, Hawke had made, in his words, 'one of the strongest and bitterest attacks I ever made on my colleagues in the Cabinet' because he was 'annoyed beyond measure' by the attitude of many of his colleagues and their 'cynical dismissal of the beliefs of the Jawoyn people'.

He said at the release of the Cabinet papers in 2016 that the pro-mining ministers had shown 'innate prejudice . . . unconsciously, I think, in some cases'. He reserved his strongest comments for what he saw as the 'mind-boggling, monumental hypocrisy' of the pro-mining stance and arguments. 'The same people who denigrate blacks in this way can easily accommodate and embrace the bundle of mysteries that make up their white Christian beliefs. The virgin birth, the holy trinity, God in his question-mark-heaven. Where is he? This supercilious supremacist discrimination is abhorrent to everything I hold most important and what, in the end, this party stands for. We can argue about some things but surely in the end we are at one against discrimination.'

The many pro-mining ministers were livid, and told him so in no uncertain terms. Their offices briefed gallery journalists that Hawke 'was losing it', and had been seriously damaged by his insistence on this matter.

'There is no doubt this was one element in my loss of leadership, as there was a great deal of antagonism amongst my colleagues as to the intensity of the remarks I made. But this was something I felt very deeply about.'

Significantly, the Cabinet discussion had originally been scheduled for May, but had been deferred until after the (first) challenge by Paul Keating against Bob Hawke's leadership. Consequently, Paul Keating was not in Cabinet when the discussion took place. So, the PM's Cabinet victory, with another leadership challenge from disaffected colleagues looming, came at a political cost. His stance on this issue was construed, or painted, as showing he had become much 'too green' and captive of conservationists.

In 1988, with the land rights issue still simmering, Bob Hawke, as part of the Bicentennial celebrations in 1988, visited the Barunga Festival in the NT. There, a group of Aboriginal leaders presented him with the Barunga Statement, a major declaration of rights and objectives. The Statement concluded by saying:

> We call on the Commonwealth to pass laws providing:
>
> A national elected Aboriginal and Islander organisation to oversee Aboriginal and Islander affairs;
>
> A national system of land rights;

> A police and justice system which recognises our customary laws and frees us from discrimination and any activity which may threaten our identity or security, interfere with our freedom of expression or association, or otherwise prevent our full enjoyment and exercise of universally recognised human rights and fundamental freedoms.
>
> And we call on the Commonwealth Parliament to negotiate with us a Treaty recognising our prior ownership, continued occupation and sovereignty and affirming our human rights and freedom. [Thirty years later, what has happened?]

Bob Hawke responded by saying that he wanted to conclude a treaty between Aborigines and other Australians by 1990.

The Barunga Statement, Hawke's 'promise' and the inaction afterwards by government, led to the song 'Treaty' by Yothu Yindi.

On the morning of 20 December 1991, the last day of Bob Hawke's prime ministership, he hung the 1.2-metre-square Barunga Statement painting in the central hall of Parliament House. He stated that 'its presence here calls on those who follow me . . . it demands of them that they continue efforts, that they find solutions to the abundant problems that still face the Aboriginal people of this country.'

As Bob Hawke and I walked back into his office, it was a minute to midday, when his term as Prime Minister would officially end. 'That was the last official thing you do as PM,'

I said. 'But can you quickly sign my copy of *The Light on the Hill* [Ross McMullin's 1891–1991 history of the ALP]. He wrote an inscription, and dated it. We shook hands, and it was noon, and all over.

Simon Balderstone was a senior advisor to Prime Minister Bob Hawke.

Steve Dubois

Bob was a good listener, a rare virtue, and he always respected the opinions of others without belittling them.

I remember him visiting a senior girls' high school in my electorate, the only one that went on to the HSC level, where he received a rock star reception from the students, much to the surprise of the principal, a nun. Later, at the principal's reception, the conversation was about accepting the traditional beliefs of others, and soon Bob, the agnostic, and the principal, a Catholic nun, were on a unity ticket on the importance of accepting Aboriginal history and values. Both agreed that the Dreamtime and stories about the Rainbow Serpent were an essential part of Australia's culture.

Bob never rammed his views down anyone's throat; he valued the opinions of others and, perhaps, that was one of the reasons he was held in such high regard. I will always remember him for his enlightened attitude towards all.

Steve Dubois was Member for St George, 1985–93.

Col Parks

It was August 1991 when Professor Fred Hollows was ushered into the Prime Minister's Parliament House office. Bob had been briefed that Fred would ask for federal funds to help his foundation expand its eye surgery work among Aboriginals and in Third World countries.

Both men knew each other and there was some laughter-rich banter before Fred got down to business. Fred made the request: memories are vague as to the figure, but recollection is that it was $500,000.

'Half a million dollars!' exclaimed a stony-faced Bob. His voice dropped to a growl and he then proceeded in salty language to lecture Fred along the lines that he was not Santa Claus, that times were tough, that as Prime Minister he had to be careful with taxpayers' money—on and on (for about thirty seconds, but feeling like five minutes).

Concluding, the Prime Minister said, 'So Fred, $500,000 is just not on, absolutely not on.'

Pause.

'Could you manage a million?' said the Prime Minister.

Laughter all round.

Col Parks was senior advisor to Prime Minister Bob Hawke.

Postscript from Simon Balderstone

Advising Bob Hawke on Indigenous issues and the environment at that time, I had been liaising with Fred and the founding head of the Fred Hollows Foundation, Mike Lynskey, regarding government support. I had arranged this meeting.

Midway through it, I began to have second thoughts as to the wisdom of organising the meeting, as these two forthright, self-confident men began to butt heads. Fred started to strongly suggest to Bob some serious policy changes and initiatives. 'Listen Fred,' said Bob, 'I don't tell you how to fix peoples' eyes, so don't you tell me how to run the country!'

But they then got on with business, to very good effect.

Simon Balderstone was a senior advisor to PM Hawke, and is author of Seeing is Believing *(McGregor Publishers, 1994), about Fred and the Fred Hollows Foundation.*

Pam Tatz

I immigrated from South Africa at the end of 1988. My Australian family adored Mr Hawke, as did I. Coming from a restrictive, racist police state, I found his policies and personality intriguing and engaging, positive and productive.

I was a high school teacher, and to supplement my income, I worked for a husband and wife catering business. The husband ran the cafe at the then-new ABC studios in Ultimo. The building was opened on 22 June 1991 and I was on coffee duty in the VIP room where refreshments were served before the official opening, which was done by the late great PM Bob Hawke.

It was an honour to serve him his coffee. After the official proceedings, I was cleaning up in the VIP room which was deserted at that stage. In walked Bob Hawke, he came up to me and said, 'Is it possible to use the phone?' I was absolutely amazed and replied that of course he could, he was the Prime Minister! A true man of the people!

Garry Sturgess

I spent a lot of time with Bob in the tidying up and finessing of parts of his memoir, *The Hawke Memoirs*, published in 1994. I remember going with Bob and Richard Super to a Double Bay chocolatier, where Bob bought a box of chocolates for Hazel. Richard and Bob drove me to my mother's place in Watson's Bay. We stopped outside and I turned to Bob with a request, knowing that everyone wanted a piece of him and I was no different.

'Bob, would it be an enormous pain in the arse for you to come in and meet my mother?' He bounded out of the car and up the stairs to the front door, thinking nothing of it. My mother, a dyed-in-the wool Coalition voter who had hosted fundraisers for Malcolm Fraser and told Lee Kuan Yew how to handle striking unionists, was beside herself when she opened the door. Bob's easy charm began by handing her the box of chocolates. At her overjoyed invitation, he entered the lounge room where my sister was sitting on the couch with a mud pack on her face. She screamed like she was at a rock concert and couldn't quite believe her eyes. My mother never tired of telling the story of Bob visiting her home and giving her a box of chocolates.

Thereafter, one prime minister stood above the rest. 'He may be Labor but he was the best!' And my sister Alex was an instant fan. She gifted him a portrait she did of him, which is recorded in the national gifts register. I've seen that ability Bob had to strike a lasting chord with people many times. He knew instinctively that life was like a box of chocolates and that the key was in reaching out and giving.

Garry Sturgess worked with Bob on The Hawke Memoirs *and on the BBC's* Republic of Oz. *He also recorded oral history interviews with Bob for the National Library of Australia.*

Anne Vans-Colina

My late husband, Jeff Dobell, invited Mr Hawke to be patron of Engineering Aid Australia in 1999. He accepted the invitation and attended almost every event that we organised for the next twenty years. The advice he gave the Indigenous students stuck with them. It gave them encouragement and confidence to ride through the difficult times when the study demands seemed overwhelming.

He suggested to Tasmanian school student Levi Dance in 2015 that he should follow his dream of becoming a professional engineer and then consider politics! Levi had just presented an excellent speech of thanks at Admiralty House at the conclusion of the Indigenous Australian Engineering School (IAES).

Levi writes:

> Yes, it was also a sad time for me here in Hobart after hearing about the passing of Mr Hawke. It brought back memories of IAES and the impact that it made on my career.'
>
> Mr Hawke used to say to us: 'No project that I have been involved in since I left public office has given me more satisfaction than the Indigenous Australian Engineering Schools.
>
> He was very dear to us and we will miss him.

Catherine King

I was preselected to run for the federal seat of Ballarat in 2000 and Bob came to help me campaign. He was picked up from Melbourne airport by Ari Suss, a Labor volunteer from Melbourne Ports who jumped at the chance to drive him. As we walked down Sturt Street people could not stop coming up to him and grabbing his hand. The warmth with which people responded to him was amazing—but the warmth that he responded with was equally wonderful. He lit up like a candle with every interaction.

We later toured Wendouree Village (now Stockland) and the reaction was the same. He was full of good humour and patience with everyone he met. As we were walking, he suddenly darted off into the bookshop. He had spied the *Guinness World Records,* and to the delight of a growing audience he looked up his beer drinking record and, laughing, told them that it was still there! He then grabbed my husband Mark and waving a Richard North Patterson book, he told him, 'You have to read these—they are great political drama.' *We have both read everything he has published ever since.*

Before he headed down the road home, he of course wanted to have a cigar. My campaign office was in a very old bakery—he headed up the stairs and amongst the 100-year-old ovens held court with all of the young Labor volunteers, dispensing advice and regaling them with anecdotes.

He rang me on the night of the 2001 election, while I was at Ballarat Trades Hall. While we had been successful in Ballarat in taking the seat off the Liberal Party, *Tampa* and 9/11 saw Howard back in office and Kim Beazley step down as Labor leader. I remember saying to him, after I thanked him for his call and congratulations, 'I don't think Kim needed to step down.'

'No, he surely did not,' was his sad reply. He loved Kim.

I saw him many times again over the years but never quite as up close. What I take from my interactions with him was that Bob thrived on the personal—he wanted to see and hear and talk to everyone. He was extraordinarily generous to me as a young candidate, to the young Labor volunteers that he spoke with, and the many people who stopped him in the street. He was generous to the party and to our movement—I know often to the detriment of those who knew and loved him the most. We are so grateful and blessed to have had him in our lives.

Catherine King is federal Member for Ballarat, and shadow Minister for Infrastructure, Transport and Regional Development.

Roger Ellis

In around 2004, my partner and I were at the Sydney Opera House to see a show. We were in a large crowd waiting for the start when I spotted Bob Hawke on the far side of the foyer standing on his own. I said to my partner, 'Oh look, there's Bob Hawke over there on his own. Let's go over and talk to him.'

My partner was a little shy. 'Oh no no,' she said.

'Well,' I said, 'I'm going over.' So I strolled over, introduced myself, and we had a delightful chat.

Then Blanche arrived, possibly from the car park. Bob said, 'Oh Blanche, I'd like you to meet a good friend of mine, Roger Ellis.' Indeed.

We shook hands and I said, 'Now, Blanche, you nearly ran into me in Northbridge car park the other day.'

'No, no,' she exclaimed. 'You nearly ran into me!'

Not true, but Bob said in his best gravelly voice, 'Give it away Roger, you won't win this one!'

With warm goodbyes we parted.

I never indicated that I had never voted for his side, but I admired him and valued our brief encounter.

Ged Kearney

Soon after the Bracks government came in, in 1999, they had an Economic Summit. It was probably early 2000, in the Victorian Parliament's House of Assembly chamber. Bob chaired with good grace and humour. Dinner was at the Windsor Hotel. Bob told a story to those of us at the table about playing cricket for Oxford (I think in the First XI*). As a talented cricketer he had been making a few solid innings for Oxford. However, as Bob confessed, he was also a prodigious and well-known drinker.

So, when they played Cambridge, the dean or chancellor had clearly done his homework. Before the game scheduled for the afternoon, he invited Bob for lunch. At lunch he offered Bob a drink. One drink became two and two drinks became three.

Before he knew it, Bob was opening the batting for Oxford in a fairly dazed state. Suffice to say, his innings came to an

* As twelfth man in the First XI, Dad got to train and travel with the team and sometimes to play.

abrupt end after three lucky runs. Bob said he trudged all the way back to the pavilion vowing never to trust anyone from Cambridge again, especially anyone bearing gifts!

Steve Bracks

Bob Hawke was a great support to me as Premier of Victoria. Not only did he provide regular advice and support to me, he also agreed to chair the Growing Victoria Summit at Parliament House, Victoria early in my first term. This summit brought together Victorian industry, union and community leaders to agree on a path forward on growth and development for our state.

And chair it he did, never relenting over two days and nights to find consensus for a communique. Indeed, he moved overnight to the Windsor Hotel with key industry leaders, locking them into his room until agreement was reached. And, of course, he achieved this agreement, which was used by our government for the next three terms. Only Bob could have achieved this. Always committed to the Labor cause across Australia.

The Hon. Steve Bracks AC was Premier of Victoria, 1999–2007.

John Murphy

I was the Labor candidate for Lowe. Bob launched each of my federal election campaigns in 1998, 2001, 2004 and

2007, and every one of his visits to Lowe was truly very memorable. I will always remember the spontaneous and rapturous receptions given to Bob by the locals as he led me down Burwood Road, Burwood, and Great North Road, Five Dock, stopping to shake hands with shopkeepers and the public, kissing the ladies and waving to everybody, all the time being pursued by an equally enthusiastic media pack! None of these street walks was scripted.

In 2007, after going into every type of shop to say hello, Bob took me into the Five Dock Hotel. He was given a rock star welcome at the bar by the regulars who immediately invited him to have a beer with them. Bob obliged and promptly pulled a $50 note out of his wallet, placed it on the bar and said, 'Have one on me!' The locals loved it, as the former Prime Minister downed a schooner with them. Bob then headed for the TAB (next-door to the pub) and the punters thrust a form guide into his hands, requesting a tip.

(A week after Bob passed away, a local resident stopped me to express his heartfelt sympathy that 'Australia has lost our greatest Prime Minister'. I agreed. The resident then promptly recalled Bob's 2007 visit to the local pub and the TAB and remarked, 'What other Prime Minister, past or present, would be game enough to go into a pub or TAB during an election campaign?')

In my campaign office in Five Dock, Bob would always stand on a milk crate, putting an arm around me like a father, while speaking passionately to the party faithful and the locals about the Labor Party platform and explaining why they should vote for me and the ALP. I will never forget him.

John Murphy is former federal Member for Lowe and Reid.

Robert Dane

Where's my fax?

I was in Hainan with Bob when he was chairman of the inaugural Boao Forum for Asia.* Bob met me at the airport and we were whisked though the city in a VIP convoy with flashing lights with Bob screaming at the driver to 'turn that bloody music down.'

We arrived at the hotel where Josh Klenbort, Bob and I were staying in a villa within the grounds of the hotel, separated by a lake from the main hotel.

The next morning at 7 a.m., Bob hosted a meeting at the villa (with Josh translating) with the Boao Forum organising committee who were panicking—there was a huge press scrum outside wanting a statement from the committee but Bob said they couldn't give one until the committee was elected at the conference that started at 9 a.m. But the 'to be elected committee' were insisting on a press release, with Bob saying, as a lawyer, that under their own constitution

---

* The Boao Forum for Asia is a non-profit organisation that hosts forums for government, business and academic leaders across Asia and other continents to share their vision for their region.

they could not give one. This went around in circles for about an hour with frantic discussions. Bob stood firm, of course, giving a press release to the media saying only that the committee was yet to be elected.

While all this was going on, we were served breakfast in the villa by a maître d' and a waiter. I made the mistake of saying that the coffee was cold. The maître d' shouted at the poor waiter, who was sent back to the hotel, racing through the media scrum down to the lake and across the bridge. I then watched him hurtle back, sweating and panting with a tray of hot coffee.

Bob then asked the maître d', 'Where's my fax?'

The waiter was sent back again, running across the bridge like a madman. This fax was obviously vital for national security. The media scrum parted for the waiter, sprinting back with an envelope. Of course, it was the cryptic crossword that his office faxed him every morning.

Bob's brain

We were flying to Ningxia Province, 400 miles west of Beijing. Josh and I were sitting behind Bob, who had completed the cryptic crossword before the plane took off. When the pilot gave his speech—flying west, 30,000 feet etc., Bob said loudly, 'For Christ's sake, we don't care. Just fly the bloody plane.'

When we arrived, we were ushered into a press room set up in a horseshoe arrangement with the mayor and Bob separated by a huge vase of flowers. The room was crowded with people—an interpreter crouching behind the mayor, officials down one side, myself and Josh and Austrade people down the other side, and the local press kneeling on the carpet in the middle.

The mayor gave a twenty-minute welcome speech, and each sentence was then translated. Themes of friendship and the importance of relationships, planting the seeds in the winter for growth in the spring, and so forth. It was a fulsome, one could say rambling, speech and Bob appeared to be looking around and not particularly paying attention but when it was his turn to speak, he gifted back to the mayor his twenty-minute speech, replying to his sentiments and points word for word, chapter and verse. It was astounding.

The tea ceremony

We were in Beijing. Our hosts had invited us to the original Peking duck restaurant where on the menu you got a photograph of the duck you were going to eat (dead on a hook and numbered 1 millionth ++duck).

We had a family friend in Beijing, Simon Espie Greenacre—the Australian youth ambassador in Beijing—and I asked Bob if he could join us.

We were seated in the VIP room but before we could eat, we had the VIP tea ceremony, prepared by a young woman with much bowing, explanations, translations and hand flourishes. It took nearly fifteen minutes. There was unhurried pouring of tea from a small teapot into the bowls and then, using special tongs, from one bowl to another. The bowls were then emptied and tea was added to the smaller teapot, leaf by leaf, each leaf representing different qualities: harmony, strength, vitality etc. Hot water was added to the smaller teapot from a larger teapot, the tea was poured into the bowls, and then the bowls were emptied yet again. Finally, the bowls were filled with tea, not emptied, and after more bowing, the tea was ceremoniously served to us.

Bob turned to Simon and me, announcing: 'This is why we invented teabags.'

Susan Dane

I picked Bob (Hawke) and Robert (Dane, my husband) up from a meeting in Sydney's CBD to drive them to the airport. Bob was sitting beside me and giving directions.

'You need to get in the right lane,' he said.

'I can't, Bob. It's a bus lane.'

'Christ, don't worry about that.'

I moved into the bus lane, the lights turned red, and immediately a bus pulled up behind us and blasted its horn. Three times, each time longer and louder. It then pulled out and alongside, next to Bob. The driver was sliding the window open; this time we were going to receive a verbal blast—until the driver saw who was in the passenger seat.

The bus driver's face transformed from fury to surprise, then to pure delight. She waved wildly out the window at Bob as the lights turned green and we drove away.

Ian Buchanan

As a non-Muslim who had lived and worked in the Islamic nations of Southeast Asia for thirty years and who happened to be in Manhattan on 9/11, on my return to the region I became a co-founder, and advisory council member, of The World Islamic Economic Forum (WIEF). Former PM Hawke graciously accepted our invitation to speak at our second annual forum, hosted in Islamabad by President Pervez Musharraf in 2006.

As a WIEF advisory council member, on arrival I was met by a minister, assigned a government car plus two jeeps of AK47-equipped Special Forces guards for the duration of my stay. As this was an 'Islamic'—rather than a formal 'government'—event, some quirk of protocol meant PM Hawke received no official government facilities. On my first morning I saw 'PM Bob'—who I knew but not well—uncomplaining, and like any other invitee or citizen of Islamabad—walking from our hotel to the conference venue. I stopped our three-car convoy and offered him a lift. From then on, he became part of our small WIEF/ Special Forces 'team' as we attended events and explored Islamabad. We had some fascinating discussions with our young Special Forces team leader as he arranged several local tours for us, including Army HQ near Abbottabad and the Kashmiri border areas.

'PM Bob' had the very special capacity to be as comfortable chatting with a young Pakistani Special Forces corporal as he was with me or with President Musharraf. I enjoyed his company and was fortunate to have the opportunity to continue these occasional informal discussions on a wide range of global and regional issues with him over the years following this meeting.

His combination of intellect, strategic vision and common touch will be sorely missed.

David Bartlett

I was elected leader of the Tasmanian Labor Party and therefore Premier of Tasmania in May 2008. Soon after that, the twenty-fifth anniversary of the saving of the Franklin River came around. Bob Brown had organised a large celebration at Hobart's waterfront Grand Chancellor.

I had decided to go, much to the horror of many of the Labor Party elders (in Tasmania, the Labor Party is split, and half of the party is very anti-Green.) I grew up in a house where my foster father was staunchly conservative, anti-Green and pro-dam. However, I will never forget the day of the High Court decision that effectively ended the planned destruction of this precious part of the planet. Much-loved

Taroona High School (where I was in Grade 9) teacher Mark Healy ran from the staff room leaping and cheering down the main A-block corridor. Such joy was in direct contradiction to the grumpiness that would be expressed at my home that night.

In so many ways the Franklin River was the moment of my political awakening. So, to attend the celebration of the saving of this mighty river as premier was a no-brainer. Quite aside from acknowledging my own political awakening, to attend this event was a signal that we were going to do things differently—to build the clever, kind and connected Tasmania that I had been speaking of.

Right up until an hour before the event, I was getting pressure from Labor Party stalwarts to decline the invitation. But as we worked our way through a stunned crowd of over 2000 to the table at the front of the room, one face appeared that made me realise in an instant that I had made the right decision.

'Ah David, welcome. I'm Bob.' He extended a warm hand.

It may have been Bob Brown's party but it was Bob Hawke's night. I knew it was Bob Hawke who saved the Franklin, and to be there amongst Labor company to celebrate not only the saving of the Franklin, but in so many ways the saving of the nation by that Hawke government, was special beyond belief.

We sat down as Bob Brown took the stage, and began to talk. A freshly minted, ambitious and energetic young premier with his hero, the saviour of the Franklin, saviour of the nation and Australian legend. The conversation rambled across national economic reform, the price of power, the cost to young families of fathers in the spotlight, my aspirations for Tasmania, sport, and Bob's journey through the Australian psyche.

At all times Bob Hawke, the most important person in a room of thousands, made me feel like I was the most important person in the room to him. I came to learn that Bob had that very rare talent of being deeply loved but at the same time exuding love without question. Without effort, he could reflect his care, courage and charisma upon the person he chose to—on this night me. He filled me with courage, aspiration, energy and confidence. He explained to me that it is the catalytic decisions that change the place for the better for decades to come, and that this is what leadership and politics are all about.

Bob followed the night up a few days later with a call to my mobile. 'Ah David, it's Bob, just checking in and letting you know anytime you need help I am here.'

It was early in 2013, as the Gillard prime ministership was under relentless negative pressure, that I wandered into an airport lounge in Melbourne. 'Ah Premier, come and join me . . .' rang out that familiar voice across the cavernous Qantas lounge.

Hmmm, is Bob slowing down, I thought to myself? I had stepped down as premier two years prior. So, for a moment I was frozen between wondering if I should break the news to Bob or just play along. As I arrived at his table and pulled up a chair at his insistence, he clearly clocked the confused look on my face.

He leaned forward and said, 'Ah David, I like the American tradition of calling a leader president for life.'

'My Prime Minister,' I exclaimed. 'Great to be with you!'

For about an hour, people filed in and out of the lounge, most staring wide-eyed at the rock star Prime Minister and many simply saying 'G'day Bob' as they shuffled by for a blessing from the great man.

Again, for that whole hour Bob made me feel like the most important person in the room to him. He asked after my family, my health, my post-political life, the state of the Tasmanian economy, the seemingly impossible resolution to Tasmania's forestry wars, and the Gillard prime ministership.

As he stood to head to his plane, again the warmest of handshakes, a cheeky twinkle in the eye: 'See you soon, Premier. You've got my number. Call anytime if I can help with anything.'

'Goodbye my Prime Minister,' I replied, as Bob strode from the room with all eyes on him.

Goodbye, my Prime Minister, and thank you for everything.

David Bartlett is a former premier of Tasmania.

Dennis Lillee

Like most Australians, I have a warm and deep regard for Bob. It's not just the fact that I believe he was possibly our greatest Prime Minister but that he was one of us. I can't think of another PM for whom that can be honestly said.

As President of the West Australian Cricket Association, it was traditional to invite guests along to the test match days in Perth. As Bob was a known cricket tragic, a few years back I invited him along to enjoy the cricket in the President's Room. A great day was had by all, and Bob was in his element talking and watching the day's play.

It was when he left that I saw something that still amazes me. My PA, Ros Heal, and I escorted him downstairs and to the main entry gate to see him to his car. That's when it happened! Word must have got around that he was at the ground. There must have been 200 people around the car, calling his name at the top of their collective voices while he smiled and waved to them. This brought goose-bumps to the neck and, let me assure you, this scene would not have been played out if it was most other Prime Ministers!

Anthony Marano

I have lived in Sydney all my life but I love going to the races and whenever I can I head to Melbourne for the Spring

Racing Carnival, as I love the atmosphere and excitement of Derby Day at Flemington.

In 2008, I was at Derby Day with both Melbourne and Sydney friends and after a long day at the track we headed to the CBD for dinner. We ended up at Becco, an Italian restaurant and bar in Crossley Street, Chinatown, which is a Melbourne institution.

After dinner we went into the bar for a drink and who should we find sitting there having a beer, but Robert J Hawke himself. Only in Australia could you walk into a bar and find a former Prime Minister sitting alone without any security or minders, having a beer.

My friends and I gathered at the bar to order drinks, and in a matter of minutes we were invited by Bob to join him for a drink. The excitement was palpable and we enthusiastically surrounded him, and the night was about to get interesting.

We had some pretty women in our group and Bob was enjoying their company and they his. He explained that Blanche had left him in the bar after dinner as she was tired, and went back to their hotel across the road. Bob had intended to follow not long after, but our arrival changed those plans.

After a couple of hours of great storytelling and drinking, we mentioned to Bob that we had been invited to a party in Brighton and he needed little encouragement to come with us.

The next thing I know we are piling into a maxi taxi van in the rain with our freshly 'kidnapped' Prime Minister. The van was a nine-seater but I think we had thirteen people packed into it, which the driver had noticed.

We were so busy squealing with laughter at Bob's running commentary and with the van rocking and the windows all fogged up, nobody noticed that after ten minutes we still had not left the kerb. When someone called out that we were not moving, I asked the driver why he was not taking us to our destination and he said angrily that there were too many people in the cab and he would not leave until four people got out.

Bob, who was sitting near the front, yelled out, 'Mate, I am the fucking Prime Minister of Australia, now take us to fucking Brighton.' The driver turned around to confirm whose voice he had just heard, and immediately said 'Yes sir' and pulled away from the kerb with much haste. I thought that we were in the presence of greatness!

When we arrived at the house in Brighton, we walked into what was a fairly subdued gathering at 1 a.m., but our arrival caused much excitement when they saw who we had brought with us.

As all the men in our group were in suits, a woman asked me if we were Mr Hawke's security detail, which I happily went along with. She asked me what it was like looking after Mr Hawke and what sort of hours did we work? I explained that looking after Bob was very exciting as we never knew where we could end up, and that we only finished our shift when Mr Hawke was ready to go home.

My new job of being part of Mr Hawke's security detail was

doing wonders for my ego and my popularity with the opposite sex, so I remained in character for the rest of the night.

Bob was holding court by the swimming pool with both men and women listening intently and beer flowing freely. I have never seen someone so popular with young people wherever we went.

Before I knew it, it was 5 a.m. and we were all exhausted, so we suggested to Bob that we would head back to the city to call it a night. He said he was happy to leave if we were, so three of us shared a cab with Bob and dropped him off at the Sofitel Hotel in Collins Street. He told us that he had a wonderful night and now he had to explain to Blanche where he had been for the last eight hours.

Even though I am a long-term Liberal voter, I have always admired Bob Hawke as a great Australian and a true embodiment of the Australian spirit, the likes of which we will probably never see again in political life. Politicians today seem so dull when compared with Bob and meeting him by accident in a Melbourne bar will always be one of the highlights of my life.

I don't think I have ever laughed so much as I did that night, nor did I learn so much in such a short time, from a funny, charismatic and intelligent man who charmed the pants off everyone who came anywhere near him.

Bob Hawke, I will miss you and I will never forget our chance meeting which turned into one of the best nights ever. You are a great Australian.

Michael Yabsley

Bob and I forged an unlikely but special friendship. We were from different backgrounds, different generations, and different sides of politics. All of that became irrelevant as we forged our friendship.

When we were travelling together in Saudi Arabia in 2010, I had a serious eye problem that required emergency surgery. Bob took me to hospital and stayed with me for hours, making sure I was being properly looked after. Bob then visited me repeatedly over the following days. He was nothing less than brotherly, even fatherly.

Bob was, to me, the personification of the words of the celebrated American poet Maya Angelou who said: 'I've learned that people will forget what you have said; people will forget what you did; but people will never forget how you made them feel.'

Peter Lino

'Thanks for being a great Prime Minister,' I told Bob Hawke after he had just sat down opposite me in a lunch tent at Woodford Folk Festival.*

---

* Dad started attending Woodford Folk Festival shortly after he married Blanche, and they continued to go and enjoy it every New Year. He became good mates with its founder, Bill Hauritz, and although it was out of character with anything he had done previously, he loved the vibe, the diversity of people and events, and soaked up the warmth many there showed him.

'Jeez, thanks mate,' Bob replied. He was waiting for his food. So I asked, 'Can I tell you a little story?'

'Yeah, why not?'

I began. 'In my mother's last days, she was in hospital and family were at her bedside. At one point she seemed semi-awake, so I reassured her, "It's okay Mum, you're safe, in hospital in Lismore."'

'"Liberal? No, I voted Labor all my life!" She replied.'

Hawkie exclaimed, 'You bewdy!'

'But she actually voted Liberal all her life.'

'Ah, a deathbed conversion. The best type,' he replied.

Thanks for being a great Prime Minister, Bob Hawke. One of us.

Samantha Regione

Back in 2011, I was a relatively new staffer in Canberra and quite shy, when I saw Bob Hawke sitting in the courtyard. I had previously met Sue Pieters-Hawke through her work as a campaigner for dementia awareness (I was working for the Minister for Ageing at the time) but had never met the great man himself.

I ventured out into the courtyard, nervously introduced myself, and asked if I could take a photo of him to show my mum. Hawkie was seated, wearing a three-piece suit, a newspaper spread across his lap, and smoking a cigar. He exuded statesmanship and confidence but most importantly, despite the extravagance of his attire, he had a friendly down-to-earth approachability; he had been a king and yet I was not a lowly subject. We had never met before, but I was his mate because I lived in his kingdom. The Kingdom Downunder. Hawkie broke out that big larrikin smile, a mouth full of gleaming, white teeth, and ordered a nearby friend to take a picture of the two of us together, draping his arm around my shoulders. 'For your mum,' he said.

Suddenly there was a scurry of movement at the large glass doors to Parliament House. Tony Abbott, Opposition leader at the time, had also seen Hawkie in the courtyard, and thought he would pay him a visit. Abbott must have just finished a press conference because he was surrounded by the entire Press Gallery, and the press, sensing a performance ahead, turned on their cameras and followed in a great throng. Abbott loped over, his signature strut growing stronger with his approach, chest out, arms wheeling, like a machismo tornado bent upon destruction.

Hawkie stood up, grinning from ear to ear. The then 82-year-old former Prime Minister fronted up to the then 54-year-old soon-to-be Prime Minister, positively relishing the opportunity for a fight. The two alpha males circled one another, the air around them choked with masculine malice. It was an 'You all right, mate? Ha ha ha,' kind of dance. They spoke politely with curt tongues and fake smiles, laughing with feigned joviality for the cameras, every peal ringing with threat and challenge. I was half expecting someone to begin chanting 'fight, fight, fight'. It was both enthralling and terribly frightening.

I had been knocked out of the way by the cameras and had wanted to flee but I was too amazed by the circling peacock show in front of me to move. Mid-dance, Hawkie appeared to remember that I was there. He glanced over and winked at me. His wink told me that he was having an extraordinary amount of fun. His wink reassured me that he was okay and that I was okay, and this was all a great laugh. It was like we shared a special secret. The larrikin king reminding me I was his mate and this was his kingdom.

Samantha Regione is a staffer with the Australian Labor Party.

Joel Fitzgibbon MP

Some of the more successful fundraisers held in my electorate are those held at the Singleton Rugby Club. Held in the local clubhouse, a couple of hundred people usually gather to eat, drink and enjoy the guest speaker. More often than not, the guest is a sporting legend, but occasionally the club invites a politician.

The day that Bob was the star attraction, the event had to be moved from the clubhouse to a huge marquee on the football field. The proportion of women present was also at least twice the usually modest number. I marvelled at the number of women flooding to have a selfie with Bob.

The drinks were being served that day by young women dressed in what can best be described as a swimsuit emblazoned with the Hahn beer logo. They too were keen for a selfie with Bob. But selfies weren't enough: yours truly was recruited to take a shot of Bob and a group of Hahn girls. The next day, the *Newcastle Herald* ran a photograph of the local federal member taking a shot of Bob and his Hahn admirers. Only Bob could pull off that one!

Vivienne Skinner

In 2013, I was a political staffer working for Anthony Albanese and had been assigned to Melbourne to work on the election campaign. It was a dire time. We were almost certainly facing defeat, we'd had a cavalcade of leaders, and the Murdoch press was at us every day. Despite this, jammed elbow to elbow we loyal staffers worked twelve-hour days for six days a week for six weeks trying desperately to hold onto whatever political furniture we could.

A couple of weeks out from the poll on a lonely weekend afternoon, in walked Bob Hawke to rally the troops. You should have seen it. It was like the place had been showered in ecstasy. Some of the staffers were so young, they wouldn't have been born when Bob was in office. But it didn't matter. Everyone—male, female, young, old, idealist or cynic—we all surrounded him while he roused us, reminded us that what we were doing mattered, and that Labor was the greatest cause of all. Some of us got photos with him. Like Bill Clinton, Bob radiated that 'onwards and upwards good feeling'. And that is what that dispirited team of staffers needed that day.

David John Orzechowski-Yacaginsky

It was a fiftieth anniversary of the National Press Club (NPC) event: Bob Hawke and John Howard speaking at a luncheon. I quickly bought my ticket and emailed my friends, Scott Thompson and David Hughes (great-grandson of Billy Hughes PM), to see who was attending.

Living forty years in the USA until migrating to Australia, I had little knowledge of both prime ministers' exceptional records of achievements. After the luncheon, I stayed around to meet John Howard downstairs. I then walked upstairs and was introduced to Bob Hawke by the Press Club board members and the CEO, who he was sitting with. Walking away, I thought: what a great afternoon. I then went to my car to bring out some cigars.

When I returned to the club, I found my friends busy talking. Remembering multiple photos of Bob Hawke with a cigar in-hand on the NPC walls, I walked toward the group sitting with Bob. My cigars were top-notch that day, so as a gesture of goodwill I interrupted saying: 'My friends and I are going to enjoy one on the balcony, would you like to join us, Bob?'

Surprising me (and all), he jumped up with a big smile and said, 'Damn will!' Seeing me with Bob Hawke, my friends quickly came out to take their places and their cigars, alongside the former PM.

It was amazing the friendliness and familiarity Mr Hawke had with the group. He quickly focused on me being from the USA. He then told us a story of leaving an event early in Melbourne and walking back to the hotel. He was stopped by a car full of Americans who praised him. As they spoke, he interrupted and said, 'If you like me so much, would you like to give me a ride back to the hotel?' In shock, they took him there. They were busy, he said, on their phones, trying to tell everyone they knew who they were with!

Then Bob took a good puff on his cigar, looked straight at me, and said, 'Damn Good Cigar. What is your name again?' He would end up saying this at least three times during our almost three hours on the balcony.

Bob was great answering the many questions we had and adding more stories. He told of his greatest accomplishments and how in some cases he had wished he had done even a little more. He told us of the relentless studies of economics, quitting drinking and other items to make sure he did a good job as PM. In my opinion, he was a very, very conscientious man who gave the role he was honoured with his best effort. He was extremely sincere and humble, but aware and committed to maximising his God-given abilities.

That afternoon we even each took turns telling a joke. Bob told us a great golfing one. People entering the Press Club were shocked to see Bob Hawke on the balcony, smoking a big Churchill cigar. Many came out and interrupted our talks. No one was disappointed, as he stopped, answered questions, and allowed pictures of himself with numerous well-wishers.

Bob again turned to me and said: 'From the USA, what might you like to hear about?' Before I said anything he answered: 'Let me tell you about the first time I met with President Ronald Reagan.'

I quickly answered, 'Yes please!'

It was another great story, with special meaning to me, as I believe Reagan did a lot for the world during his presidency.

Bob was told he had to go. My friends said: 'You haven't fully finished your cigar!' With that, I pulled out a metal cigar tube and gave it to Bob. He tried to extinguish his cigar without ruining the last bit but I believe it went in the tube and into his pocket still lit (and would have been fairly warm until the lack of oxygen fully extinguished it). We laughed about this later.

It was a wonderful and special afternoon. After that talk I could easily see how a country had fallen in love with Bob and trusted him with their destiny. A man who had time for all, enjoyed life and people, and had an intelligence and drive worthy of the role he undertook. I and my friends will always feel privileged to have met such a special man.

John S Batts

Maybe no more than two years ago, I found myself in the Concert Hall of the Sydney Opera House for a Sydney Symphony Orchestra evening seated immediately in front of Blanche and Bob.

At the beginning of the interval, there was a gentle tap on my shoulder. Blanche had lost her 'only lipstick'; it had fallen and rolled beneath my seat. When I turned around to return this item, I received a broad smile from Bob, who made a remark I shall always treasure: 'Ah mate, you're a saviour!'

Polite, over the top (of course!) but, I suspect, genuine.

Ron Edwards

The Kimberley Prawn fishery, off the coast of Broome, was holding a fundraising event and Bob was the star guest, as always. The main food on offer was WA-sourced seafood, with Kimberley prawns in abundance.*

Bob tried the prawns. 'These are the sweetest prawns I have ever tasted. They are like small school prawns, delicious and tender.'

In his Perth days Bob would have tried a lot of school prawns, as the locals pulled prawn nets in the Swan River.

---

* Dad loved fishing off the Western Australian coast. He often asked if he could join Theo George Kailis, heir and part-owner of Austral Fisheries (the world's first carbon-neutral fishery) on his boat.

It became commonplace when seafood was on the menu that Bob would turn to me and say, 'Are these Broome prawns?'

'Of course, Bob. Only the best from WA for you.'

Sally McManus

I was lucky enough to meet Bob just before I became ACTU Secretary when I sought his advice about the job. Bob's number one bit of advice was to take on journalists in interviews!

It was interesting. I was having this discussion with him, and one moment he had the watery eyes of a grandfather, and then in the next moment there were these piercing blue eyes just looking at me and he was straight to, 'How big is your budget now? What are you doing with this? What are you doing with that?'

That was just two years ago. We were talking about his union legacy, and to be honest—not to be unfair to any ACTU leader who came before him—he really re-wrote the job and he was the person who actually put the ACTU on the front pages. He was a giant—a complete giant. He stood above all others.

There are two big things I think he achieved when he was ACTU leader.

The first was he was an advocate, such a smart man. He was obviously a Rhodes Scholar, with a law degree—going in and presenting arguments himself in the minimum wage cases. He was very successful and achieved really good increases for workers.

The second thing, which people often don't know about, is that under his leadership the union movement played an important role in the bringing down of Apartheid in South Africa. He led a boycott of goods from South Africa when Nelson Mandela was in jail. Union members and ordinary working people wouldn't handle goods if they were flown in, or if they arrived at our ports, which put a lot of pressure on that regime, and it was one part of the global effort that led to Nelson Mandela getting out of jail.

Bob could walk the path between business and workers seemingly with ease. He could bring those divided parties together so easily. What was his skill? I think it's the common touch. It didn't matter who you were, he never put himself above anyone. He never had tickets on himself. He could relate to you if you were a young bloke in a car driving to the pub, or if you were the CEO of a large business. But also, on top of that, was his intellect. He was a really smart, sharp man.

Sally McManus is Secretary of the ACTU.

Peter FitzSimons

When I interviewed the late, great Robert James Lee Hawke thirty years ago at the height of his prime ministership, specifically on his Greatest Sporting Moment, I was knocked out by both his garrulousness and the joy sport gave him. At the tender age of nineteen, and still only a twinkle in the nation's eye, our Bob found himself keeping wicket for the University of Western Australia in a first-grade match against Subiaco.

'A fellow called Ray Strauss was bowling,' he recalled. 'He was a medium-fast swing bowler and occasionally I used to stand up to the stumps for him. Bill Alderman, the father of present-day Terry Alderman, was at the crease for Subiaco. I said to Ray at the end of the over: "Now look, I think this bloke's a bit ambitious. I reckon we might be able to stump him. On the third last ball of the over, give us one down the leg side."'

'The moment came. I was standing up. He bowled it down. The greatest moment of my sporting life then occurred. He went forward, snicked it, I caught it, and stumped him. "Howzat!" I yelled at the umpire. "Bloody marvellous!" came the reply. "He's out twice." It was just one of those rare moments of your sporting career when all the co-ordination was there and everything just clicked.'

As to his most famous moment as Prime Minister, he reminisced fondly about the day Australia achieved a remarkable sporting summit.

'It was very funny, you know. I had actually arranged to have a Cabinet meeting in Perth many, many weeks prior to the America's Cup, so it was just quite coincidental that I was there when the final moment occurred. I was watching it there in Perth, sitting up through the night and early morning. Gradually all my staff went off to bed. They thought we'd had it. One of them, though, stayed sitting with me, making the tea during the night and, if you remember, our fellow went out on the starboard tack on the second last leg. He was way, way out and the Americans were out on the port tack and it was very, very difficult to tell because they were just so far apart.'

'Then I said to Graham: "I think our man's made up a lot of ground here," and we started to get more and more excited. Then when he came back in and tacked across in front it was just . . . !! Just . . . !'

So were you, Bob. A great Prime Minister. And a very great Australian. Vale.

•

On the occasion of Kim Beazley's swearing in as WA Governor six months ago, His Excellency newly-anointed asked me to sit with the wheelchair-bound Bob afterwards in the ballroom filled with 500 of WA's fine society, chat to him, and make sure that none of the many well-wishers coming to shake his hand and chat stayed too long to exhaust him, etc.

For the next hour, thus, as people came and went, I sat as protector to the great man, using as the spine of our conversation all the Australian prime ministers he'd known, the

Opposition leaders, and for the hell of it, American presidents. It was one of the great privileges of my life—with Hawke on his last night in his home-town, *last drinks, please, gentlemen*—and I wish I had it on tape, but perhaps it was the informality that made him so revealing. What struck me, though, was both the extraordinary richness of his life: the people he'd known, things he'd done, mind-blowing things he'd accomplished—and the generosity of spirit towards all. On everyone, he saw the bright side not the dark side, and—this is what particularly interested me—kept his warmest words of all for Paul Keating and what they had achieved together.

Late in the night when we were back in Kim's private residence with a couple of dozen of the hard-core, Bob wanted to have a cigar with Kim, and I wheeled him out onto the balcony where Kim awaited. I ached, I mean *ached*, for one of them to say, 'Would you like to sit with us, too, Peter,' where I could just sit and listen as one of the titans of his political age talked to his greatest supporter and most faithful friend, but of course, I don't think it occurred to either of them. I retired thus to the pavilion whence I came, out for a duck on the second ball of the day.

No matter. Any time at all spent with Hawke was a privilege.

•

If politics makes strange bedfellows, you can believe that the memorial service at the Opera House on 14 June for the most iconic politician of our lifetimes, Bob Hawke, brought together more long-time adversaries than has been seen this side of the Black Stump, since forever.

Malcolm Turnbull observed the entire proceedings from the third row, looking right over the shiny pate of Peter Dutton, perhaps the man in politics he most detests, though it is a crowded field. To Turnbull's left John Howard and the one-time Kevin 07 express train—*toot! Toot! Coming through!*—sat companionably side by side. David Marr, meantime, sat just a few seats along from Alan Jones. Though not adversaries, Paul Keating has been apart from his long-time wife Annita for well over two decades now and yet—just as they charmingly did for the Gough Whitlam memorial service at the Sydney Town Hall in 2014—they sat warmly side by side, her occasionally touching his arm when warm reference was made to the father of her children.

Twelve rows back, relatively anonymous but serene—given he must sometimes feel like the *world* is against him—Bill Shorten sat with his wife Chloe, the two flanked by Tanya Plibersek and Penny Wong. Had things turned out differently, it would have been him on the Opera House stage, claiming the Hawke mantle, promising to live up to his legacy, but . . .

But it was not to be as, ladies and gentlemen, please welcome Prime Minister Scott Morrison, who proceeded to make a strong and generous speech, perfectly pitched to the truth: though Bob Hawke was a warrior for the opposing side of politics to his own, Hawke's iconic status transcended politics and not even his strongest critics could dispute the impact he had on his nation. Say it, Prime Minister.

'Today, I come to speak on behalf of a nation Bob Hawke loved and that deeply loved him in return. It was a great romance played out in the shopping centres with journalists tripping over cables, sporting ovals, grandstands, schools, town halls, beaches, parks, outback stations and, of course, Indigenous communities all around the country. It was a passionate and affectionate relationship between Bob and the Australian people. Today, we will rightly honour his many achievements for our economy, for our security, for Indigenous Australians, for our society and Australia's place in the world and, as a Liberal, I'm honoured to acknowledge these achievements as I know others would be.'

In the crowd we shifted . . . comfortably. We weren't quite sure what to expect from him, but this was great. And right on the money.

The photo tribute to Hawke, as the Sydney Symphony Orchestra played 'The Hallelujah Chorus', was so moving that Victorian Premier Daniel Andrews not only doused his own handkerchief in tears, but was surely tempted to take the one Anthony Albanese proffered him, before Albo, too, made his way to the podium as Chloe Shorten placed a light hand on her husband's shoulder. The Opposition leader's tribute was heartfelt, and offered a quote that brought the house down. 'Bob once said, "Do you know where my credibility comes from? It's because I don't ooze morality."'

And so it went. Bill Kelty spoke from the heart, without a single note. Kim Beazley gave the perfect eulogy, filled with love, humour and praise for the man, the politician, the sheer *force* of his character. Sue Pieters-Hawke spoke with great love and eloquence on behalf of the family, about Hawke as father, husband and grandfather.

All was building to the climax, the final formal speech, before Blanche D'Alpuget's wonderfully moving farewell—that of Hawke's great political partner and rival, Paul Keating.

For once, it was not Keating's words that made the impact. I can't quite remember them. It was really just his presence, his warmth, the fact that as Hawke departed the national stage the man seeing him off was the very man with whom he had achieved so much. Had he not been there, it would have been a jarring lack of presence. The fact that he was there paying tribute was perfect.

Yes, they had fallen out, and Keating made no bones about that. But they had also been close, and accomplished great things together to make their nation stronger. Most importantly, they had reconciled before his death. As Keating finished, the sails of the Opera House shimmered and shook with the applause. The perfect finish.

Vale Bob Hawke. You did the nation proud. And the nation did you proud, farewelling you, our favourite son, in wonderfully moving fashion.

Martin Porteous and Rebecca van Bilsen

Inala is committed to providing support to individuals living with disability. Blanche and Bob have given generously of their time, care and enthusiasm to support and improve the lives of the wonderful individuals supported by Inala.

Larger than life, Bob would often rally support for Inala unbidden and entertain everyone with his well-known larrikin nature and quick humour. Many will remember his stirring rendition of 'Waltzing Matilda' at the Kurri Burri Mother's Day polo event, and his signed Prime Minister XI cricket bats and offers of attendance at board room lunches were always sought after.

Ever willing to help, Inala was privileged to have had such a longstanding engagement with Bob and his involvement with Inala will be missed.

Martin Porteous and Rebecca van Bilsen are joint CEOs of Inala.

Brianna Roberts

Let me tell you about the time I spilled an entire glass of red wine in the lap of the former Prime Minister. I was out with Bob and Louis (his stepson and my partner). Bob was in his eighty-eighth year. Blanche was away for the weekend, and we had all far exceeded the usual one glass of wine that Bob was (for medication reasons) permitted with dinner.

The restaurant staff had been giving us the royal treatment, as was usual whenever we went out with Bob. They kept coming over to offer him things—more water, napkins, the wine menu, and were we ready to order?

Given a choice between the fish or a cheesy pasta, Bob decided he wanted both. The fish—with a creamy gorgonzola sauce. The waitress's eyes widened when he said this, but he insisted. She scurried away and emerged minutes later looking embarrassed.

'The chef says he cannot do it. He says he simply cannot serve cheese and fish together.'

This made Bob rather cross. 'What's his problem? He doesn't have to eat it! He just has to cook it.' And so it was done.

When Bob's meal arrived, it came on separate plates. One for the fish, with another, smaller plate, full of cheese sauce.

(As a disclaimer to what happened next, I should say that I am a generally clumsy person. On my first date with Louis, I had accidentally emptied an entire glass onto his white shirt. He took it with good grace, like a proper gentleman should. He zipped up his jacket and said, 'I'd better go get you a fresh glass of wine.')

When I knocked the wine onto Bob, it sent the over-attentive waitstaff into overdrive. We were quickly surrounded by dozens of people, clutching napkins, trying to dab Bob's crotch dry. I wanted to slide under the table, but Bob took it reasonably well.

'It's not the first time,' he said with a smirk. 'I'm going to have to call you "Chucker" from now on—the wine chucker.'

The commotion had drawn the attention of the table next to us who, mortified, had offered to pay for our meal. 'It's the least we can do, given how much you did for our country,' they said. Bob thanked them and asked for their names, before insisting on a cheers 'to our new friends'.

I couldn't stop apologising, and heard myself say a phrase I'd only ever heard in American romantic comedies: 'Please send me the bill for the dry cleaning!'

'Don't worry,' he said, with a twinkle in his eye. 'Still love ya,' he added. '—Chucker.'

SPH

Alcohol post-Canberra

Some of us waited with bated breath to see how this one would play out. In the months after Paul deposed Dad as PM, Dad retreated into family a lot of the time, understandably subdued. It was like having a severely wounded beloved beast in your midst–all we could do was quietly include him, get on with life, have the grandchildren around as much as possible, and give him time to heal, knowing he would, as he did.

I talked with him about whether he thought he would drink again, and he thought he would, but for pleasure, not to hide in. He felt he'd learned a lot being sober and often observing folk drinking. 'It just really strikes you how silly it can all be.' I kept a straight face.

The handful of times he ventured back into drinking in this early period after Canberra were pretty ugly, before life settled. Mum had health scares but pulled through, their new home was 'renovated', and the alcohol use largely settled too. But I knew something was 'off' when they moved into the rebuilt house—his drinking escalated, and clearly all was not well in paradise.

When he first told me that he was contemplating leaving Mum, the renewed turbulence suddenly made sense. There's nothing much good to say of that transitional period—all involved were understandably pretty upset and f---ed up. Dad was back in love with Blanche, and yearned to be with her, but did not want to leave the family, and was utterly ripped up over it. There were a few years across this transition when he could either enjoy a glass of wine and be perfectly pleasant, or not. But as he settled into his new life, and was profoundly happy with Blanche, he (and she) gradually 'tamed the beast'.

So for most of his remaining years, he would enjoy a drink (now usually red wine), occasionally 'too much'—but he was more like any other over-indulged bore. I don't recall the drunken nastiness of yore raising its head at all in latter times.

In his last few years, with heart issues, blood thinners, and frailty, the amount of alcohol he could consume daily was medically mandated—it was carefully matched to his meds and was, he was told, important to observe. Many an evening over dinner together he contentedly sipped a glass of red. But he still had that 'naughty little boy' streak in him and enjoyed the occasional chance to flout rules he hadn't made for himself and thus wasn't a fan of. If he was away from anyone who he saw as an enforcer of this irritating limitation, he would get that twinkle in his eye and say quietly to one of us, 'Hey fill it up again, won't you?' We would try to keep it limited, but the odd hilarious night ensued.

John Brown

This is a note of thanks for the support Bob gave me as a minister, which he obviously appreciated. Upon receipt, Blanche rang me to say that Bob was reading the letter with tears running down his cheeks.

> Dear Bob,
>
> I note that you have been very unwell (welcome to the club).
>
> As you may know, I am doing a function with our mate Paul Hogan for Barbecure, which is, of course, raising money for research into children's cancer. The purpose of the night is to emphasise how this group is altering the status quo as to how medical research

has been traditionally conducted. Paul is an ambassador of this group and he asked if he and I could do a public presentation as to how together we altered the status quo of the way in which Australia's image was promulgated. I don't think that Paul and I deserve the credit we are sometimes given. The truth is that in fact it was a trio who organised this miracle which has given Australia its booming tourism industry. Without your help at Cabinet level, particularly with the fabled Hogan tape at the expenditure review committee, the whole proposition would not have got off the ground. No other Prime Minister ever supported a Minister against internal opposition at the level at which you supported me. Every legislative move I made from obtaining Paul's services to fascinating the world to a huge increase in budget to the 4% depreciation rate we obtained from the building of tourism infrastructure against the wishes of some—it was me and you against the world. Thank God you had the vision and the courage to back your crazy Minister against the view of the balance of the Cabinet.

When I think about the size and the extent of the tourism industry in Australia, particularly the infrastructure that has transformed the Australia and the Sydney of 1983 to be one of the most advanced and lauded destinations in the world, I think of you. Together, we have given Australia this hugely successful industry with a turnover in the hundreds of billions and an employment rate the highest of any industry in Australia, and a country whose physical beauty cannot be over-estimated. I appreciated, at the time, the journey we undertook from Surfers Paradise through the Whitsunday passageway up to Bedarra Island. I venture to say that no other Prime Minister experienced at first-hand the extraordinary potential, almost ignored and under-estimated, of this beautiful country that you enjoyed on that particular trip.

The truth is, Bob, amongst your huge achievements as Prime Minister, I reckon your support and encouragement in those early days when tourism was but a dream has given this country from almost nothing in 1983 to what possibly is Australia's biggest industry and the one with the most potential now that China and India have opened their doors. I just want to put on the record my appreciation of your unstinting support of your Minister's dreams of a tourism industry when you were my lone but very powerful supporter. Paul and I at this function will be acknowledging generously your support for Brown and Hogan in opening Australia to the world and in most cases also to Australia.

P.S. I could write a very similar note about your support for your Minister for Sport. Again, a very powerful support against some of those pessimistic Members of the caucus. Keating said to me once, 'no good fighting with you, you've got God on your side.' May I say, many generations of sports lovers and practitioners are very pleased I had God on my side.

Kindest regards,

Hon. John Brown, AO

Chairman, Sport and Tourism Youth Foundation

Ann Morgan

Bob was always a keen supporter of the Hawke Library, and popped in regularly to have a look at the items in the collection. You could tell that viewing his collection brought back memories of his public life, in the ACTU, on the campaign trail and also as a politician. He was always keen to learn more about the archives and our work, and to discuss in detail what our plans were for his archives, displays etc.

You could tell that he was also proud to show off memorabilia to others. One day, out of the blue we had an unexpected guest—Mr Hawke was in Adelaide with one of his grandchildren. He brought them to the library to show them the replica of his motorcycle. He told them about the accident that he often says changed his life.*

He often did this quietly and without any fuss. 'Just call me Bob' he said to me during our first meeting, and we quickly struck up a friendly relationship. It was always a pleasure to host him in the library. For me, Bob was the first politician I got to know, but he will always remain one of my favourites. He was a very kind and humble man, always generous with his time, and willing to speak to anyone

---

* When I was quite young, I remember Dad telling me about this accident and the effect it had on him at the time. 'While I was lying there, not knowing if I would survive, I resolved that if I did, I would no longer cruise through anything. I would live at 100 per cent of my abilities . . .' Every so often I felt I could see that the accident had, as he said, changed him for life, and helps to explain the intensity with which he lived.

who approached him inside and outside the library. It was a pleasure to work with him and to curate the Bob Hawke Archival collection.

Ann Morgan is the Manager, Research and Data Management Support, at the University of South Australia.

Jane Angel

On 21 May 2019, in a wave of activity following the death of Bob Hawke, I received the email—excerpted below:

> Dear Hawke family,
>
> With fondness I recall the genuine warmth and smile former Prime Minister Hawke had for people. My and my family's sincere and heartfelt condolences on the sad passing of Mr. Hawke, a kind, down to earth, jovial and good ol' mate, a true Australian.
>
> I lived and grew up in Papua New Guinea between 1989 and 2004, when Prime Minister Hawke, in 1992, paid a visit to the once colonial territory of Australia where, he, in an exemplary fashion as a leader, went out of his way, disregarding protocol and security, to reach over and across the airport fence in Port Moresby, to shake the hands of the common man who came to greet him with Papua New Guinean warmth and hospitality.
>
> The genuine love, rapport and concern he SHOWED for the grassroot man at the airport, was real, it was from his big and warm Aussie heart.

David Bandua had a story to tell and it is now connected to ours, and to Bob's, embedding itself in an evolving national narrative.

The Bob Hawke Prime Ministerial Library (BHPML) is tasked with identifying, collecting and conserving the Prime Minister's papers and memorabilia and making them accessible for research and public access. At the heart of the library is a person, and as such, the BHPML is a living biography. Our role is also to preserve the memory of the Prime Minister. Hence David Bandua's email to us.

I have spent many hours with Bob—and yet, I never met him. In late 2018, when I was appointed to the university, Bob was too frail to travel to Adelaide. However, my daily interactions with Bob make me feel as though I know him well. It is a deep privilege to have the opportunity to study and consider his life and times, to handle items that he valued, and to read speeches that make me marvel at his determination or delight in his sense of humour. Sometimes, unexpected connections will surface. Even my own.

In the 1980s I was a boarder in England when my parents were posted to Cape Town. In the holidays I needed a visa to visit them, which meant that at the height of anti-Apartheid feeling, I had to cross a picket line of protesters to enter the high commission.

I moved to Australia in the summer of 1987. Decisions that the Hawke government was making at the time contributed significantly to the end of Apartheid, and to the release of Nelson Mandela. In 1990, I was in Cape Town on the day Mandela walked free from Victor Verster prison. I celebrated with the rest of the world, largely ignorant of the role Bob had played.

Nearly thirty years later, in December 2018, the BHPML took delivery of a large number of books from Bob's personal library, including *Portrait of a Leader: Nelson Mandela*, gifted to Bob on the passing of this celebrated statesman and freedom fighter. It is inscribed by the then South African High Commissioner to Australia, Sibusiso Ndebele: 'To the honorable Bob Hawke, We will always cherish your role in the struggle for a South Africa free of Apartheid.'

Alone in the archive, the book connected me to a moment in history, to oppression and liberty, to a kid wanting to go home for the holidays, and to Bob.

Jane Angel is the manager of the Bob Hawke Prime Ministerial Library at the University of South Australia.

Tanya Plibersek

In 1983, when the Hawke government was elected, I was in the early years of high school. I couldn't remember a time when I wasn't a feminist: even before I knew the F-word, I strongly felt that boys and girls were equal. So when the newly elected Hawke government legislated on gender discrimination and affirmative action I was delighted.

It seems impossible to believe, but that election in 1983 saw the first woman from NSW elected to the House of Representatives. In 1983, it was legal to sack a woman who got married or became pregnant. Jobs were advertised for men or women. Women found it difficult to get a home loan and unless she wanted to be a teacher or a nurse, she probably wouldn't have gone to university.

Bob Hawke and his government changed that. Bob's reforms were controversial, hard-fought, but most importantly, enduring—like the *Sex Discrimination Act 1984*, which is still providing working women with protection from harassment at work.

In the 2013 election campaign Bob was his usual generous self, campaigning with me on Medicare (another great Hawke government legacy). When it looked like we would not win, he took me aside and urged me to run for the leadership after the election. At the time, my youngest child was only three. I didn't want to be on the road seven days a week. So that's what I told him.

Little did I suspect, however, that the night before the election David Speers would ask Bob who he thought should take over the leadership. When my name was raised, Bob simply repeated what I had told him. The internet went berserk. Sexist. Misogynist. Chauvinist. Anti-feminist. Everything that anyone who had met him knows is the exact opposite of who he was. As soon as I saw the reports I called him to apologise and all he did was laugh. Classic Bob.

The Sex Discrimination Act. The Affirmative Action Act. Huge increases in support for childcare. Medicare.

I am only one of the millions of Australian women who benefitted from Bob Hawke's enormous contribution to public life.

Thank you, Bob—for your leadership and your friendship.

Jennifer Thomas

I was a health practitioner/nurse/massage therapist who saw Bob through April and early May 2018. He had a profound effect, beyond anything that I realised at the time. Thirty minutes prior to the news that Bob had passed away, I was in the park with my dog, with Bob strongly in mind, and I began spontaneously practising the Qigong movements that signify letting go and releasing! The spirit works in amazing ways, as Bob and I had said once in each other's company.

He was a true father of our nation and must be remembered for what he represented.

Stavros Yiannoukas

My name is Stavros Yiannoukas—I'm the national sales director over at Hawke's Brewing, and extremely proud to be selling beer in honour of Mr Hawke while raising money for Landcare.

On a trip back from Canberra earlier this year, I began to appreciate that I may never get the opportunity to meet Mr Hawke, in spite of the fact that I talk about the great things he did, every day. As a result of this disappointing realisation I wrote him this letter.

Fortunately, I did get the chance to meet Mr Hawke once earlier this year. I'm truly grateful for the honour.

Sunday 3 February 2019

Dear Mr Hawke,

I hope this letter finds you well.

My name is Stavros Yiannoukas and I'm the new Head of Sales at your company—Hawke's Brewing.* I am writing you this letter in part to say thank you, and in part to make you a promise.

I would firstly like to thank you for the opportunity to represent you, while I sell delicious beer. More importantly, I would like to thank you for the opportunity that you (and Mr Whitlam) gave my parents, Dr Yiannis and Mrs Georgia Yiannoukas, who arrived in Australia as refugees in 1976 from war-torn Cyprus.

My father worked for decades as a general practitioner on King St in Newtown before he passed in 2009. My mother still works in hospitals around Sydney as an interpreter for Greek and Cypriot patients. My parents

* Dad didn't own the company—he allowed use of his name and image, and the brewery supports Landcare.

created a better life for me here in Australia, and this would not have been possible without your open-armed policies to new Australians, so I owe you a debt of gratitude for this.

As a way of saying thanks, I would like to make you a promise, Mr Hawke—we will sell enough beer at Hawke's Brewing that we will raise at least $1,000,000 for Landcare. I can never truly repay what my parents have done for me, nor what you have done for my parents, but it's the best I can do.

Stavros Yiannoukas

Bill Crews

I vividly remember Bob and Blanche carrying trays of Christmas Day lunches to the homeless and needy at our special Christmas Day event. People would often stop and stare. They were really impressed that a former Prime Minister would care enough to serve meals to the homeless. Bob and Blanche were quite happy to just be volunteers with everybody else.

Hansard excerpts, 3 July 2019

Scott **Morrison**

We saw the totality of the man, his authenticity and imperfection. He never hid it. I'm told of a story—it may be apocryphal;

I'm not sure, but I'm pretty convinced it's true—that on one occasion at Kirribilli House the AFP officer on duty on the day, who was tasked to bring forward the papers and put them in the vestibule at the entry to Kirribilli House, one morning got to see all of Bob Hawke as he opened the door in all his glory. The AFP adopted a different protocol for launching the submission of those documents each morning with greater care so as not to be exposed to the full glory of the great Robert James Lee Hawke. He did never hide himself, physically or otherwise, and Australians loved him for it.

Greg **Hunt**

I do remember, in September of 1983 whilst I was in my final year of secondary school, watching the America's Cup. We were all enthralled with the whole back and forth of the races and the way Bob Hawke, as the Prime Minister but also as the cheerleader of the nation, captured that spirit. For so long afterwards, it wasn't the jacket—of course, the jacket is hard to forget—it was the ethos, the passion, the joy and the fact that he was able to articulate the mood of the nation to capture it and add to it. It was such a powerful moment in Australia—a unifying moment.

Sussan **Ley**

Bob Hawke was a larrikin Australian whose laugh would stand out in any public bar and whose voice would echo powerfully on the world stage.

Pat Barblett AM

Bob was a lifelong friend of Alan's, their friendship spanning seventy years. I know how much Alan appreciated Bob's visits in the last year of his life.*

Dimity Pond

We were talking about Bob Hawke at my aquarobics class on Saturday. A few of us remembered the America's Cup. There is a lot on the net about that, but not so much what we were remembering—what we remembered was Bob Hawke asking us all to 'blow' to help our boat along. He said he reckoned that every Australian 'blew'.

He had a great gift for pleasure and for bringing people together, as a nation, to share that pleasure, didn't he?

Heather Roberts

The crowd of friends and family gathered in the sitting room with panoramic views of Middle Harbour, Sydney, to celebrate the engagement of our daughter, Bree, to Louis. [Bree's story is on page 302.]

---

* Pat's husband, Alan, and Dad met at Perth Modern School and then studied together at the University of Western Australia in the early 1950s, were both sports mad, and thick as thieves. Alan was Best Man at my parents' wedding, about which, bemoaning my grandmother's influence, Pat said: 'It was over a hundred degrees in the shade, and only warm orange juice to drink!' Alan represented Australia in Olympic hockey and pursued a distinguished career in law, becoming Deputy Chief Judge of the Family Court of Australia. Pat and Mum remained lifelong friends.

Louis' stepfather began his speech with all the charm and skill of a seasoned public speaker. It was clear to see that the couple were very dear to him. As I looked upon this rather surreal moment it was hard to believe the speechmaker was Bob Hawke, the former Prime Minister of Australia, the most well-known and popular of all past prime ministers. It was a very good speech that received a rousing applause and then there was some music. My husband, Geoff, played the keyboard while Anastasia, a dear friend, sang the old standard, 'Can't Help Falling in Love'. At just the right moment, all the guests joined in spontaneously. It was as if we were the cast of a Hollywood musical; without any obvious direction, we had all joined in then quietened again when the verses were sung. The most enthusiastic singer of all was Bob.

True love sometimes happens quickly, and it was hard to believe we had first met Bob and his wife, Blanche, for the first time here at their home just a few months earlier. I was looking forward to meeting them. I had watched their lives unfolding over the years on TV programs and in magazines since I was fourteen.

The steep road curved up and around the cliffs where grand homes were perched to take advantage of the stunning views. I briefly wondered what my mum would have thought about this meeting. She was born the same month and year as Bob, in 1929. They would have grown up in a similar household: God-fearing, teetotalling and hardworking people with a great heart for the community. My dad was a minister just like Bob's dad. I think they would have been surprised and chuffed.

'It's good to meet you at last,' Blanche smiled as she greeted us in the kitchen. Dressed in casual but elegant clothes, she led us to a sitting room with its wonderful view. We sat down a little stiffly on a white leather sofa—Geoff, our son Isaac and I all sat in a row.

'You sit here,' Blanche said, guiding me onto the matching sofa that was placed at right angles to the sofa we had been sitting on. 'You're too squashed there.'

Bree and Louis helped Blanche to bring out the white gold-rimmed china and the silver service—real silver that had been her mother's—and placed them on the glass coffee table in front of us.

'We bring these out for our VIP visitors,' Blanche said.

She disappeared for a moment through the sliding doors that lead to the balcony and we heard her call: 'Bree's folks are here.'

'It's so nice in the sun, couldn't they come out here?' Bob replied.

'No, Bob, they cannot,' his wife insisted.

And then he was there, sitting beside me, chatting like we were old friends. He was quite frail, having just recovered from a serious illness, but yes, it was unmistakably Bob—the hair that was a thick silvery mane and his piercing blue eyes that noticed everything. He told me how lovely our daughter is, and that Louis was like a son to him.

'And which electorate are you in?' Bob asked. Geoff and I looked blankly at each other, panicked for a moment, and then I remembered.

'La Trobe, I think.'

'One of ours,' Bob said, with a quick nod and a smile at Louis.

Moving to a safer topic, I told Bob about our beautiful granddaughter, and his face lit up. He said that he always loved to see his grandchildren. There were cakes and tea and then he was off, shuffling back out to his balcony and a quiet puff of his cigar.

Our meeting was over with the man who was friend of the Queen, prime ministers and presidents past. Included among them now, our daughter, given a glowing report and welcomed as family.

I would have liked to have had more chats with Bob, but it wasn't to be. We had our moment with the man, in the twilight of his memorable life, which we will always treasure.

The next time I spoke with Bree she gave me Bob's report. 'Your family are lovely, lovely, people.'

Penny Wong

When Bob Hawke was confronted with the threat of race being used as a political weapon, he responded by demonstrating decency and the commitment to an Australia that was culturally diverse, accepting and open.

I'd been living in Australia about a decade at the time John Howard tried to turn community sentiment against Asian Australians like me. It was pretty harrowing to see the racism I had experienced blithely bandied around in the national debate, as if the idea of rejecting a whole group of people based on their ethnicity were just a regular policy suggestion. Bob made it an opportunity to unify. He led the Parliament—and the nation—in affirming Australia's commitment to a non-discriminatory immigration policy, affirming that we are a multicultural nation, and that that is a good thing.

Aside from the injustice of it, it would have made no sense to Bob to have antipathy toward Asians. After all, to Bob, we were part of Asia. This was part of his foresight in building a modern Australia; an open Australia. He knew the world's future was in Asia and so ours must be too. Yet he was also unwavering in his projection of Australian values in the region, never more so than his compassion and humanity in the wake of Tiananmen.

His embrace of multiculturalism, his passion for reconciliation, his activism on Apartheid—was him signalling to Australia that we were all equal and equally worthy. All of us who in some way felt marginalised felt included by Bob.

I always felt welcome with Bob, always valued. One of my greatest fortunes in being a Labor senator was being able to see him from time to time, especially on the campaign trail.

Every time I met Bob, he was optimistic, ebullient, and telling me what to do. I recall, after the 2013 loss, going to see him in his office. He asked, 'How are you, love?'

'Oh, it's pretty hard being in opposition,' I said.

He replied, 'Ah, well, I wouldn't know.'

Andrew Denton

'Would you like to hear a joke?' Bob Hawke looked at me with a twinkle in his eye.

It wasn't what I'd expected to hear from Australia's 23rd Prime Minister. I'd just finished interviewing him about voluntary assisted dying for my podcast series *Better Off Dead*. Without hesitation he'd put himself on the record in support: 'I think it's absurd that euthanasia is not legal in this country. It doesn't meet any requirements of morality or good sense.'

I was packing up my digital recorder, thanking Bob for his time, when the offer of a joke came out of the blue.

'Sure,' I said, always keen for a laugh.

What came next was a performance delivered with all the aplomb of Dave Allen, complete with Irish accent.

'So,' says Bob, sitting behind his big desk in his private office right next door to the old Boulevarde Hotel, 'two Irishmen are having a beer outside a pub across the road from the local brothel. Suddenly, they spy the local Anglican priest making his way furtively into the house of ill-repute.'

'Will you look at that?', says Seamus. 'The feckin' hypocrite. All week he's in the pulpit teaching us morality and there he is, sneaking into the brothel!'

'The feckin' hypocrite', says Paddy in agreement.

Ten minutes later and—what do you know—the local rabbi sneaks into the same place.

Seamus is outraged. 'Will you look at that?', says he. 'All week he's in the synagogue, preaching to us about how to lead our lives and there he is sneaking into the brothel!'

'The feckin' hypocrite', exclaims Paddy.

Ten minutes later and, you wouldn't believe it, but the local Catholic priest sneaks into the very same brothel.

Seamus and Paddy look on in amazement, then Seamus turns to Paddy and says: 'Ooh look. There goes Father O'Neill . . . Ahh, some of the poor girls must be sick.'

I don't know if Bob told me that joke because he was wise to the cant and hypocrisy from the leadership of the Catholic Church about voluntary assisted dying. Or because he just thought it was a good joke.

That he did tell it, was a reminder of why Australians were drawn to him: the steel-trap mind married to a larrikins' soul.

I've re-told Bob's joke many times since, always to a decent laugh. Each time I do, I see that twinkle in the prime ministerial eye.

The Hon. Bill Shorten MP

When we are young, we are warned not to meet our heroes, because they are destined to disappoint. My experience with Bob was quite the opposite. It is amongst the great privileges of my life that not only did I get to meet my hero, I had the honour of knowing him as a friend and learning from him as a mentor.

But I never lost that sense of wonder that comes from turning to your hero for advice. Just as I could tell that Bob never tired of his deep interest in national political debate, his deep affection for the trade union movement, his profound belief in the Labor Party and its values, and his boundless love for the Australian people.

I last saw Bob just days before he passed away. He was sitting out on his beloved balcony. He had a crossword in front of him. There was a dictionary, a strawberry milkshake and a cigar.

The sun was on his face. He was at ease with himself.

I understood that this visit was most likely goodbye, although he had a sturdy constitution, because I had visited him twice before in previous months thinking that that too, perhaps, would be when I last saw him.

I tried to tell him then what he meant to me and what he meant to all of us. I'm not sure I found the right words for the weight of that moment. Yet—still—I think Bob knew.

He wanted to talk about everything else, not himself. But he knew what he meant to Australia. He knew what he had achieved for our country. He knew that he was loved by his family, by his friends, by his former colleagues, by the people, right to the end.

We will miss you, Bob. We will carry on your unfinished business. We will recall your lessons, but we understand that there will never, ever again be another Bob Hawke. You were one and you were unique.

Jan Pieters

1 May 2019

Dear Bob,

I have been stewing a while to write to you ever since Ben left after a wonderful stay here. It then dawned on me that I will probably not meet you in person again—your life on this planet coming to an end. I am writing to say goodbye and so long . . .

I, and my family, have been so lucky and fortunate to have you, Hazel and Blanche as my in-laws; your boundless generosity, your loyalty, your passion and commitment, to never hold any grudges, your sense of fairness, your ability to assess and decide, your love. You taught me so many lessons, you have been a father-in-law one could only dream to have.

In a strange way, it was not until I witnessed your love for Blanche that I started to discover more what it means to love and be in partnership—the B&B love story was and continues to be an inspiration for me.

All I could do when you and Blanche got together was to tell the family that I saw people madly and deeply in love—and this love has lasted! You are both so amazing together, and I will never regret our secret meeting in the coffee shop of Westfield Towers (and I had to keep that secret for a very long time).

I have so many amazing memories of you: your incredible support of my family, you paid for the deposit of our first house, kids' school fees, through the 1987 financial crisis—material support, but it was mostly your wise advice over the years, your moral support and wonderful family gatherings I treasure the most (The Lodge, Pebbly Beach, Gold Coast, and of course Northbridge).

You gave me the opportunity to meet so many interesting people: Sir Peter Abeles, Frank Lowy, your mates from the union, artists, friends like Colin from Melbourne and the eccentrics like Richard Super and Dick Smith. Your talented ministers, Gordon the Scotsman, your secretary Jill, only to name a few.

It was an honour and a privilege to sit next to you at Sophie's wedding, to have you as my father in Oz, grandfather of my children. While Sophie and Ben may not carry the Hawke name for future generations, they will surely represent your passion, wit, commitment, loyalty, love.

I salute you, I honour you, and when the day of your passing comes, any boss who doesn't declare a holiday to honour one of the greatest Prime Ministers of Australia is a BUM!

Adieu, I love you and will deeply miss you.
Jan

This letter now sits in the archives at the Hawke Centre at the University of South Australia.

Louis Pratt

It is difficult for me to think of just one story to describe Bob. What comes to mind is a series of moments, over days, months and years, all blurred in together. It's fishing together off the end of the jetty, the animated conversations about politics over dinner, or the moments he'd spontaneously burst into song, his loud voice booming and his eyes twinkling as he made his own fun.

The first time I met Bob was at his wedding to my mother. I found out about their engagement when it was reported on the 6 o'clock news. I was on holiday in Queensland and it was in the days before mobile phones. I turned on the TV to see Mum and Bob taking a long walk down a beach holding hands—the perfect image of their private love story, played out in public.

On their wedding day they both seemed like excited teenagers, despite the fact that Mum was in her fifties by then and Bob was even older. Outside the wedding venue, protestors with loudspeakers blasted aeroplane noise, taking advantage of the media presence to protest the development of a second Sydney airport (still no closer to a reality today than it was twenty-five years ago).

I didn't really know Bob at the time, beyond his public image. But when I saw how much he loved my mum, it was impossible for me to dislike him. We had a sort of unspoken understanding, we accepted each other as an inevitable part of each other's lives and were respectfully civil.

When I moved into the boatshed at Mum and Bob's place, we really got to know each other, and once we did, we were thick as thieves—staying up late, playing snooker, making bets and generally carrying on—while Mum shouted for us to be quiet.

Gradually, as his body failed him, our list of activities grew smaller. When his skills declined, I started deliberately throwing snooker matches until, quietly, we stopped playing them. When he could no longer get around a golf course, we resorted instead to watching it on TV, making bets, and him yelling at the screen his mantra for any golfer: 'A short putt never goes in!'

Old age mellowed him, until what was left was his sweetness. I can see him holding Mum's hand and looking up into her eyes with adoration. He'd tell anyone who would listen how much he loved his 'beautiful wife'. He used to say she looked just like Zsa Zsa Gabor, and even composed a little song for her which he would serenade her with. '*Zsa Zsa Gabor, I love you more and more.*'

When I introduced him to the woman who would become my wife, he pretty much insisted I marry her immediately. Luckily, he did live to see me marry her. We danced our wedding waltz for him in the living room, as he was too weak to make it to the wedding reception

He smiled. I kissed him goodbye. A few days later, the great man was gone.

Laura Panetta

My mum told me about former Prime Minister, Bob Hawke, and how he made education something that everyone could access by increasing the number of students who finished Year 12 in high school, and by making university affordable to everyone. [Laura is the daughter of Catia Malaquias, who features earlier in the book on page 210.]

I have a little brother Julius, who has Down syndrome, and I know how important education is, especially to children who need a little more help in school.

Next year, I will be a student at the new Bob Hawke College in Subiaco, Western Australia. The school is only a few hundred metres from Bob Hawke's high school, Perth Modern, where my mum also went much later. I even know one of Bob Hawke's high school friends, Dawn Barry. She lives a few doors from my auntie and used to live next to Mum.

I am proud to live in a country where I can dream to be anything I wish to be. I know that Bob Hawke helped make Australia a land of real opportunity.

On TV, I watched our WA premier, Mark McGowan, announce that my new high school in Subiaco would be called Bob Hawke College. He said that maybe a future Prime Minister of Australia would come through its doors.

I dream of lots of things.

Sometimes good things happen. I am probably the shortest girl to be voted head girl of my primary school, Wembley, in its eighty-year history.

Who knows, one day I can help make Australia even better for everyone. I would love to be Prime Minister of Australia.

Laura Panetta, age 11 years, Wembley, Western Australia

Sue Pieters-Hawke

I first thought of Dad as getting old when I looked across at him at eighty and saw a shift. He had always been remarkably resilient, and general perceptions of ageism, which are objectionable anyhow, didn't affect my perceptions of my parents—age did not diminish them in my view, and they had been unfussed anyhow about getting older—life simply continued as they aged, as it does. They were never whingers. Mum's dementia, which is a chronic disease, not normal ageing, brought a new set of concerns, but no less love or respect. Besides which, Dad retained his vigour and his radiating energy for long after he left Canberra. However, in this glance I noticed something subtle in his face and movements that had me realise, slightly surprisedly: *Oh!, Dad's getting old . . .*

The next eight-odd years saw a slow progression of ageing to a point where Dad was clearly becoming frailer. This was complicated by a couple of heart-related episodes and then, most limitingly, by a peripheral neuropathy of his feet that rendered movement extremely slow and painful. It wasn't until further into his eighties that his feet were a near constant pain and he started to be really frustrated by his aging. He needed more sleep. I asked him about his legs and feet one day and he dismissed the pain with a grimace but said, 'I fucking hate it. It makes people think I'm old and dithery and I'm not.' I don't think the downsides of ageing bring anyone much pleasure, but you can imagine that someone with the vigour, self-belief and drive that Dad had, found all this especially frustrating. Slowing down had never been part of his nature.

I felt sad for him but not profoundly stricken as I also knew that Dad had an immense capability to adapt to necessity when he could not fully shape it himself. But as he aged, there were two essential problems with this. Firstly, he was bloody minded and didn't want to f---ing adapt to being frail. It simply refused to meld comfortably into his identity or sense of himself—a common issue for many people later in life. And secondly, too many of the numerous interactions and sources of joy in his life were gradually becoming less available to him. He was going to too many funerals, he said. He lived with a lot of pain in his last years, which was better managed towards the end but nevertheless did wear him down—as it would anybody. This and the diminishment of opportunities for the enormous relishing of life that was so much of his character brought him to a place two or three years before his death where he first started saying occasionally, 'I think I'm ready to die', and it was neither particularly dramatic nor mysterious. We had discussed death in different ways at different times over the course of my life and he repeated what he'd always said: that he wasn't scared of it. He wasn't, and it really did seem so until the very end, and I think in that unconscious way that you often hear of, it's almost as if he hung on despite himself for key events: my daughter's wedding, my step-brother's wedding, a return to decent government.

As this frailty progressed it was matched by a slow, subtle but clear turning of focus inwards. It wasn't that Dad cared less about the world or people—he still watched the news assiduously—but he didn't pay the immensely absorbing and energetic attention to the detail of it all as he once had. Some say this 'turning in' is a natural part of late ageing when approaching death, is its own natural preparation, and it certainly seemed natural and gracious in Dad's last few years. The mellowing was very real. Frustration at times was the only 'negative', for which we had nothing but empathy. His fondness was more likely to be expressed in a slight smile and twinkle of the eye or touch of the hand than in lots of words. I think that by this late stage he really was ready to die. One of the very salient factors was that he no longer felt that he had anything to contribute—and that had been at the core of his existence and purpose in life.

His last few years were characterised by a palpable tenderness from him and towards him. Family gatherings for Christmas or birthdays, or regular popping in there for dinner—these were now organised to take less time and make fewer demands on him and on Blanche. When he could no longer sit at the table he would lie back on the couch and nap, and half tune in, especially if the kids were present. There was this gathering in him and around him of the enormous love that had so characterised his whole life. There was a distilling of essence. And I suppose we just naturally adjusted to what was happening. There was some sadness but nothing really maudlin. Less taxing conversations still happened, and I enjoyed sitting up alone with him many an evening after dinner watching cricket or golf. For me, it was simply the chance to sit quietly with him in a silent house, treasuring the unspoken companionship.

He spent much of each day outside, on the balcony near the kitchen. He had always loved being outdoors, and it is where he was often happiest. He developed a routine where he would sit at the table, either well out in the sun (he'd always been a lizard who loved sunning himself at any opportunity) or tucked back in a more protected spot if the weather was foul. Blanche would wrap him in warm layers of clothes and a blanket, and there was an outdoor heater if required. His table would be set up with all he needed—the papers, his cryptic crossword, notepaper, cigars, water, ashtrays and so on, and the much thumbed dictionary. We would take him an occasional cup of tea, chat for a while, but mostly leave him in peace. It was usually here that friends who visited him in the last months would sit with him. [See the photo of Dad and Bill Shorten.]

He'd glance out at the water, the birds and bush and light, and seemed content, although he was also a bit bored and frustrated. He'd always been good at relaxing—could switch seamlessly from being totally focussed on work, to lounging in the sun with the form guide or a cryptic for a while, then back to work again. It was, I believe, one of the keys to his enormous productivity. But now there was not much switching back to any productive tasks that demanded his full engagement, it was as if part of who he had been was no longer in play, and I felt it irk him.

At times in his last year he needed people to be there overnight for him but Blanche also needed sleep, so various male family members and friends stayed over in case assistance was needed during the night. As often happens through the caring process, it's a constant adjustment. I was touched seeing Blanche make the adjustment from being not at all the carer-type to confronting the reality that her best friend and husband had become frail and was approaching his death. I was moved to see her transformation into the most tender carer imaginable. And the rest of us, as you do around a person approaching death, the rest of us just made adjustments with all the knowledge and sensitivity we could muster to meet changing needs and sensitivities. As some have said in their contributions, sometimes in his later years Dad could seem a bit remote or not fully there, but I experienced this as part of his withdrawal from a complete presence in the world at all times, and he would always tune back in when it mattered.

Dad had been very attuned to Mum's dying and death six years previously. He saw her just before she died and attended the private funeral and public memorial with us a month later. Although a bit unconventional, we all felt it had been a really good way of letting go of Mum, her body and her presence in our lives, and of then celebrating her legacy and who she had been. I'd also discussed this with Blanche, who hadn't attended.

A couple of years before Dad's died, when I was at dinner with him and Blanche, I initiated a conversation with him about his death: 'You know you're going to cark it before too much longer, you're talking about it already, and once you do, who knows what happens to you, but there is sure as hell going to be a lot of feeling and fuss left for all of us to handle. And there's the whole State service aspect to consider, and having done one, I figure doing yours in a week would be like a nightmare on steroids when we will need simply to be grieving and may well need some privacy for that. So I reckon it would be good if we could talk about what you might want or not want to have happen then.'

Dad raised his eyebrows, but was very open to it. We talked about how well it had worked that we'd had a small private farewell after Mum's death and then took the time to create a public and celebratory memorial that was personal to her. We discussed it further, and I asked him some details about where he might want it to be, what music he would like, and so on, and agreed generally on an outline. In fact, I got a message from him a couple of days later saying that he'd really enjoyed dinner, which he thought was pretty funny given that we'd talked about him being dead! Blanche and I talked further about how it would be good to get his indication on some more details, and have a rough planning meeting so that when it happened, especially if it was sudden, we had a rough plan in place with which Dad and Blanche were happy, and felt would be appropriate and satisfying for others.

About a year before he died, we had a low key meeting. We tossed around logistics, talked about music and people and speeches and atmosphere, and whether Dad might want, despite being agnostic, the sacredness of a church, and referred this all back to him. We now had an agreed outline we could put aside. There was only one small problem—now that the subject had been broached, Dad was rather enthused, and seemed to have asked two hundred people and their pet goats to speak at his memorial! It was a very delicate job dealing with it when the time came.

As it happened, all that preparation was most valuable—within twenty-four hours of his death the Sydney Opera House was booked, and we more or less knew how we would proceed.

But it's funny this dying thing. Unless some clear accident or incident has precipitated an abrupt death, the body can take days to shut down and die (as I witnessed with my mum). So you've come to terms with the idea that death is no longer far away—you just don't know actually when it's actually going to happen. It might be tonight or in months, but you know you're on the eighteenth hole, and that it won't go on forever; 'the end' is approaching. In Dad's case it happened fairly quickly after a sudden turn for the worse—in less than 24 hours he was gone.

He had made it to Lou and Bree's wedding the weekend before—he was thrilled to do so, but it was tough for him, and it was the last thing he attended. I then received a gentle phone call from Blanche on the afternoon of Thursday16 May and was not surprised but still deeply shocked. From Blanche's delivery of the news and from conversations I've had with her and others since, I feel absolutely confident that Dad did indeed die without fear or fuss and went peacefully surrounded by love. This was an enormous comfort. I was very sad that I wasn't there to sit with him for a while near the end, especially as I hadn't seen him for a couple of weeks, but I know that when it did happen it progressed so quickly that having someone supporting him through it was all that mattered.

During the last year or so I'm sure he occasionally felt it was a bit of a useless tail-end he was enduring. In the end his timing was perfect. He had made it to Louis' wedding and died a few days later before the shock election loss that would have broken his heart. On election night, two days after his death, we still gathered as planned for the counting and results, but were subdued, and commented more than once that we were glad he wasn't there.

The private funeral was organised by Blanche and led by a wonderful celebrant who is a close friend of hers. It was beautiful, but an important luxury to have the safe and private space with only close family and friends and no intrusion by media or protocol or crowds we couldn't have coped with at the time. I had surprised myself by wanting to see Dad before he was cremated. Not having been with him for a couple of weeks, there was part of me that needed to do that in order to process his death, so a viewing was kindly arranged. And when at the conclusion of the private service he was placed in the hearse and slowly driven away from us, it's as if I saw through the coffin to him, his feet in shiny black shoes slowly receding from us forever. It was the most vividly awful moment.

To have that and then the memorial about three weeks later did truly prove to be a satisfying way to deal with many things, including both the privacy of our grief and the widely shared nature and the widespread desire, including our own, to mark his passing and celebrate his life. It somehow all worked perfectly.

THE FINAL WORD

Sue Pieters-Hawke

So, at the end of the day, what is all of this for? Simply put, it is a celebration of my dad—who he was and what he stood for.

Beyond that, in celebrating his and his colleagues' values and achievements, by implication it interrogates the future. One of the themes that emerged most forcefully during the public memorial for Dad was a vivid sense of a time when politics was practised intelligently for the good of the whole nation. To borrow from an old Jewish proverb: whenever there are two people in a room, there will be at least three opinions. There will always be fierce differences of opinion across humanity, and 'spin' is in our nature, but we are living in a time when some of us raised in relatively secure and (relatively) democratic societies are observing somewhat fearfully the concerted undermining of much of what underpins us.

'Back then', the future mattered, respect and integrity mattered, and facts, imagination, science, accuracy and honesty were all valued. 'Truth' as the basis of debate mattered. Our diversity flourished and was celebrated. All manner of pursuits—cultural, educational, imaginative, innovative, traditional—were considered worthy alongside our sport.

Economics was important, and economic policy was transparently approached by government as crucial in enabling 'a fair go for ALL', so people could make a decent life, and be secure in knowing that their children would be educated and other foundational needs would be met. Aspiration was understood as being not only personal, but also communal—a shared concern that we were part of a decent society that did right by all its citizens and as part of the international community. Economic matters had not become the abstracted and supposedly apolitical creature that rules us today, whereby all imperatives must themselves suit the mythical beast, 'The Economy'. This inversion of reality is itself dangerous and delusional, a myth that has to a large degree obscured our choices, our humanity, concern for others and the care we show 'our' planet. Economic activity and policy is always purpose-driven—it is simply a question of what purposes it serves. A decent social democracy requires free, open, informed, rigorous and mostly respectful debate about purpose and vision and means—and Dad was an outstandingly committed, articulate, skilled and compassionate social democrat.

There was an optimism, a coherence, a vision to it all, and a tangible sense that the enterprise of government was on behalf of the whole population. This enterprise was not flawless but was inherently positive and 'caring'—and it could in degree be realised; indeed, it was happening. With Dad's death and at the memorial came a sense of grief that that's not how it is now. At depth, we were mourning more than Dad. But rather than despair that those times have inevitably gone, the true thing to do is to understand from history that the pendulum always swings, to take heart from these memories, and to grow that vision and act inclusively with others towards a society and future that serves all who live in it.

If we look to the future with a vision inspired by the values of those governments applied to our world now, I see three overarching areas of 'unfinished business'.

First is climate change. Dad's governments were the most environmentally progressive the world had seen until then, but so much more is required of us now. As my daughter said at his memorial regarding climate change: 'We must stop delaying the cost of change now, for all we do is load our future citizens with a debt that they cannot repay. Let us listen to the children and young people who parade their courage and conviction, because their tomorrows will be affected by our actions today. Truly honouring my grandfather means reflecting on his achievements and applying his values to the future choices we make. Let us take to heart his courage, borrow his optimism and mirror his love for the brotherhood of humankind. So, we live in unparalleled times, and must act with urgency and scale and optimism and co-operation appropriate to the crisis, or our kid's kids, or their kids, may face a planet rendered near uninhabitable for humans.

The next major piece of 'unfinished business' concerns true reconciliation, justice, inclusion and opportunity for Indigenous Australians. On the morning of 20 December 1991, the last day of Dad's prime ministership, he hung the 1.2-metre-square Barunga Statement painting in the central hall of Parliament House. He stated that 'its presence here calls on those who follow me . . . it demands of them that they continue efforts, that they find solutions to the abundant problems that still face the Aboriginal people of this country.' We have a chance right now to respond positively to the Uluru Statement from the Heart, to move decisively forward towards that purpose. To irreversibly elevate the status of Indigenous people in their own country to one of full equality and inclusion, to replace the relics and aftermath of colonisation with respect, looking to them for leadership in solving the problems we've all inherited but of which they bear the burden. This risks being undermined by today's reactionary wing of politics and society—much as happened in Dad's time with the push for a treaty—and must not be allowed to happen again.

The third chunk of unfinished business is what we could call the 'social contract' between a people and their government. The details and issues that lie under this umbrella are vast, but at their heart is the principle that good government is about serving the whole population, about supporting the conditions that allow all its people the opportunity to be safe and to thrive. As we are a comparably affluent nation, there is no reason why good healthcare, good education, work, leisure, housing and a sense of belonging should be unavailable to anyone by virtue of their circumstances. This includes the robust commitment to well-designed, sufficient and readily available sets of supports and 'safety nets' for people who need them.

As well as the pleasure in remembering Dad, my hope for this book is for us to be in a small way reminded that everything that drove him, all he achieved, is available to us now. He *was* outstanding, but not at all unique in the arc of human history. There have always been great leaders and potential leaders—but for what do they lead or we follow? Do we empower and listen and learn and co-operate, or do we blinker, demonise, exclude and divide?

We are not isolated from the rest of the world, but we are a country of a size that can transform itself, for better or worse, in less time than some. And when we participate in life—our families, communities, and institutions—doing so with an inspired vision and commitment that values the wellbeing of all, it can bring out the best in us and in those beyond us. We could be the Australia we like to think we are. So, my ultimate hope is that the readers and leaders of today and tomorrow will see that the value, possibility and personal satisfaction of engagement beyond ourselves and our own is not a story about personal power, but is a story of commitment to a bigger picture both now and for future generations. It is in us as human beings.

There's no such thing as perfect—it is all about reaching deeply into ourselves and out to each other, and doing what is needed. Dad was so loved, I feel, partly because he did exactly that, and did it with warmth and humour and flair.

In reading this book, I hope you have had some of the warm and fuzzy feelings I had when putting it together. And perhaps you will also be reminded that the past never gets us off the hook for the future, and thus be inspired by the many glorious people who've gone before us, who are around us and who are still to be born, to make the best lives that we can, for ourselves, each other, our country, our world and for future generations.

That's how Dad would want to be remembered.

Acknowledgements

First and foremost, I'd like to thank all of the contributors who generously gave of their time and insights, affection and wit. In many cases they went 'above and beyond', nudging friends and colleagues and chasing stories for me (gotta love the Glee Club . . .). I know many contributors had time and other constraints, and that it was pretty emotional for them, so getting this done was not easy. The timeline overall was a nightmare, given that it wasn't until some time after Dad's death that the project came back to mind. I obviously could not have done it without a pile of fabulous people swinging behind it. My thanks also to those who tried to put something together but weren't able to in time, and apologies to those who for some stupid reason (chaos, probably) we failed to reach out to. There are so many folk with great stories of Dad, but who for one reason or another are not included.

I want very much to thank my esteemed publisher, Tom Gilliatt. This is the third book I've done with Tom and my first with Allen & Unwin. In the earlier stages of formulation, the book kept shape-shifting, complicated by Dad's illness and then death, but the depths of Tom's patience and humanity over this time reflects the kind man that he is.

At Allen & Unwin, my thanks also go to the rest of the team who made all of this happen: Rebecca Kaiser as editorial director, Lou Cornege and Patrizia di Biase-Dyson in publicity and others I've yet to meet.

And to Louise Swinn, project manager extraordinaire—kudos, respect and affection in spades. If you ever have anything bookish that you need support to get done, look no further!

A special note of thanks to my step-mum Blanche, who has been supportive since I first started talking to Dad about doing 'something'. She is mostly better than Google for facts and dates about Dad, and much more fun. Our publishers understandably see this book and the publication of Blanche's two updated biographies of Dad as rivals in the Christmas book market, but maybe they don't get that in the Hawke-world family affections and loyalty trump commercial interests. We've been cheering each other on and see our books as utterly different and both very much worth purchasing!

Everyone should have a village . . . I do, and I thank the folk there for daily laughter, friendship and support.

My kids—well I just thank them for everything, for being the amazing people I adore, for being there if/when I need them, and 'cos simply by being themselves, they drive home to me the point and love and value of 'family' and the future.

And of course, the ultimate thanks and acknowledgement are for Robert James Lee.

Contributors

The *Exodus* Foundation

Bob Hawke was a keen supporter of the Exodus Foundation.

Recognised as a leading frontline charity, The Exodus Foundation meets the needs of Sydney's poor and homeless by connecting each guest with the professional services they need to break their cycle of poverty.

The Exodus Foundation provides free meals to the needy every day of the year, and counselling and outreach services to guide their futures.

Food parcels are distributed to disadvantaged families and our health professionals deliver primary healthcare.

Thousands of homeless and needy people rely on The Exodus Foundation each year and the community trusts it to make their futures better.

Donations can be made at
www.exodusfoundation.org.au